*f***P**

Also by David Walsh, Ph.D.

No: Why Kids—of All Ages—Need to Hear It and Ways Parents Can Say It

Why Do They Act That Way? A Survival Guide to the Adolescent Brain for You and Your Teen

Dr. Dave's Cyberhood: Making Media Choices that Create a Healthy Electronic Environment for Your Kids

Selling Out America's Children: How America Puts Profits before Values and What Parents Can Do

Designer Kids: Consumerism and Competition—When Is it All Too Much

Smart Parenting, Smarter Kids

THE ONE BRAIN BOOK YOU NEED TO HELP YOUR CHILD GROW BRIGHTER, HEALTHIER, AND HAPPIER

David Walsh, Ph.D.

FREE PRESS
NEW YORK LONDON TORONTO SYDNEY

NOTE TO READERS

Names and identifying details of most people portrayed in this book, including all those counseled by the author, have been changed.

fP

Free Press
A Division of Simon & Schuster, Inc.
1230 Avenue of the Americas
New York, NY 10020

First Free Press hardcover edition June 2011

Designed by Julie Schroeder

Manufactured in the United States of America

10 9 8 7 6 5 4 3 2 1

Library of Congress Cataloging-in-Publication Data
Walsh, David Allen.
Smart parenting, smarter kids : the one brain book you need to help your child grow brighter, healthier, and happier / David Walsh.
p. cm.
Includes bibliographical references and index.
1. Children—Intelligence levels. 2. Cognition in children. 3. Child development. 4. Child rearing. 5. Cognitive learning. I. Title.
BF432.C48W35 2011

649'.1—dc22 2010051303

ISBN 978-1-4391-2117-7
ISBN 978-1-4391-3733-8 (ebook)

to my wife, Monica,
my partner in parenting and life

CONTENTS

Smart Parenting, Smarter Kids

ONE

Our Children's Amazing Brains

The phone rang as I returned to my office.

"Hello, this is Dr. Dave Walsh," I said as I sat down at my desk.

"Hi, my name is Eleanor Stephenson. My husband and I were at your seminar in Lake Crystal, Minnesota, a few weeks back. We found it helpful, and I wonder if you have a minute to give me some advice."

"I'll try," I replied.

"Thanks," she said. "Our son Jeremy is in second grade and we are having a problem with his teacher. I really need help knowing what to do."

"What problem are you having?" I asked.

"Well, we had parent conferences the other night," she began, "and Jeremy's teacher told us that Jeremy had difficulty paying attention in class. I didn't say anything, but I knew this couldn't possibly be true. Jeremy can play video games for hours on end without blinking. It's clear Jeremy can pay attention, so I think the problem is with his second grade classroom—it's too boring. Do you have a suggestion for how I can handle this?"

"Well, Eleanor, there may be another explanation for what's happening. It may not be the teacher's problem. As a parent," I said, "you, too, have probably noticed how hard it is to get your kid to pay attention to math homework, while he has no problem sticking with a video game for hours on end. This is explained by the way the brain pays attention. The brain is equipped with two attention systems. One, reactive attention, is located deep within the brain's emotional center, automatic, instinctive, and involuntary. When something moves or is very stimulating in our environment, we automatically react and focus our attention, very handy when our ancestors needed to watch out constantly for danger.

"The second system is called 'focused attention' and is located in a different part of the brain, called the prefrontal cortex or the executive center, right behind our forehead. We use the focused attention system when we *decide* to pay attention. Unlike reactive attention, this one is not automatic. Focused attention is only developed with a lot of practice. It's very important because we need focused attention to learn things that aren't naturally stimulating. For example, word rhyming, a second grade reading skill, is not particularly exciting, learned only by listening closely, paying attention to word endings, and practicing words."

Eleanor and her husband realized that their son's reactive attention was engaged with video games, while his classroom work needed focused attention.

The distinction between reactive and focused attention is important to keep in mind—really important when we listen to teachers talk about their struggles to keep kids' attention these days. We'll explore in chapter 4 the important relationships between attention and memory and learning. For now this one example illustrates how recent brain science discoveries can help parents, teachers, coaches, or anyone interested in kids do a better job of raising healthy, successful children in the 21st century.

Parenting and our children's amazing brains—that's the focus of this book. I'll explain what brain scientists have learned about children's brains from prenatal development through the teen years. Whether you're pregnant with your first child or trying to figure out why adolescents act the way they do, you'll find important information and practical advice. The emphasis throughout will be on science made practical. The chapters will include checklists, tool kits, sample dialogues, conversation starters, and lists of dos and don'ts.

Unlocking the Brain's Secrets

Consider a newborn's three-quarter-pound brain and the teenager's three-pound wonder: their brains control everything they do and who they are. As director of mundane but critical tasks like regulating body temperature and heart rate as well as higher functions like solving quadratic equations and falling in love, the brain works even when we're sound asleep. While it occupies only 2 percent of our body mass, the brain burns 20 percent of our body's energy. Only recently have we begun to discover how the brain really works or develops.

The brain is a particularly difficult organ to investigate. We can't easily observe it, so we have to try other methods to explain the activity inside our heads. For centuries scientists devised theories, based not on direct observation of a living brain, but indirectly, on how people acted.

Sigmund Freud, for example, developed a very elaborate theory of brain functions from the behaviors he observed. After Freud's ideas were published in the early 1900s, many others advanced their own pro- or anti-Freudian theories. Theories on the mind got so confused that mid-20th-century psychologist B. F. Skinner declared all these theories a waste of time. He called the brain the "black box" and claimed that behavior, not the mind, should be a scientist's focus because we could measure behavior directly.

At the time, Skinner, the "father of behaviorism," may have been right, but in the 1970s scientists invented machines including CT scans, MRIs, PET scans, and SPECT scans, that allowed researchers to peer inside the brain without harming it or its owner.

In the past forty years these machines have greatly improved and now provide high-resolution images, pulling back the curtain in front of the brain and enabling physicians to diagnose brain problems and dramatically improve treatment. We've also gained a wealth of information about the development and function of normal brains.

The new information about children and youth brain development is especially exciting. My book *Why Do They Act That Way? A Survival Guide to the Adolescent Brain for You and Your Teen* is entirely about how the teenage brain works. My previous book, *No. Why Kids—of All Ages—Need to Hear It and Ways Parents Can Say It,* pays special attention to the critical importance of self-discipline—how children learn to balance and manage the brain's hardwired drive to seek pleasure. The book you are now reading expands my inquiries into children's behavior to cover a wider range of brain-related topics.

We learn new brain secrets every day, and in the process even correct some mistaken beliefs. As recently as the mid-1990s, for example, students of the brain were taught that the only brain cells we will ever possess are the ones we are born with, that we never grow any more. Today, we know that isn't true. The 1998 discovery of adult neurogenesis, the birth of new brain cells later in life, overturned that long-held theory.

Brain Science Saves the Life of a Teenager

Our friends Austin and Pam, parents of fourteen-year-old Jacob, benefited from this new brain information. The surprise neuroscience lesson happened one night while we visited over coffee and dessert.

"How are the kids?" I asked, as my wife, Monica, and I sat talking with them.

"Jenny is fine but Jacob's driving us nuts," Austin replied. "It's almost like he's had a personality transplant. He's become more and more sullen, withdrawn, and grumpy. Our trip to Des Moines last week for my nephew's wedding was miserable. All Jacob wanted to do all weekend was to listen to his iPod. He was downright rude to half the relatives."

"Last night," added Pam, "I asked him to take the garbage out after dinner. You'd think I asked him to clean the entire house. Jacob rolled his eyes, sighed out loud, and mumbled about doing everything around the house. I bit my tongue because I didn't want to say something I would regret. He acts so annoyed whenever we ask him to do anything."

Having survived three teenagers ourselves we had a pretty good idea of what was going on with Jacob. "Welcome to adolescence," I tried, to lighten the mood a bit.

"Your kids were never like that," Pam said as she looked at Monica.

"That's just because you didn't see them at home," Monica replied. "Teenagers can be a little surly with adults, but they usually reserve the vintage collection for their own parents. I still remember all three kids' predictable response when I asked for help: 'Why do I have to do it?'"

"Parenting teens can be really difficult," I chimed in. "It helps to try not to take it personally. Realize that right now his feelings probably confuse him as much as you. The issue is not really you," I said. "It's what's going on in Jacob's brain."

"You mean hormones?" asked Pam.

"Hormones are only part of the picture," I explained. "There's a lot more going on in the teen brain than hormones. Brain science now tells us that adolescent brains are works in progress, a series of major construction zones. The changes going on inside their brains explain a lot of the moodiness, impulsivity, risk taking, and anger."

Our neighbors' response echoed that of many parents when they discover what brain science has learned about the teen brain. As Pam joked that night, "This little brain lesson might have saved the life of a fourteen-year-old. I was beginning to weigh a prison sentence against putting up with Jacob's surliness. So do we just put up with him until his brain finishes growing?"

"Well, yes and no," I responded. "Knowing what's going on in Jacob's brain can help us not take everything personally. On the other hand, we can't become doormats for disrespect. Cutting teenagers some slack doesn't mean a free pass for bad behavior. Adolescents need to learn accountability, too, and it's our job to teach them. It's a real balancing act." We'll explore more about the teen brain and how parents can strike that balance in chapter 10.

Brain Science 101

Austin and Pam had a ringside seat to one of the brain's many growth spurts. A few brain basics will help us understand these spurts. The brain is essentially a vast electrical system. Right now, as you read this book, your brain is generating enough electrical power to light a twenty-watt lightbulb. That familiar lightbulb-over-the-head cartoon image turns out to be accurate after all. The basic unit of this electrical system is the brain cell, or neuron. While brain cells come in different sizes and shapes, they share a common structure, including a cable or axon with branches at each end. One set of branches is called dendrites and the other synaptic buttons. Electrical charges enter the neuron through one branch, zip down the cable, and exit out a branch at the other end.

The number of brain cells is quite impressive. An infant arrives in the world with about 100 billion brain cells, each with an average of ten thousand branches. A quick calculation reveals that the possible number of contact points in a newborn baby's brain is one quadrillion. Trying to compute the possible number of match-ups with these quadrillion connections would stymie the most brilliant mathematician.

Consider this comparison. A piano has eighty-eight keys. How many possible songs or tunes can be composed with those eighty-eight keys in different combinations and sequences? Of course, the answer is "Who knows?" So if we can't figure out the potential number with eighty-eight keys can you imagine the possibilities with one quadrillion? The late Nobel laureate Francis Crick, one of the co-discoverers of DNA, once said that the possible number of neural network configurations in one brain exceeds the number of atoms in the universe. The possibilities are limitless.

When a baby arrives in the world, however, only 17 percent of her brain cells are wired together. That leaves the rest—the vast majority—to connect in the days, weeks, months, years, and decades that follow. Two forces drive the wiring: genetics and experience. I like to think of genetics as the hard wiring and experience the soft wiring.

How a baby learns language provides a good example of the combination of hard wiring and soft wiring in action. As new parents know, their bundle of joy arrives perfectly capable of making noise. Vocalizing is hardwired. However, which of the world's 6,500 languages a baby will eventually speak is not hardwired. Her language is shaped by her experiences, that is, the sounds she hears. (A whole chapter on how she acquires language follows later in this book.)

A child's experiences are a key factor in how her brain gets wired. Neuroscientists have a phrase to underline the importance of experience in brain wiring: *the neurons that fire together wire together.* The more often neurons fire together, the stronger the connection becomes. Or as University of California, Los Angeles neuroscientist Jeffrey Schwartz puts it, "the survival of the busiest." An elementary grade teacher drilling her students on basic math facts is an everyday example of this important brain principle in action. After a pupil repeats that 3 plus 2 equals 5 often enough the connection is made, and that fact becomes fixed in memory for easy retrieval.

I was explaining brain basics to a group of third graders at the Park Tudor School in Indianapolis recently and asked one little girl what her favorite sport was. "Tennis" was her immediate reply. "That's a great example," I said. "Tell me," I continued, "what was it like when you first tried to play tennis?"

"I could barely hold the racket," she said, smiling. "And I couldn't even hit the ball."

"Well, now that you're in the third grade, how is your tennis game?" I asked.

"My dad says I'm getting pretty good," she answered.

"How did you get from not being able to hold the racket to being pretty good?"

"I practiced."

This little girl is a brilliant neuroscientist, because when we "practice," the scientific principle "the neurons that fire together wire together" goes into action. Here's my rule: *Whatever the brain does a lot of is what the brain gets good at.* That's true whether we're talking about studying math, playing the trumpet, or working on our tennis game.

Mental Experience Counts, Too

The brain isn't just shaped by our actions. Even thinking wires the brain. When Alvaro Pascual-Leone was a scientist at the National Institutes of Health, he invited people who had never played the piano to be part of an experiment. After teaching them all how to play a simple tune, he randomly assigned them to two groups. The first group kept practicing the tune for two more hours. The second group just imagined playing the piece without so much as laying a finger on a keyboard. He mapped the brain activity of both groups before, during, and after the experiment and amazingly, the ones who had imagined playing the tune exhibited the same brain changes as those who had actually played. A pianist still needs to practice, but thinking had rewired their brains. When world-class athletes imagine their performance before the competition starts, they aren't just concentrating. The neurological starting gun has already fired.

The Brain's Growth Spurts

However, all experiences aren't equal in wiring the brain. Some experiences are more important than others. Experiences with the greatest impact on brain wiring are those that happen during a brain's growth spurts. "What's a brain growth spurt?" you might wonder. Well, we know that our billions of brain cells wire together into circuits. We don't know our total number of circuits, but we do know they develop in spurts at different times and speeds. While some spring to life, others are less active.

University of California, Berkeley neuroscientist Marian Diamond describes exactly what happens during a brain circuit's growth spurt. A hardwired trigger sends the neurons' branches, the dendrites, into a frenzy of growth. At the same time, experience swings into action. The branches that fire together connect while those that don't fire eventually wither back and die like neglected, unwatered flowers in a garden. Scientists call the hypergrowth "blossoming" for obvious reasons, and they call the withering process "pruning."

What's doing the pruning is, of course, experience. Our experiences during a brain's growth spurt affect the brain's wiring more than at any other time during our life. The two nicknames "window of opportunity" and "window of sensitivity" highlight this importance, as a child's brain's greatest potential as well as its greatest vulnerability lies during these critical growth spurts. For example, the Japanese language doesn't have the same "l" sound that we have in English, so young children learning Japanese don't hear the "l" sound as we speak it in English. They don't have a circuit wired to recognize or vocalize our "l" sound, and the circuit that does fire sounds like our "r" sound—so, when learning English, they might say that they pray, rather than play, video games.

Glial Cells

Although I will use the terms *brain cell* and *neuron* interchangeably throughout this book, neurons actually only make up about 10 percent of the cells in the brain. The other 90 percent are called glial cells, which comes from the Greek word for glue. We are only beginning to appreciate their roles. Until recently, scientists thought that glial cells did nothing more than provide structural support and a transportation route for raw materials and waste products for their more important neural neighbors. That thinking is beginning to change as glial cells' role in the production of neurotransmitters, the chemicals that fills the gaps between neural branches, becomes clearer. I wouldn't be surprised if further research reveals that glial cells are much more than supporting actors.

The Brain's Chemistry Set

Neurotransmitters are one of two important groups of chemicals—the other is hormones—that play roles in how the brain works. My friend Pam mentioned hormones earlier when she was describing her adolescent son Jacob. Our body produces more than sixty of them in glands located throughout the body. Their job is to bring messages to various organs both inside and outside the brain. The technical name for the hormone system is endocrine, and since the brain is the master control center the entire network is often referred to as the neuroendocrine system.

Here is an example of the neuroendocrine system at work. You're walking down the street when a huge snarling dog leaps a fence and races toward you with teeth bared. Nerve impulses from your eyes travel to your brain, and your brain immediately gets to work alerting the body to the danger. It instantaneously sends signals to the adrenal glands located way down by your kidneys, and these glands begin pumping out the well-known hormone adrenaline. The surge of adrenaline courses throughout your body increasing your heart rate and blood pressure and sending massive supplies of glucose to your muscles. This adrenaline rush is the classic "fight-or-flight" response, an inborn survival instinct. Seconds later the dog's owner yells his name. The dog immediately screeches to a halt, reverses direction, and retreats back over the fence. Your cortex realizes the danger has passed, but because of the survival instinct unleashed by adrenaline, it may take a couple of minutes for your body to return to normal. Even though it turned out to be nothing, your neuroendocrine system has used hormones to ensure your survival. And it all happened in a fraction of a second.

The most commonly known hormones besides adrenaline are testosterone and estrogen. At last count scientists have identified sixty-seven hormones, and they are essential to everyday life. Part of the brain, the hypothalamus, serves as the master control for the endocrine system, telling the glands when to ramp up production of hormones and which ones the body needs. We'll discuss hormones' roles in later chapters.

The second group of brain chemicals, the neurotransmitters, is located in a microscopic gap left between the branches of two connecting neurons—also known as a synapse, the Greek word for gap. There is a stew of more than one hundred different chemicals, collectively known as neurotransmitters, swimming around in the synapse. They bear this name because their job is to transmit the electrical charge across the gap. They also bear the nickname "molecules of emotion" because they play such critical roles in our emotional life. I'll explain the roles of different neurotransmitters like dopamine and serotonin as we encounter them.

Brain Growth Throughout Life

My friend Al Peichel is ninety-five years old. Among his many interests are card games. A visit is never complete without a match of nickel poker or gin rummy. I learned long ago that I'd better pay close attention if I ever wanted to win a game. His mind is quicker, more agile, and more engaged than those of people half his age. I've learned to call ahead before dropping in for a visit because, likely as not, Al would be out or busy with his many social, service, and volunteer commitments.

Al Peichel is a living example of another brain principle: "use it or lose it." While hardwired growth spurts are completed in the mid-twenties, the brain doesn't grind to a halt once the blossoming and pruning are over. Brain cell branches continue to sprout the more we use them. Even though this book focuses on kids' developing brains, adults can be encouraged by the fact that, the more we use the three-pound marvel on top of our shoulders, the healthier, sharper, and happier we will be—even into our nineties like my friend Al. That's why renowned Swedish neuroscientist Torkel Klingberg says, "Our brain maps are forever being redrawn."

It's Not All Experience

Michael and Nancy have nine-year-old fraternal twin sons. Although the boys, together since conception, share a bedroom, are raised in the same way, attend the same school, and eat the same food, they couldn't be more different from one another. "It never ceases to amaze me," said Nancy during a recent conversation. "Kevin is outgoing, adventurous, sports loving, and loud. Paul is a quiet introvert who prefers a book to a football game on TV."

I've highlighted the importance of experience in brain development, but Kevin and Paul remind us that hardwiring is a big part of the equation as well. Temperament and many personality traits are hardwired, and a growing body of evidence shows additional traits that are innate and not the result of experience. Take Tommy, for example.

Sheila, a single mother, struggles to cope with seven-year-old Tommy. Within minutes of our first counseling session together it was clear she had her hands full. "I'm exhausted," Sheila sighed after reciting the litany of issues Tommy presented and listing all the parenting books she'd read and seminars she'd attended to learn about "spirited children." "I spend ten times more energy handling Tommy than I do with his older brother and sister combined," Sheila said.

After two sessions with Tommy and reviewing reports from his teacher and school social worker, I had a good idea of what to recommend to Sheila at our next session.

"After talking with him and reading the reports from his school I think that Tommy may have an attention deficit hyperactive brain. A lot of experts call this attention deficit hyperactivity disorder or ADHD. However, I don't like the word *disorder* because it suggests Tommy has a defective brain. The latest brain research shows that kids like Tommy have a brain that's wired a little differently, but it's not a bad brain. In fact, some very successful people had brains just like Tommy's, including Abraham Lincoln, John Kennedy, Winston Churchill, and Albert Einstein."

"What makes you think Tommy has ADHD?" Sheila asked.

I looked at the page of notes I wrote before Sheila arrived. "Well, I see Tommy is very bright but impulsive. He has trouble sitting still, is impatient, easily frustrated, and frequently forgets or loses things. His teacher wrote that he often interrupts other students, is easily distracted, and has a lot of trouble paying attention. You also told me in our first session that Tommy was like this long before he got to school," I asked.

"Absolutely. He came home from the hospital that way," Sheila remembered. "So what should I do?"

"I'm not an expert in ADHD," I responded, "but I know someone who is. I'd like you and Tommy to visit her and see what she thinks. If I'm right, she can help you with some specific strategies and possibly prescribe a medication that will help."

Tommy's problems didn't mean Sheila wasn't a good parent. "Your son is very lucky to have you as a mom," I told her. "You've turned yourself inside out to be as good a parent as possible. Tommy was born with a brain that's a little different. Once he learns how to manage it he might end up with some real advantages over other kids."

Practical Brain Science

The purpose of this book isn't just to describe new scientific findings or to explain interesting brain facts. My goal is to equip you with solid scientific information, over a range of topics, like exercise, nutrition, play, sleep, emotional intelligence, connection; information you can use in the most important job in the world: raising kids. Some discoveries in neuroscience confirm thousand-year-old parental wisdom while other discoveries will prompt us to make some changes tomorrow. Still other brain information helps explain behaviors that have puzzled parents forever, such as why friendly, easygoing kids like Jacob can turn into withdrawn, sullen, fire-breathing dragons overnight when they enter adolescence.

I will also separate sound science from urban myths. Brain science has spawned an entire industry of "brain products and programs" aimed at anxious parents. Some are good while others are modern-day snake oil.

Parent Tool Kits and Dos and Don'ts

I've included two items in each chapter to help you use the new scientific information: Parent Tool Kits and lists of Do and Don'ts. The Parent Tool Kits are sets of questions about knowledge, attitudes, and tips you need to parent with the brain in mind. The more you answer "yes" the better equipped you'll be. When you don't answer "yes" very often, you'll find information in the chapter that will help you get to yes. Here's a short sample set of questions to give you an idea of how the Parent Tool Kits work. Of course, the kits in the following chapters will be longer and more specific.

PARENT TOOL KIT

Parenting with the Brain in Mind

Yes No

☐ ☐ 1. I believe that scientific information can help me be a better parent.

☐ ☐ 2. I keep up with new information about children's brain development.

☐ ☐ 3. I'm open to new ideas to help me be a better-informed parent.

☐ ☐ 4. Raising kids is the most important job in the world.

You'll also find a list of Dos and Don'ts at the end of each chapter. These are suggestions—good starting points. Following the lists you'll find a place to write down the things you want to continue and the things you want to change. The result will be your personal plan to nurture your child's intelligence.

DO

- ✓ Talk with your spouse, partner, or as a single parent develop an agreed-upon list of desirable traits, qualities, and behaviors that you want your children to have.
- ✓ Learn as much as you can about your child's brain development to gain realistic expectations of your child's behavior.
- ✓ Relax. Parents have been doing a great job raising kids for many thousands of years.
- ✓ Get support from relatives and friends. Parenting is hard work.
- ✓ Remember that raising kids can be a delayed-gratification activity. The rewards we get along the way are bonuses. The real payoff comes when our kids turn out to be the kind of adults we can be proud of.

DON'T

- ✗ Don't get taken in by every product or program that guarantees to turn your child into a genius.

- ✗ Don't lose your sense of humor. Raising kids is too serious a responsibility to be taken too seriously.
- ✗ Don't be too hard on yourself. All of us parents have times when we look back and wish we had handled a situation differently. Kids are resilient.

What do I want to continue?

____

____

____

What do I want to change?

____

____

____

TWO

How to Raise Your Child's IQ

Just as all children in Garrison Keillor's mythical Minnesota town, Lake Wobegon, are "above average," we all hope that our children will reach the bell curve's upper limits, especially for intelligence, whether we say it aloud or not. It's no surprise that when I ask parents to imagine their children in the future, words like *smart* and *bright* inevitably make the list.

Many of my readers are anxious to learn if the secrets of brain science will guarantee smarter kids. You will happily discover that we have found the keys to intelligence, and *you* can have a major impact.

FAE—the Fundamental Attribution Error

Let's start to unwind what intelligence means. I think you can easily answer these three questions:

Question 1. Why is Bill Gates so wealthy?
Question 2. Why were the Beatles so successful?
Question 3. Why do kids in Asian countries often outperform American kids in mathematics?

If you're like most people, you probably answered something like this: "Bill Gates is a genius who figured out how to translate his natural talent into a profitable business." "The Beatles were incredibly gifted musicians." Or "People from Asia must have a genetic advantage for math."

We all know that extraordinary natural talent is required for amazing accomplishments, right?

The problem is that all these conclusions are wrong. Why? We all tend to overvalue innate, inherited traits and undervalue external causes when we consider behaviors or accomplishments. Psychologists call this the "fundamental attribution error," or FAE for short. We assume, for example, that a woman who sits in the front church pew every Sunday must be a very religious and spiritual person. We know her boss is a deeply involved congregation elder, but we see her behavior and conclude that she must be a deeply religious person—we don't consider that she may simply be attempting to curry favor. Our strong predisposition assumes that innate or inborn traits explain the behavior we see. We're surprised, or even shocked, when we are wrong.

Outliers

Malcolm Gladwell doesn't use the term *fundamental attribution error,* but he describes this phenomenon in his bestseller *Outliers.* He fills in important—but little-known—details behind the success of Bill Gates, the Beatles, and Asian students. Extraordinarily successful people do possess underlying talent. However, we tend to *overestimate* talent's contribution to achievement while we simultaneously *underestimate* the role of luck and effort.

No doubt Bill Gates possesses plenty of talent and ambition. However, there are many people with those two traits. A series of fortunate circumstances enabled Gates to capitalize on his inherited gifts. When he was a youngster in Seattle, Bill's parents enrolled him at a private school, Lakeside, at the same time that the school's Mothers' Club decided to buy equipment for a brand-new club just getting off the ground. The year was 1968 and the new extracurricular activity was a computer club. Few people had even heard the word *computer* in those days, and there probably wasn't another elementary school in the world with a computer club!

Bill's luck continued. A couple of start-up Seattle companies offered the Lakeside kids free programming time if they would test their software. On top of that the young Gates could walk from home to the University of Washington, where he could "steal" computer time late at night when no one was around. Then in his senior year Bill talked his Lakeside teachers into letting him do an independent study project writing code for the technology company TRW, where a brilliant programmer named John Norton took Bill under his wing. So by the time he graduated from high school Bill Gates had benefited from a string of coincidences that provided more time and exposure to computers, programming, and coding than perhaps any other teenager had in the world.

Good luck, however, is not the whole story behind Bill Gates's success. He took advantage of all these unusual opportunities and, more important for our discussion, put enormous *effort* into honing his skills. Sure, he could walk to the University of Washington physics lab to use the computer, but how many teenagers would "steal" computer time between 3 and 6 A.M. night after night? When he was fifteen years old he ran up 1,575 hours of computer time in a seven-month period. That's eight hours a day, seven days a week. People make a lot of the fact that Gates dropped out of college to start Microsoft, as evidence of his inborn genius. They overlook the fact that by the time he quit Harvard he had already been programming nonstop for over seven years.

The story of the Beatles is similar. The four Liverpool, England, lads took the musical world by storm in 1964. Few people know that they'd played together for seven years in a Hamburg, Germany, nightclub that required them to perform as many as eight hours straight, seven days a week. To fill all those hours the Beatles improvised and fashioned a whole new musical sound. By all accounts, they were an ordinary struggling rock band in 1957, but unusual circumstances forced them to play hour after hour, honing their skills and developing their signature style. Actually, no one coerced them to play for thousands of hours. Most other groups would have quit under those working conditions. But the real secret to their success mirrors the founder of Microsoft: hard work.

Thomas Edison, dubbed the "Wizard of Menlo Park," streamed an amazing string of inventions out of his laboratory. Edison himself, however, knew he was no wizard, as his inventions required hard work and many ended in failure. He wasn't joking when he famously said, "Genius is one percent inspiration, ninety-nine percent perspiration."

Many Asian-descent students perform well above average in mathematics. The key to their success is *effort*, just as it was for Bill Gates and the Beatles. I saw that effort firsthand when Thuy Nguyen, a thin, quiet girl who arrived with her family as refugees from Vietnam, enrolled in the high school where I was the counselor. She sought me out to talk about war trauma and her family's escape and for help with the cultural challenges of fitting into a new school where the only other Vietnamese students were her two brothers. Fortunately Thuy spoke good English, and before long she was at the head of her class, getting straight A's. "Thuy is such a brain," her classmates said, but they didn't appreciate that besides being smart, she worked hard. She never walked away from a class confused. She either waited politely to ask a clarifying question or made an after-school appointment if she was really lost.

Thuy always looked for suggestions to improve her writing and felt comfortable from our counseling sessions to stop by my office before classes to ask if I had time to look over an English or social studies paper. When Monica and I visited her parents' popular restaurant, Thuy was always there waiting on tables, clearing dishes, or helping out at the counter. She graduated with honors, received a scholarship to the University of Minnesota, and has a successful career in medicine. I had the good fortune to teach, coach, and counsel many wonderful young people during my high school counseling career, but I can't think of anyone who worked harder than Thuy.

PARENT TOOL KIT

Raising Smart Kids

If there is one thing that we all associate with our brains, it's intelligence. We even call smart people "brains." Use these questions to test your knowledge about what contributes to raising smart kids.

Yes No

☐ ☐ 1. I understand that effort is as important as genes in determining IQ.

☐ ☐ 2. I realize that the way I praise my children has an impact on their IQ.

☐ ☐ 3. I know that talking to my child and including them in adult conversations is important.

☐ ☐ 4. I realize how important it is to steer my child to stimulating after-school activities.

☐ ☐ 5. I know how important physical exercise is for intelligence.

☐ ☐ 6. I realize it is more important for my child to wrestle with challenging classes than to just get good grades.

☐ ☐ 7. I know how important memory and attention are.

☐ ☐ 8. I know self-discipline is even more important than IQ when it comes to success.

☐ ☐ 9. I understand that teachers and schools do make a difference.

☐ ☐ 10. I try to avoid telling my children how smart they are.

The more yes answers to the questions in this tool kit, the more likely you are to foster intelligence in your children.

What Is Intelligence?

Since intelligence is so important, you would think we could explain it exactly. It turns out there are almost as many definitions of intelligence as there are experts. Some include capacities like creativity and empathy while others leave those traits off the list. Harvard psychologist Howard Gardner believes that our traditional notions of intelligence are too narrow and so he has proposed a theory of multiple intelligences, which include linguistic, logic-mathematical, musical, spatial, bodily kinesthetic, interpersonal, and intrapersonal abilities. In his bestseller, *Emotional Intelligence*, Daniel Goleman also makes a convincing case that emotional intelligence is more important than what we measure with IQ tests. Gardner, Goleman, and others know there are many ways to "be smart." Indeed we all know people who aren't necessarily "school smart" but who have more common sense than university professors with half the alphabet after their names.

Sidestepping this never-ending argument, almost all experts agree that *intelligence* is an umbrella term for:

- The ability to acquire and retain information,
- The ability to apply that information to different situations (i.e. solve problems),
- The ability to reason abstractly, and
- The ability to do these things with reasonable speed.

Traditionally, we measure intelligence with a variety of tests, mostly to produce an IQ score. The *Q* in *IQ* stands for quotient because in the early days of intelligence testing we divided a child's mental age by his chronological age. Today statisticians set the average score at 100 with scores between 90 and 109 considered normal. People with IQ scores between 110 and 119 are deemed bright and those with scores above 120 very bright. On the other end of the spectrum, those whose scores fall between 80 and 89 are scored dull and below 80 very dull. Although, as far as we know, Albert Einstein never took an IQ test, scientists have estimated his IQ to be somewhat north of 160.

Is Intelligence Important?

I was a high school counselor before the era of mass testing began. Even in those days, though, we administered the California Achievement Test every year to see how our students stacked up against the national averages for different grade levels. In addition, most juniors and seniors took the Scholastic

Aptitude Test (SAT), the test from the American College Testing Program (ACT), or both. It was not unusual for parents to ask me if these were IQ tests—and after I explained that they weren't, some inquired if I could give their kids an IQ test. Although trained to administer these tests, I never used them in my counseling and was struck by parents' interest in them.

Something about numbers fascinates us. We love them and track all sorts of statistics from pedometer readings to sports statistics to weather data. IQ scores, in particular, get our attention because they not only give us a measure of intelligence but also are predictive of important future outcomes. Even though there are too many life variables at play to prove a direct causal link, IQ scores measure something that predicts potential academic success, future income, occupational achievement, and social class. No wonder parents are interested. There's a lot at stake.

Hard Wired or Soft Wired?

What is the connection between genetics and intelligence and academic success? This is my own personal testimony to the fact that intelligence is not all hardwired.

I believed for a long time that "my brain is just not built to do math." Upon reflection, however, I started to doubt my own conclusion. After all, both my parents were good at math. My older sister, Joan, had a successful career as an anaesthetist so she was good at math and science. My older brother, Philip, is an engineer, and my "little" brother Kevin taught graduate-level statistics for years. Where was I when they dispensed the math neurons?

Eventually, I realized a series of unfortunate experiences had derailed my mathematical development. It started in eighth grade when my class spent the entire day with one teacher, who must have had a math phobia. We spent a lot of time on reading, writing, spelling, geography, and history, but we didn't go near math or science.

When I entered high school the next year, like every other freshman I had to enroll in algebra. The teacher we were supposed to have disappeared from the scene and at the last minute the administrators recruited a man in his eighties to come out of retirement to teach the class. Poor Mr. Leary was hard of hearing and quite infirm so it was all he could do to keep a room full of testosterone-hyped fourteen-year-olds from tearing apart the classroom. Suffice it to say, my classmates and I didn't learn any algebra.

I entered tenth grade without having had decent math instruction for two years, and I knew I was in trouble the first day with Father Oliver, whose pedagogical approach was based on fear and intimidation. Every day he strode into the room, pushed a chair to his favorite spot in the corner, and then ordered a student up to the board. He called on us at random, one at a time, so you never knew when your moment of reckoning would arrive, and we all quaked in our chairs afraid we would be that day's target for ridicule and put-downs.

After the public humiliation segment of the class, Father Oliver would quickly explain that day's lesson while scribbling rapidly on the board. Upon finishing he would turn to the class and toss the chalk at anyone who looked bored. "Any questions?" he asked without waiting for an answer. "No? Good. For your homework, do all the problems on pages such-and-such." We were too terrified to ask questions. Our only hope was that someone had figured out what was going on and could fill in the blanks for the rest of us after class.

This class routine continued for the rest of the year. Then came my junior year and you'll never guess who I had for Algebra II. Father Oliver for another year of shock and awe!

You might wonder why I couldn't see that my math problems had very little to do with innate traits and more to do with a two-year hiatus followed by two years of math terrorism. The answer is that I, like many others, believed the experts who preached that intelligence and specific cognitive skills were genetically determined and hardwired. I made the same "fundamental attribution error."

Judith Harris published a bestselling book in 1998, *The Nurture Assumption: Why Children Turn Out the Way They Do*, trumpeting the importance of genetics. Her popular book reinforced the notion that family experiences played a distant second, third, or even fourth fiddle to DNA. Although Harris popularized this view she was backed up by many scholars who believed that as much as 85 percent of intelligence was determined by our genes. Today, however, as we learn more about how the brain is designed to interact with the world, we have a much better appreciation for the role of experience. University of Michigan psychologist Richard Nisbett conducted an exhaustive review of current research and concluded that less than 50 percent of our intelligence is inherited.

The new research should not really surprise us, since we have instinctively acknowledged the role of experience for thousands of years. Many readers will recall the New Testament parable of the sower who scattered seeds on a path, on rocky ground, among thorns, and on good soil. The hundredfold difference in the yield from the seeds planted in good soil is consistent with our intuitive sense that environment makes a big difference. There is also abundant evidence about the impact of environment on all sorts of traits that have genetic components. For example, improved nutrition added seven inches to the average height of Korean boys in just forty years. More germane than height to our interest, French scientists conducted a convincing study on how experience affects intelligence. They tracked down sets of twins who were raised separately and found that siblings adopted and raised in more advantaged environments had IQ scores twelve to sixteen points higher than their unadopted twin siblings.

If intelligence really were 85 percent inherited, I would end this chapter right now, since the genetic roll of the dice is beyond our control. But we now understand more than ever about young, developing brains and how experience plays a major role in wiring. Before we consider the factors that do foster intelligence, however, I'd like to issue a cautionary warning about the things that don't.

Beware of Quick Fixes

It all started innocently enough with some fascinating research. University of California, Irvine neuroscientists Frances Rauscher, Gordon Shaw, and Katherine Ky found that college students performed better on spatial reasoning tasks after listening to one of Mozart's sonatas. The media got hold of the findings and quickly trumpeted, "Listening to Mozart makes you smarter." Not long afterward guarantees floated that any classical music would boost IQ. In 1998 Georgia governor Zell Miller asked the legislature to approve funds so that every new parent in Georgia left the hospital with a classical music CD. After playing a short Beethoven piece he asked the assembled lawmakers, "Now don't you feel smarter already?"

Parents trying to enhance the intelligence of their young children were quickly barraged with advertisements for CDs, DVDs, music boxes, toy pianos, and music cubes. What almost everyone ignored was that the Rauscher, Shaw, and Ky research was done with college students, not children, and the improvement was on specialized spatial tasks, not overall intelligence. Even more importantly, the improvement vanished within fifteen minutes.

We nonetheless saw the growth of lines of merchandise such as Baby Einstein and Brainy Baby, whose names implied that the products might impart brain developmental advantages. After all, what parents wouldn't want their baby to grow up with a brain like Einstein's? And doesn't the name Brainy Baby say it all?

Brain science provides exciting insights, but no one should make any assumptions based on product names or any marketing that might suggest a particular thingamabob boosts intelligence. Do some research to see if there's any truth to your assumptions or to any marketing claims that may be made by a company.

Effort and Intelligence

Talent plus luck plus hard work is the recipe for exceptional success. While we parents can't control the confluence of circumstances we call luck, we can teach our kids how important effort is and motivate them to work hard. That's the secret behind the performance of Asian students on international math tests.

In 1983 most Americans were confident that we had the best schools and the smartest students in the world. That all changed when the secretary of education at the time, Terrel Bell, examined a study comparing American students with their peers in other countries. He was shocked to find out American students had finished dead last on seven different international tests in the previous decade. He was so concerned that he called the report *A Nation at Risk*. That report was an alarm bell calling Americans to wake up from their complacency before it was too late. Concern about the academic performance of American children relative to their foreign peers has grown stronger ever since.

Currently, there are two widely used international tests that compare countries. The PIRLS, or Progress in International Reading Literacy Study, is the test that measures reading and language skills. TIMSS, in full the Trends in International Mathematics and Science Study, evaluates performance in math and science. Every four years the fourth and eighth graders from more than forty countries take TIMSS. And every four years students from Asian countries come out on top. Interestingly, before the students actually look at the questions or puzzle over the problems they need to answer 120 survey questions that collect data on everything from their attitudes toward school to family demographic information. As you can imagine, many students get tired answering question after question, so many give up before completing the survey. University of Pennsylvania professors Erling Boe, Henry May, and Robert Boruch wondered if there was a relationship between the number of background questions that students from different nations answered and how they performed on the test itself. The results of their study were amazing. They found that when they ordered the countries according to the number of background questions the students answered, the order matched the test results. In other words, why give the test? All we have to do is ask students from different countries to complete a long survey. The effort and persistence required to finish the survey is a reliable proxy for the test results themselves.

To put it another way, it takes a lot of effort to get smart. As I was reading the Boe, May, and Boruch study, I couldn't help but remember how hard my Vietnamese student Thuy worked.

Praise—a Double-Edged Sword

A twenty-eight-year-old man named Keith sought my help to understand and tame the fear and apprehension that crippled him. "I'm in graduate school, and I'll bet that half my professors can't fathom how I was admitted since I'm too scared to ever say anything in class. I dropped a course last semester as soon as I read on the syllabus that half the grade would be based on class participation. I can write a great paper, but I dread being called on in class."

Keith shared an insight as we began one of our sessions. "The last time we met," he said, "you asked me if I had any idea where the fear came from. I thought about that question, and a memory from the second grade popped into my mind.

"I still recall the day my second grade teacher called me into the hallway. I had taken a test the day before to see if I would qualify for the school's gifted and talented program. When Mrs. Lincoln asked me how I thought I had done I told her that the test was fun and not that hard. She smiled when she heard me say that. 'Well, Keith,' I remember her saying, 'I can see why you enjoyed it. Last night I scored the test. You got the highest score I've ever seen. You are really smart.'

"Dr. Dave," Keith continued, "I remember as if it were yesterday that I didn't know what to say. I recall fidgeting, looking away, and waiting for her to tell me I could go back into the classroom. She probably thought I was embarrassed by the compliment. I wasn't embarrassed. I was terrified."

"Do you have any idea why Mrs. Lincoln's compliment scared you, Keith?" I asked.

His answer was instant and adamant. "I didn't want to be the smartest kid in the school! I didn't want that pressure."

"So her statement that you scored higher than anyone else became your burden?"

"Exactly," Keith said as his own reaction sank in.

"Is this the first time you heard that you were very intelligent?" I asked.

"Oh, heck no, I heard it all the time. My parents, my grandparents, even my nursery school teacher told me how smart I was. But this second grade episode stands out because I remember it so clearly. Maybe I'm weird. Maybe I should have been happy. But I wasn't. I still remember how scared I was."

"So, Keith, how does this help you understand the fears that keep tripping you up?"

Keith thought for a long minute. "See if this makes sense. I've always *known* that I'm smart but also have always been *afraid* that it's not really true. Case in point: in high school I refused to take AP classes even though my parents and teachers all wanted me to. I never told anybody the real reason was that I was afraid. I just came up with really lame excuses hoping they'd get off my back."

"Did your excuses work?" I asked.

"Well, if you look at my high school transcript, you won't see any AP classes," Keith replied. "My parents and teachers thought I was 'unmotivated.' I told myself that, too. Now I realize I wasn't unmotivated. I was scared. If I avoided really tough classes I avoided my fear of failing."

To make sure he was connecting the dots I asked, "What was so scary about failing, Keith?"

He hit the nail on the head. "It would mean that I wasn't really smart after all. Why would I risk that if I didn't have to?"

"So being smart was important to you after all," I offered.

"Absolutely," Keith replied. "So important that I didn't want to risk losing it."

Keith wondered if this meant he was weird. The answer is no—there are millions of people just like Keith, people who were actually hurt by the praise they received. Unfortunately it has taken us a long time to figure out that *how* we praise kids is very important. Some kinds of praise are helpful to kids while others are not.

The New Way to Look at Praise

I began my high school teaching career the same year Nathaniel Branden's book *The Psychology of Self-Esteem* hit the bestseller lists. Although the concept of self-esteem dated to the 19th century, Branden's book popularized and launched what became known as the self-esteem movement. As it gathered steam in the 1970s and '80s, psychological theory morphed into a cultural movement equating self-esteem with feeling good. As it spread, millions were told the key to success and happiness was "feeling good about yourself."

I had an interesting conversation not long ago with a Scandinavian educator. "I've always been puzzled by how you Americans go out of your way to tell children how special and unique they are," she told me. "In Scandinavia we have a tradition called Jante's law. Some of the 'laws' are 'Don't think that you are special' and 'Don't think that you are smarter than others.' We teach these laws to children and they don't seem to have any self-esteem problems."

Unfortunately, I along with millions of other teachers and parents had never heard of Jante's law. We believed it was our job to make sure kids felt good about themselves. One obvious way to accomplish this was to heap generous helpings of praise upon them and their every accomplishment. Before long we were praising kids regardless of their performance. We all did this, of course, with the best of intentions, not knowing that we weren't doing them or their self-esteem any favors.

It turns out praise is very tricky. Some forms of praise are helpful while others aren't. An experiment by psychologists Claudia Mueller and Carol Dweck illustrated the difference in a very striking way. They gave a group of children a task that almost all the students successfully completed. Then they randomly assigned the kids to two groups. They told the first group that they were really smart for being successful in the task. They told the second group the reason for their success was that they had worked so hard. Both groups were then told that in round two they could choose between two more tasks. They described one task as very difficult and the second as easy, reminding the kids that they could choose either one. The children who were praised for being smart were much more likely to opt for the easy task while the "hard workers" were more likely to go for the difficult one.

How can we explain this? Like my client Keith, the kids who were praised for being smart didn't want to risk that identity by tackling a problem they perceived as difficult. After all, if they attempted and failed the hard one, it would mean that they weren't so smart after all. On the other hand, by choosing the easy way out they could keep their smart identity intact.

This experiment highlights a growing field of research on praise and motivation that points to three unintended consequences of praise:

First: Praise for an innate ability can lead to risk-avoidance. Keith gravitated to situations involving little risk of failure. Carol Dweck's research shows that Keith's reaction is the norm, not the exception.

Second: Insincere praise leads to doubts about competence. That's what happened to a young client, Hilary. Her parents never missed an opportunity to shower her with praise while she grew up as an only child. They constantly told her how smart she was, what a good athlete she was, what a marvelous dancer she was, and how gifted she was at whatever activity she tried. Like millions of parents infected by the misguided self-esteem virus, her parents believed they were instilling confidence and setting their child up for success. It's hard to definitely say whether it was her parents' overprotection, the insincere praise, or other factors, but Hilary struggled with self-doubt throughout her childhood and teen years and is an example of what the research says about children who receive undeserved praise. She grew very dependent on her parents and lived with them during her college years. She has since moved into her own apartment but still visits and talks with her parents several times each day.

Children as young as seven years old can figure out if praise is warranted or not. When they don't merit praise kids eventually come to two conclusions. First of all, they start to doubt the praise and mistrust the source. We can almost hear them saying, "I can't believe my parents because they applaud me for everything." Second, they begin to doubt their own competence. They begin to think, "I must really be bad if they think *this* is so great."

Praise Addicts

Third: Constant praise decreases persistence and encourages the child to constantly ask questions to check if he's okay.

Zachary's mom was a lot like Hilary's parents. She was a single parent and, try as she might, she was unable to persuade her ex-husband to take an active interest in their son after her ex moved to another state. She wanted Zack to be strong and confident, so, with the best of intentions, she overcompensated for an absent father by praising her son for everything he did. If he brought home a picture, drawn at his daycare center, his mother would exclaim, "Zachary, I never knew you were such a wonderful artist," as she taped the picture to the refrigerator. On the way home from a T-ball game in which five-year-old Zack had hit the ball out of the infield she marveled at his athletic ability. "You are one heck of a ballplayer, my little man," she told him. When he started school, she made sure that all of his teachers heard how gifted he was.

The constant stream of affirmations, however, did not instill confidence. Zachary grew more hesitant, often checking for verbal or nonverbal feedback from his mother and other adults. The phrase "Right?" became a standard feature in his conversation as he searched for approval. He was disappointed if his teachers didn't tell him how wonderful his projects or test results were.

It seemed he was addicted to praise. He constantly sought it and became anxious if he didn't get it.

Zachary has a lot of company. *Wall Street Journal* senior columnist Jeffrey Zaslow wrote about the impact that the millions of Zacharys have had on the workplace as they arrive needing constant feedback. "Bosses, professors, and mates are feeling the need to lavish praise on young adults, particularly twenty-somethings, or else see them wither under an unfamiliar compliment deficit. Employers are dishing out kudos for little more than showing up," Zaslow claims. In addition to the thirst for accolades and praise, many young adults from what Zaslow calls the "Praised Generation" have a very difficult time handling negative feedback. Unless we're perfect—and none of us is—we need constructive criticism to grow and improve. That was a lesson that Randy Pausch, author of *The Last Lecture*, wanted *his* children to learn when he told them, "When you see yourself doing something badly and nobody's bothering to tell you anymore, that's a very bad place to be. Your critics are the ones telling you they still love you and care."

Tips for Helpful Praise

So, it turns out that praise is tricky. We all want to reinforce our kids in ways that are helpful. Try these four research-based tips to praise kids in ways that will encourage their effort and success while avoiding unintended damaging consequences.

1. *Praise the effort. It is more helpful than praising an underlying ability.* While an innate ability is not something a child can control, effort is. Kids are empowered when they realize their efforts can make the difference. This is clearly shown in Claudia Mueller's and Carol Dweck's further experiments in which they gave students a very difficult problem to solve after having praised some students for their intelligence and others for how hard they work. Afterward the researchers asked the students why the problem gave them so much trouble. Students who had been told how intelligent they were said that they just weren't smart enough to solve the problem, while the "hard workers" responded that they just didn't try hard enough. Those kids had a real sense of competence and, like the Asian students we discussed earlier, knew that perseverance and old-fashioned stick-to-itiveness were keys to success.

So rather than saying, "You're really smart," it's more helpful to say, "You really worked hard. Way to go." There are lots of ways to encourage effort, like "Way to stick with it," "Nice try," and "I'm sure you can figure it out."

2. *Specific praise is more helpful than generic.* Rather than saying, "You're really good at math," it's more helpful to say, "Nice job on those multiplication tables." This helps children focus their efforts.

3. *Praise should be sincere.* I still remember the conversation Monica and I had with our daughter Erin after she made several errors and struck out in a softball game that her high school team lost. She was understandably upset with her performance and quietly seethed in the backseat during the ride home. Wanting to be helpful, I glanced at her in the rearview mirror and said, "You lost, but good game, Erin." Seconds went by before she replied, "Dad, either you know nothing about softball or I must be really bad if you have to compliment me for *that* game." She knew my praise was undeserved and hollow. I would be much more helpful if I said, "I know you're disappointed, Erin. That was a tough game. You've got the next one to try again."

4. *Praise should not be overdone.* We don't want to turn our kids into praise addicts who need regular reinforcements to keep going. Intermittent reinforcement is more helpful than a steady stream.

There's More We Can Do to Raise Our Kids' IQ

We've explored two important elements of intelligence over which parents have a lot of influence: effort and praise. We can also develop language, foster self-discipline, provide healthy nutrition and play, encourage physical exercise, build attention and memory, ensure adequate sleep, use media and technology properly, monitor stress, and choose good childcare and schools. We will explore what brain science tells us about each of these topics in separate chapters.

DO

- ✓ Teach your kids that effort counts. It takes effort to be smart.
- ✓ Let your kids struggle with problems that are not overwhelming.
- ✓ Solve larger problems with your children.
- ✓ Understand that acquiring skills takes practice and hard work.
- ✓ Teach your kids that effort is the key to success.
- ✓ Reward your children for sticking with a task to the finish.
- ✓ Praise your children for working hard.
- ✓ Praise your children when they really deserve it.
- ✓ Help your children accept constructive criticism.

DON'T

- ✗ Don't undervalue the importance of effort in intelligence.
- ✗ Don't do for your kids what they can do for themselves.
- ✗ Don't let media products wire your baby's brain.
- ✗ Don't just tell kids they are smart.
- ✗ Don't constantly praise your children.
- ✗ Don't give insincere praise.

What do I want to continue?

____

____

____

What do I want to change?

____

____

____

THREE

How the Brain Listens, Speaks, Reads, and Writes

My son Brian's childhood pal, Andrew, stopped by the house this afternoon for a visit. To my delight, his son Ravel was with him.

"I can't believe how big Ravel is getting," I said as Andrew put him in my outstretched arms.

"Yup, he's growing like a weed," Andrew replied to me. His voice changed when he spoke to Ravel a second later. "You're really getting soooooo big, aren't you, Ravel," Andrew said in a high-pitched voice. "Can you give Dave a smile?" he added in a singsong cadence.

Andrew is big, probably six foot two and built like a linebacker. It was fun to hear this big lug of a guy switch into a different language when he talked to Ravel.

"I see you've become fluent in 'parentese,' Andrew," I commented.

"What do you mean—*parentese*?" Andrew asked.

"The language parents all over the world use instinctively when speaking to a baby," I responded. "The one where we overpronounce consonants and vowels, use a pitch that's higher than normal speech, stretch out words, and constantly repeat ourselves."

"Oh, that," replied Andrew with a hint of embarrassment. "Do I sound goofy or what?"

"Not at all," I answered. "I wasn't making fun of you. You really help Ravel when you speak in parentese. We naturally speak baby talk because it helps babies pick out the sounds more easily. It's the perfect way to talk to them. See, Ravel is 'all ears' when you talk to him. Research shows that infants as young as fifteen weeks tune into parentese a lot more than to regular adult speech."

Andrew is helping Ravel develop one of our brain's greatest abilities: language. Our capacity for language separates us from all other living things, allows us to communicate in very sophisticated ways, and is even the prerequisite for our abstract thinking. At seven months Ravel can already babble. Before long those babbling sounds will become recognizable as words, and the next thing you know Ravel will be talking his dad's arm off. At school he'll learn to read and write, and as a teen his sophisticated reasoning in an argument will make Andrew's head spin. How do children's brains develop such complicated and important skills?

Phonemic Awareness—Language's First Building Block

Ravel's first language task is to pick out the spoken sounds from all the other noise he is hearing. With only 17 percent of neurons wired together at birth, there are a lot of "free agent" brain cells waiting for assignment. As Ravel hears different sounds, some neurons get assigned to one sound frequency while others fire in response to a different sound. As that wiring happens Ravel starts to distinguish a "b" from a "d." Scientists call this "phonemic awareness," the first building block for language.

The brain's window of opportunity to wire for phonemic awareness is open widest very early in life; recall the process of blossoming and pruning described in the introduction.

So Ravel, like all babies, starts out as a citizen of the world. His brain is ready to learn any language and could pick out any of the myriad of different sounds, or phonemes, from any of the world's 6,500 spoken languages. But he won't. His brain will only wire the sounds he hears from his English-speaking parents. Wiring for language is totally dependent on a baby's environment. By nine months a baby has already begun to lose his world citizen status.

When Ravel is a six-year-old first grader trying to learn how to read, these phonemic awareness circuits will be very handy. Reading, after all, is nothing more than associating blots of ink on a page with sounds. Ravel will string these sounds together to form words, which he then connects to a meaning. The first jump, however, is from inkblots to sounds. If Ravel starts with an extensive phonemic awareness network wired into his brain, learning how to read will be easier.

This brain science information is crucial for parents like Andrew. We launch children on the road to reading success the moment they're born. Ravel is strongly motivated for this task because we are all hardwired to seek connection and, next to touch, language, including sign language, is our strongest, most reinforcing means to emotionally connect with another person. While babies want to communicate, their brains still need to learn and organize all the pieces before they can speak, read, write, and eventually graduate from school and move out of your house.

The recipe for success does not require an advanced degree. It's simple—talk, talk, talk. The more talk Ravel hears, the more his hearing circuits, in his auditory cortex, form connections. In fact, research shows that one of the strongest predictors for school-age reading ability is the amount of one-to-one communication a child has in the first three years of life, and this is because phonemic awareness is the first building block for language and therefore the first building block for reading.

PARENT TOOL KIT

Brains Listen, Speak, Read, and Write

Use these questions to assess how prepared you are to help your child to listen, speak, read, and write as well as possible.

Yes No

☐ ☐ 1. I understand the different stages of children's language development.

☐ ☐ 2. I know how important early childhood language experiences are for later reading and writing skills.

☐ ☐ 3. I use "parentese" when talking to babies.

☐ ☐ 4. I model the importance of reading by doing a lot myself.

☐ ☐ 5. I read to my child every day.

☐ ☐ 6. We visit the local library.

☐ ☐ 7. I keep media off during mealtimes so we can talk.

☐ ☐ 8. I create a reading-friendly home with lots of books, good lighting, and comfortable reading chairs.

☐ ☐ 9. I balance reading and media use.

☐ ☐ 10. We talk about what we see and hear: around the house, in the community, on TV, etc.

☐ ☐ 11. I encourage writing by having my child write thank-you notes, stories, and diaries.

Language skills are important for your child's success. Use the information in this chapter to give them a good language advantage.

Mirror Neurons—Another Key to Language

While Ravel wires his brain for phonemic awareness he is also hard at work learning how to reproduce the sounds he hears. It's curious that even though the brain reached its present size 250,000 years ago, language emerged more than 200,000 years later. A great leap forward in human evolution occurred at the same time we began to communicate with language. Use of tools and fire, art, and music all blossomed as language emerged. Did our ability to speak just happen or did something important evolve in our human brain? The answer to this question was found in an Italian laboratory in 1998.

One day, a neuroscience graduate student at the University of Parma returned to his team's lab eating an ice cream cone. He noticed that when he licked his ice cream cone, the machines measuring the brain activity of laboratory monkeys sparked to life. Every lick triggered a big response in the monkeys' brains. His mentor, neuroscientist Giacomo Rizzolatti, was amazed and, more importantly, intrigued. The monkeys weren't physically *doing* anything, but something happened inside their brains, and he determined to figure out why. The trail eventually led him to a startling discovery: mirror neurons. Rizzolatti found that when the monkeys *watched* someone eat, the same brain circuits fired as if they were actually eating themselves. Eventually his research showed that we humans have mirror neurons as well, but ours are more numerous, more complex, and more sophisticated than those found in his lab monkeys.

One of the most important neuroscience discoveries of the past twenty years, mirror neurons are critical to understanding the actions, intentions, and emotions of other people. When we watch someone throw a ball, our mirror neurons simulate the same ball-throwing action in our brain even though we don't lift a finger. Mirror neurons also explain empathy. When we see a friend cry, the mirror cells in the same emotional circuits light up in our own brains, enabling us to vicariously share our friends' sadness.

In addition to mirror neurons being responsible for social understanding and empathy, renowned neuroscientist V. S. Ramachandran is convinced that they support our ability to use language. When Andrew is speaking parentese to Ravel, his son's mirror neurons are firing away, giving Ravel the ability to later mimic the lip and tongue movements he will need to form words. Mirror neurons also explain why Ravel opened his mouth and stuck out his tongue, copying me, when I held him during our visit.

Create a Language-Rich Environment

The takeaway for parents from brain insights about phonemic awareness and mirror neurons is clear: language-rich environments are essential for children's language development. That means a lot of talk, a lot of reading, and in the early years a minimum of media interference, even from products that promise genius.

It turns out that babies cannot develop phonemic awareness from listening to audio recordings or watching TV or videos. A baby needs completely individualized language experiences delivered by a real person. Language acquisition is a social process with feedback and reinforcement delivered with smiles, giggles, and touch. All those products promising brilliant babies or infant second-language fluency don't work. The language centers in a baby's brain thrive on real-person interaction.

What Do You Hear?

A woman approached me during a break in a professional workshop I was conducting on brain development. "My son," she began, "is an example of what can go awry when the window of opportunity for phonemic awareness is open."

"What do you mean?" I asked.

"My son Jason had a lot of ear infections when he was a baby," she explained. "Unfortunately he also had a very high tolerance for pain, so he never fussed, and we didn't know his ears were infected. We weren't worried when we couldn't understand his first attempts at talking because we figured that was normal. We did get worried, however, when we understood his playmates but couldn't recognize any of the words Jason tried to say. To make a long story short, Jason is now ten and still in speech therapy. He mimicked the sounds he heard, all right. The problem was the sounds were filtered through the fluid in his ears. It sounded as if we were talking to him at the bottom of a swimming pool."

When something interferes with a baby's ability to hear clearly, his brain records a distorted sound. That's why the Joint Committee on Infant Hearing recommends universal screening for infants in the first month of life. Before universal screening, 70 percent of children's hearing losses weren't detected until a child was two and a half years old. By then, the brain's neural map, created from distorted sounds, was set, and the prospects to develop normal language skills dimmed. With newborn screening, children who suffer hearing loss can get the help they need right away to acquire language and not fall behind a hearing child's skills in communication, reading, and social development. Early diagnosis and treatment give hearing-impaired children the best chance at normal language development. Parents should ask their pediatrician to test their baby's hearing and communication ability at well-child doctor visits.

Here are language and hearing milestones from the American Academy of Pediatrics. If you suspect that your child may have a hearing loss or a language delay, check with your pediatrician right away.

Between birth and three months, a baby should:

- Startle when he hears a loud noise.
- Wake up if there is a loud sound.
- Have the reflexive action of a blink or widened eyes when there is a loud noise.
- Coo and try to imitate your sounds.

At 3 months to 4 months, a baby should:

- Quiet down when he hears his mother's voice.
- Stop playing when there is a loud sound.
- Look around for the source of a new sound.

At 6 months to 9 months, a baby should:

- Enjoy musical toys.
- Coo and babble with a change of pitch in his voice.
- Say "mamama" or "babababa."

At 12 to 15 months, a baby should:

- Look at you when he hears his name or when you say "No."
- Be able to follow a simple request like "Show me your tummy."
- Say his first few words (to the enthusiastic reaction of his audience).
- Imitate sounds that you make.

At 18 to 24 months, a baby should be able to:

- Point to parts of his body when you ask questions like "Where is your nose?"
- Play the "Where Game," as in "Where's the ball?"
- Use two-word phrases when talking, as in "all gone" or "more milk."
- Have a vocabulary of between twenty and fifty words.
- Have 50 percent of his talk intelligible to strangers.

At three years, a child should be able to:

- Say four- to five-word sentences and have a vocabulary of about five hundred words.
- Understand some verbs like "put, drink, eat, read," etc.
- Demonstrate mastery of basic grammar using plurals, past tense, etc.
- Have 80 percent of his speech understood by strangers.

At four years a child should be able to speak in complex sentences with clauses and connecting words, such as "I didn't want the toy, but she did."

Driving Our Kids Deaf

Hearing loss can also occur in older kids. Even though the negative impact on phonemic awareness is past by the time our kids are teenagers, the risks to their hearing are growing as our environment gets noisier and more kids wear earphones. In fact, the hearing aid industry is on the rise, and its long-term business prospects are getting better all the time. A 2010 study showed that rates are increasing, with 6.5 million teens already suffering hearing loss.

Been to a movie lately? It's not your imagination; those flicks are getting louder. The average decibel level for movies is now about 100. An action movie jacks the sound up to 120 dBs. But our ears aren't built for that noise level. Our ears work best at 85 dBs and lower. What happens at 120 dBs? With as little as thirty minutes of exposure we risk permanent hearing loss.

Not such a big deal if it's just an occasional loud movie assaulting young ears. But kids who attend rock concerts, hang out in arcades, or simply listen to their iPods with the volume turned up are way over the 85 dBs threshold. The electronic world is getting louder and louder. Half of the loudest sounds around us have appeared only in the last ten years.

Teens tell us to chill, of course, because they hear just fine. And they can . . . for now. Hearing loss is cumulative and gradual, so damage done by their iPods won't show up for years. By the time it does, the ringing in their ears will be constant and the hearing loss irreversible. Enter the hearing aid industry.

What's a parent to do? For starters, we should tone down the volumes we can control. If kids use headphones, the volume is too high if anyone else can hear it. Of course, it's easier to monitor sound levels for the younger ones. Getting preteens and teens to take hearing loss seriously is another matter. While we don't want to deprive them of music, it is worth giving some talk time to the risk of hearing loss—nothing preachy, just the truth. Tell them that things like loud music damage hearing and you can't tell it's happening until it's too late. By the time you notice the ringing in the ears or that you have trouble hearing everyday conversation, the damage is done and irreversible. Give them and their friends earplugs—several sets. Tell them that more and more musicians are wearing them. The choice is theirs.

Importance of Conversation

At parent workshops I always remind parents and other caregivers that the key to a child's language success is conversation. Social interaction with a child is critical for any number of reasons, and language is an essential ingredient. Everyday activities like meals, diaper changes for babies, trips, walks, errands, or playtime should all be filled with chitchat. We should never pass up a chance to explain a child's world to him and we should sprinkle in new and varied words. Watch out for your cell phone use. Times with your child are golden language opportunities.

Our friend Theresa always thought of new ways to use language with her son Alex. Every night she and her partner would bring some new object to the dinner table. One night, when Alex was eighteen months old, she put two AAA batteries and a toy car on the table. When Theresa said "battery" Alex stared at her. She immediately picked up his cue and explained, "These are batteries, Alex. They make the car go."

"Car go," said Alex.

"Yes, Alex," said Theresa. "The batteries make the car go." A demonstration followed as Theresa put the two batteries in the toy car, flipped the little switch, and watched as Alex shrieked in delight as the car sped across the table.

Theresa brought the batteries and car to dinner that night because she noticed how quickly Alex's language skills were expanding. She probably didn't know, however, what was driving her son's brain explosion. Recent brain research gives us the explanation: the myelination (insulation) of the brain cell axons (or cables) in the language center is complete at about eighteen months of age. This means electric signals can travel from one neuron to another much more swiftly and securely. It's like connecting all your home computers with fiber optic cable. That's why Alex's language skills took off. And because Theresa keyed in to her son's development, she knew it was important to introduce him to new words and ideas. Although Alex couldn't explain how the batteries made the car move, he built a huge storehouse of descriptive and enriching vocabulary words to draw upon as he grew up.

Keep It Up as They Grow Up

Jack and Patricia, a couple I counseled for a number of weeks, made good progress in a short period of time to correct some bad habits that had crept into their marriage. At the start of a session Pat asked if she could shift gears for a minute and talk about how she and Jack related to their two daughters, Hannah and Rebecca. "I feel really bad," Patricia said, "because last night as I tucked Hannah in, she told me that we never talk anymore."

"What did she mean?" Jack asked, obviously concerned.

"She said all she hears is 'Do this or do that. Get your coat on. Is your homework done? Get your elbows off the table. Did you practice your piano?' I felt sad as I listened to her because I think she's right. We get so busy that when we do talk it's all about business."

"I really want to change this, Jack," she said. Then she turned to me. "Any suggestions?"

I had suggestions, although I admitted that I wasn't always good at following them myself. "Carve out time for conversations with your kids. If we don't deliberately make catching up a priority, there is always something else to do." Then I looked directly at Jack. "Jack, I've noticed that you have your BlackBerry in your hand. Do you have it close by during mealtimes with Patricia and the girls?"

"Yes, he does," Patricia said. "That was one of the things Hannah mentioned last night."

"Jack, put it away. Don't even bring it to the dinner table. Use mealtime to really tune in. Ask your kids how their day went. Try to make mealtimes relaxed and enjoyable; don't use this time to bring up negative behaviors." I also explained the difference between open-ended and closed-ended questions. "Closed-ended questions are answered with one word. Open-ended are more likely to generate more conversation. For example, rather than asking, 'How was school?' say, 'Tell me about your school day.'"

Jack and Patricia's priority was to improve communication with their daughters as a way to maintain and strengthen a positive relationship. Our increasingly digital households more often put us in the same house, but inhabiting different worlds. These additional tips have the added benefit of enhancing their daughters' language skills.

- Make conversation. Try to introduce new words, helping your kids expand their vocabulary.
- Make a "Word of the Day" list and hang it up. Take turns adding a new word each day. These can be good conversation starters or a chance for some family fun.
- Play games together. Word games like Scrabble or Boggle are good vocabulary builders, but any game can start conversations.
- Play a variation of the I Spy game. For example, say, "I spy something that rhymes with *cable.*" Take turns so your kids get practice.
- Look up words in a dictionary or online. Try to stump one another with new words. Play the Dictionary Game.
- Read stories to your child that are a little harder than she can read herself.

Bilingual Kids

A young woman approached me after a recent parenting seminar. "Hello, Dr. Walsh, my name is Fatima," she began. "Can I ask you a question about my daughter?"

"Sure," I responded.

"My family is from Peru. My mother lives with us and takes care of my baby daughter, Alicia, while we are at work. Since my mother cannot speak English, my daughter hears Spanish all day long. My husband and I only speak English with her because we want her to know English. Is this really bad for her? Will she end up all confused?"

This is an increasingly common question, and I was glad I could reassure Fatima that her daughter was actually lucky. "If she grows up hearing both languages it is likely that she will be bilingual, which is a great skill," I said. "Children have the ability to learn more than one language simultaneously and keep them separate. The one thing you do want to avoid is mixing the two."

"You mean Spanglish?" Fatima asked.

"Exactly," I said. "That's confusing for kids. But they are capable of learning more than one language. That's why children born in Europe, for example, will often be fluent in a number of languages—because they grew up hearing so many."

"I'm really glad to hear that, Dr. Walsh. I want Alicia to speak good English, but I also want her to learn Spanish. That's our heritage."

Fatima didn't need to worry. In fact, the best time to learn another language is when children are young, so it's too bad that so many of our kids don't study a foreign language until they're in high school. It's not that high school is too late, but it would have been so much easier when they were younger.

I wished I had Fatima's phone number a few months later when I read about new research from the University of Minnesota. She would have been happy to learn that the benefits for bilingual children go beyond their ability to communicate in more than one language. They have better executive function (something we'll explore later), too, because they have to consciously shift from one language to another.

The Reading Brain

Reading is at the heart of academic achievement. It's easy to see why. Reading, whether with a book or online, opens doors to new people, places, and cultures. It stimulates the imagination as no other medium can. It also reinforces how our brain organizes itself to think. Perhaps that's why research shows that reading is one of the strongest predictors of school success.

Earlier in this chapter we discussed the importance of one-to-one conversation between caregiver and child in the first three years of life. In addition, there's another important step while baby's still in the crib: read him stories before he can even hold a book. Reading aloud promotes children's brain development, yet researchers have found that only 52 percent of parents read to their infants and babies every day.

If you recall my brain development mantra, "Whatever the brain does a lot of is what it gets good at," you can understand the importance of reinforcing patterns. That's why we read favorite stories over and over to a toddler or preschooler. Language develops with repetition and practice. Reading and singing your child nursery rhymes is a great way to reinforce the linguistic patterns. Young children's brains are geared to listen for the patterns, which is why kids love Dr. Seuss books, for instance. Their brains catch on to the patterns and even anticipate words. In addition, rhyming teaches them that individual sounds of words can change to create whole new words—a skill they will soon apply in learning to read.

I was browsing in a used bookstore recently with my adult son, Dan, when he spotted a tattered copy of *Mike Mulligan and His Steam Shovel*. His eyes lit up as he paged through it. "Remember when we used to read this?" Dan reminded me. "I loved this book."

First of all, reading aloud is fun. Tiny babies like the soothing sounds of a familiar voice reading. Even when they prefer "eating" their books, they're already making the mental association of reading with comfort, security, and enjoyment. That link is a great foundation for raising readers, and, as my son proved, it can create fond memories that last for years.

There are technical benefits as well. Children start to associate marks on a page with language. They also pick up the basics, such as reading a book from front to back and left to right. These things may not seem important, but they are all building blocks for reading.

Here are tips for reading aloud to infants, babies, and young children.

1. Read to your child every day. It becomes a great habit.
2. Cuddling is critical. This creates memories of warmth and closeness.
3. Keep the stories short. Don't force a baby or child to sit until you finish a book if he lets you know he has lost interest.
4. Let your baby take the lead. She may prefer to flip or chew on the pages. No problem. Remember that the goal is to have fun. Sturdy board books or soft cloth books can take a lot of infant handling.
5. Don't shy away from poetry. The rhyming and rhythm are great for babies and children.
6. For infants, choose books with very simple pictures or photographs.
7. Relate the words to the pictures on the page. Tapping or scratching the picture can draw your child's attention.
8. Be a ham. Read with excitement and expression. Use different voices and sound effects and don't hesitate to act out stories and nursery rhymes.
9. Editorialize. Books for babies won't have a lot of words. So don't just read what's on the page. Expand, embellish, and relate the story to real life. "The dog in the picture is black, but Mrs. Johnson's dog next door is white."
10. Make it interactive. If you ask a baby a question, remember that any sound she makes is a brilliant answer! Reinforce what your older child says with a "Good thought!"
11. Don't wait for your child to go to school before introducing her to your local library. Many have story hours and other services for preschool children. Some might even have a lap-time story for the tiny ones. These usually last about fifteen minutes and involve both the child and adult in a story as well as songs, finger plays, and other fun activities.

Reading throws open the doors to the world. The adventure begins long before a child starts to read herself. It begins with the fun of hearing stories read aloud.

Teaching Toddlers to Read?

Although the brain thrives on language and being read to, there seems to be no research that supports the formal teaching of reading to toddlers and preschoolers. Forcing a young child to spend time on learning to read may actually take away time better spent playing, exploring, and verbally interacting with their caregiver. It's more important for young children to listen to stories and have conversations than to learn from flash cards or computer programs. In fact, a study of children with speech and language disorders found that more of these children had parents who tried to teach them to read than a comparison sample of kids whose parents spent more time talking and reading with them. Preschoolers often give parents cues when their brains are prepared to unravel the mystery of reading. I still remember Erin trying to decode traffic signs. I knew then that she was fascinated by the written word. Encouraging early efforts at reading is as important as talking about colors, shapes, and letters, but just don't turn these efforts into a drill.

Once children do start formal reading education they should practice reading every day. Celebrate with your child each advancing step on their road to reading. Some kids will skip along this road with few stumbling blocks; others will advance one slow step at a time. Practice, encouragement, and reward are the keys to fluency.

Don't Stop Reading When They Get Older

Many parents stop reading to their children once they start school. That's really too bad because their kids miss out on a fun activity that reinforces family connections. Reading aloud also models fluent reading and enhances kids' other reading skills. Here are tips every parent can use to provide the right conditions for younger readers to blossom as they grow up.

1. Let your child see how important reading is by doing it yourself. Have plenty of reading material around.
2. Read to your child every day. This is one of the most important literacy-building activities we can do with our children.
3. Make library visits a regular routine.
4. Audio books can help pass the time on long road trips. Libraries

often have a good selection. Listening to stories is a better brain builder than watching videos.

5. Make reading a family pleasure. Set aside time as a family to read for fun. Make a bedtime story part of your day-end ritual.
6. Give books as gifts. Suggest that grandparents and other relatives do the same.
7. Arrange your home to encourage reading. Make sure you have comfortable places to cuddle together with a book, good lighting, and bookshelves your child can reach or baskets of books she can dig into.
8. Help your child become an author. Make a book by inviting your child to tell a story about anything he wants while you write it down. Let him illustrate the story by drawing, pasting in photographs, or cutting out pictures from magazines.
9. Use other media that promote reading. Choose entertaining online sites or video games that incorporate reading skills and problem solving. Look for videos or downloads that include a book component.
10. As children get older, read longer chapter books and poetry. Reading longer books chapter by chapter helps develop a child's listening comprehension skills. Your child actually builds his imagination while forming pictures in his mind for the developing story. Don't be afraid to read books that are a little more complicated than what your child would read himself. Your child's brain will thank you for the challenge. Remember that new experiences actually stimulate brain growth. New words and more complex sentences will have your child's neurons firing.
11. Make reading aloud interactive. Stop the story once in a while at a crucial point and ask your child, "What do you think happens next?" or "What do you think the character is feeling?" or "What would you do if you were in that situation?" It is more important to use shared reading as an opportunity for emotional closeness with your child than to tally up a number of books read. Just like with preschoolers, sharing a close, positive reading experience with school-age children helps them associate pleasure with books and reading.

When Dan, Brian, and Erin were all in grade school we took a long summer road trip out west. Monica checked an audio version of the Tolkien *Lord of the Rings* trilogy out of the library the day before we left. The next day found the Walshes traveling across the vast North Dakota prairie. It wasn't long before boredom set in, and the kids started to tease and argue with one another. Monica glanced at me and smiled. Turning to the three rascals in the backseat she asked, "How would you like to listen to a story?"

"No," replied Dan, "I just want to get out of the car so we can play."

Undeterred, Monica cheerfully said, "Let's just try it." With that she inserted the first of the series in the tape deck. (Remember, this was the eighties, long before CD players or iPods.) Within minutes the kids had quieted down, mesmerized by the dramatized voices of Bilbo Baggins, Frodo, and Gandalf. For the rest of the trip Tolkien transported us from the long stretches of road into Middle Earth and the endless adventures of the Hobbits. More than once we sat in the parking lot of a restaurant because Dan, Brian, or Erin insisted, "We can't turn it off until we find out what happens next." All three of our kids have read the Tolkien trilogy several times and their adult reminiscences about family vacations invariably include the memories of that summer spent in Middle Earth.

Reluctant Readers

Not every child takes to reading with enthusiasm. Some become discouraged and frustrated. The entertainment world of the Wii and other electronic media distracts many reluctant readers. These kids need patience, encouragement, and persistence. On the one hand, you don't want to panic if your child is progressing more slowly than others; each child has his own reading timetable. On the other hand you don't want to miss any early signs of an underlying problem that is getting in the way. Communicate with your child's reading teacher so that a reading difficulty can be identified and corrected before frustration leads to reading avoidance or behavior problems.

Some children master all the reading skills but just don't seem to be interested. Competition from video games, texting, TV, and social media are putting more kids than ever into this category. There are three keys to encouraging the reluctant reader.

1. Keep media in balance.
2. Make reading a fun and enjoyable priority.
3. Match the reading materials to your child's interest. If she loves baseball, get a supply of baseball stories. Any reading is good reading (if age-appropriate). Comic books and graphic novels capture the attention of many kids and may be a stepping-stone to other reading.

There's a great book by Emma Walton Hamilton called *Raising Bookworms: Getting Children Reading for Pleasure and Empowerment.* It's packed with more ideas for helping even the most reluctant reader to get lost in a book.

Raising Writers

A small business owner complained to me recently about the lack of writing skills among his employees. "Doesn't anybody learn how to write anymore?" he asked. "I have to read everything that goes out to make sure there aren't embarrassing misspellings, grammar mistakes, or sentences that never end." He is not alone in his complaints about deteriorating writing skills in the workplace, especially among young employees.

Is writing becoming a lost art? Kids today get ample practice in writing shortcuts with text messaging and short-description PowerPoints. The quick reply demands shortcuts. Kids themselves created handy texting shortcuts: LOL meaning "laughing out loud"; BRB for "be right back"; and the famous POS when a "parent is over my shoulder." A high school social studies teacher I know received this panicked student plea in her email box: "ms. fritz, OMG ima die. i totally thought i sent this to you on friday. ima die. OMG. please please please don't take points away. ima die. i can't believe i didn't send it."

This age of information demands that kids be skilled in multiple ways of communicating and organizing information, and writing coherently and thoughtfully will be a skill in even greater demand by employers. A survey of major corporations found that writing was a "threshold" skill needed for hiring and promotions. Two-thirds of salaried employees have writing responsibilities.

In addition to being a practical skill, writing contributes to clear and organized thinking. There is something about committing our thoughts to an empty screen (or paper) that demands coherence and organization. A writer sharpens and clarifies her ideas because fuzzy thinking does not translate well into writing. In addition, effective writing demands attention to details, like spelling and punctuation. Lynne Truss's *New York Times* best-seller, *Eats, Shoots & Leaves: The Zero Tolerance Approach to Punctuation,* humorously shows the confusion caused by poor punctuation.

Writing, emerging with other language skills, starts with drawing. If you put blank paper and crayons in front of young children they will spontaneously start to "write." Many will only be too happy to "read their stories" to an appreciative audience. Drawing becomes more formal writing as children "wire in" additional building blocks. Generations of *Sesame Street* kids have learned, for example, the phonetic sound that goes with the letter *t*. That connection paves the way for her to pick out the sound when she hears it spoken and eventually to recognize it on a printed page. If all those connections wire into her brain, then she writes the letter *t* when she hears the word *top* or when she wants to write the word *toy*.

As with every skill, writing improves with practice. (Once again, "Whatever the brain does a lot of is what it gets good at.") Try these tips to help your child's brain wire in writing skills:

- Have lots of blank paper and crayons (markers for older kids) around. Those scribbles will eventually become pictures, then words, then stories.
- Praise, reinforce, and encourage those early writing attempts. Refrigerators make great display areas for the masterpieces.
- Have your child write thank-you notes. The recipient will appreciate them whether they are a "scribble" from a toddler or a full-blown epistle from a teenager. Thank-you notes are not only a lesson in thoughtfulness; they're another opportunity to practice.
- Encourage your kids to keep diaries or journals.
- Social networking sites on the Internet get kids writing.
- Have "author's night" celebrations to reward and reinforce writing.
- Ask your child's teacher how they are teaching writing skills and what you can do to help.

These tips are just a sample. Ruth Shagoury's book *Raising Writers: Understanding and Nurturing Young Children's Writing Development* is chock-full of more.

Every time a child learns a new word, they add a new window in their minds to see the world. Words are the tools of thinking, and exposing children to a rich variety of words and experiences will help them have the brains they need for success in the 21st century.

A mom relayed this story: Her daughter was in the backseat of their car, working on vocabulary schoolwork. Her partner, Dawn, was driving and conversing with their daughter about all the words she was learning. "I realized she was playing word games with our daughter. I knew my partner liked words, but I never sat back and realized how rich her knowledge was. I asked her how she knew all these words and she laughed and said, 'I looked them up in a dictionary when I was a kid.'" Something as basic as a dictionary enriched her thoughts later in life.

So what's the best way for parents to increase their children's vocabulary? Not vocabulary flash cards. The task is much more fun than vocabulary drills. The three best ways are reading, experiences, and conversations. Good books make for good conversations, as well as experiences and doing things. And talk is free—you don't need to buy anything.

DO

- ✓ Talk, talk, talk with your children from the moment they're born.
- ✓ Read, read, read to your children from the moment they're born until they move out of the house. (You can quote a good thought to your teenager.)
- ✓ Buy books. Used books are cheaper, or borrow for free at the library.
- ✓ Get a good dictionary (online or off) and use it.
- ✓ Play word games.
- ✓ Arrange your home to be reading—and writing—friendly.
- ✓ Imitate and reinforce your infant's sounds and babbling.
- ✓ Let your child have second-language experiences.

DON'T

- ✗ Don't worry about speaking "parentese" with babies—it's exactly what they need to hear.
- ✗ Don't limit how you talk with your child. Talk about all their experiences.
- ✗ Don't try to push preschoolers to read. If you make sure the building blocks are in place, they will become readers.
- ✗ Don't replace talking with ABC flash cards with preschoolers.
- ✗ Don't miss an opportunity to chat and listen.
- ✗ Don't use your cell phone over talking with your child.
- ✗ Don't correct your child's grammar, just model the correct sentence.
- ✗ Don't let media crowd out reading.

What do I want to continue?

____

____

____

What do I want to change?

____

____

____

FOUR

Memory, Attention, and the Rule of Seven

Memory, one of our brain's greatest capacities, is the key to learning. If I can't remember, I can't learn. If I go into the kitchen and burn my hand on the stove, I need to remember to be careful the next time or I'll end up burning my hand all over again. This critically valuable brain function is also much more complicated than most of us realize. I often ask participants in my workshops how many types of memory we have. The most common answer by far is two—short- and long-term memory. We do indeed have short- and long-term memories but they are only two of dozens of different types. In this chapter we will explore different types of memory, how they relate to thinking, and how to enhance children's memory and attention skills. Along the way we'll answer some puzzling memory questions, such as, Why don't we remember our first birthday? Why do we remember years later how to ride a bike? Why do we forget? Do babies remember anything? Is it possible to build a strong memory in the same way we develop a muscle?

The Curious Case of H.M.

Students of brain science know about H.M., the man who tragically lost the ability to register new memories but in the process uncovered some of memory's mysteries. (We only learned that his full name was Henry Molaison after he died in 2008.) H.M. suffered from severe, frequent seizures caused by a childhood bicycle accident. By the time he was twenty-seven, H.M. would do anything to get relief. A surgeon recommended removing two sections of H.M.'s brain, one on each side of his head, to stop the seizures. Desperate for help, H.M. agreed to the plan. As H.M. came out of anaesthesia he awoke to a new world. The good news: the procedure reduced the seizures. The bad news: he couldn't remember anything new that happened to him. While he could reminisce about long-ago childhood events, he couldn't tell you what he ate for breakfast that morning. He would pleasantly introduce himself to a new guest even though he had just met the same person twenty minutes earlier. Curiously, he could demonstrate a newly acquired skill, such as drawing, but he couldn't tell you he had learned it. Between his surgery in 1953 and his death, H.M. was the subject of countless studies and revolutionized how scientists thought about memory. Before our new technologies allowed us to peer into the workings of the brain, scientists had vague notions how different brain areas related to memory. H.M.'s disability helped pinpoint the brain locations for various memory functions, identified discrete types of memory, and revealed memory's multidimensional nature.

Attention and Memory Work Together to Form Memories

Our brains constantly scan the environment with oceans of information pouring in through our five senses. The reason our brains are not overwhelmed is that we only *pay attention* to a small portion of the available data streaming in. When I'm reading a book, for example, I am not paying attention to my tactile sense that registers the pressure of my clothing against my body. Likewise, when I am listening to someone, I ignore other conversations going on in the room. Attention is a spotlight that picks out and concentrates on specific stimuli. It's the gateway to memory.

Once attention narrows the stream of sensory data, then the three-stage process we call memory begins. The first stage is encoding, whereby the sensory centers of the brain process the incoming data. The visual system processes and integrates the lines, shapes, and colors; the auditory system registers sound waves and volume; and so on with the other senses. The second stage of memory is storage, whereby the encoded information is transmitted via neural circuits to a destination most often in the outer part of the brain called the cortex. Neuroscientists have discovered different storage areas for various types of information. For example, we know different languages are stored in separate circuits because of cases where bilingual accident victims lose the ability to speak one language but not the other. The third stage is retrieval, the process where we bring stored information into our conscious thoughts.

Memory begins with attention, but how do we know what to pay attention to? When I ask my graduate students this question, the most common response is something like "My brain knows what's important." My follow-up query, "*How* does your brain know?" often irritates them. "I don't know, it just does," an exasperated student told me recently. I explain how attention and memory work hand in hand. Infants cannot pay attention the way older children can because they don't have enough sensory memories registered yet. As they build up more sensory memories their brains are better equipped to pick out important information and pay attention to it. Infant brains do not filter out the feel of the wind, background smells, or the soft touch of clothing. They can't recognize danger because they have no past memory to warn them. The reason parents and caregivers have to keep a close eye on toddlers racing toward a stairwell is that babies don't have enough stored memories of height, gravity, falling, and bruises to know that stairs can be dangerous and hence demand caution.

Fortunately babies build up the store of memories very quickly. As they explore the world with their senses they wire together billions upon billions of neural connections. You can help them along by creating a rich—but not overstimulating—sensory environment. You help your child develop her tactile sense when you let your baby or toddler play with water, explore smooth and rough surfaces, and feel the touch of soft or hard surfaces with bare feet. Your preschooler can play with sand, rice, finger paints, or play dough. Take your child outside. Let him feel the breeze on his face, watch the wind move the leaves, feel the touch of grass or sand, and listen to the sounds of the neighborhood. In the previous chapter on language I talked about how important it is to talk with babies so they wire together all the memories of different sounds and phonemes. Babies sleep so much because their brains, overwhelmed by all the sensory input, are in overdrive wiring together neural networks by the billions and trillions. In fact, their brains are making the most connections they will ever have. They build so many they will eventually prune back the excess they don't need. As they build their vast stores of sensory memories their brains get better at knowing what's important and what's not.

PARENT TOOL KIT

Memory and Attention

Use these questions to assess how prepared you are to help your child develop strong memory and attention skills.

Yes No

☐ ☐ 1. I know how critical good memory and attention skills are for learning.

☐ ☐ 2. I point to, name, and talk about things to develop my baby's attention skills.

☐ ☐ 3. I know that reminiscing with my child helps build his memory.

☐ ☐ 4. I play memory games with my child.

☐ ☐ 5. I know how important conversations are to foster good memory and attention.

☐ ☐ 6. Basic knowledge builds the scaffolding for future memory to attach to.

☐ ☐ 7. I understand the connection between working memory and focused attention.

☐ ☐ 8. I know that working memory's capacity is seven "chunks" of information.

☐ ☐ 9. I know memory aids like mnemonics work because they create more neural pathways to the information my child wants to retrieve.

☐ ☐ 10. I realize stress interferes with the brain memory systems.

☐ ☐ 11. I understand that multitasking affects concentration and attention.

Our memories define who we are and what we can do. Use the information in this chapter to enrich and sharpen your child's attention and memory skills.

Focused and Reactive Attention

I recently conducted a daylong in-service for the 285 teachers from a rural Minnesota school district. At one point I asked, "How many of you have taught for more than ten years?" After about 75 percent of the hands went up I said, "This next question is for you. How many of you think it is more difficult to get and keep students' attention today than it was just ten years ago?" Every single one of the veteran teachers' hands shot into the air.

There is an attention crisis among American children today. I am not talking about the clinical syndrome called attention deficit disorder. I am referring to the growing number of "distracted kids" who have an overdeveloped reactive attention system but an underdeveloped focused attention system. I described my conversation with second grader Jeremy's mother in the opening pages of this book. There are millions of children like Jeremy who have no trouble paying attention to media but struggle to maintain focus in the classroom.

Reactive attention—responding to movement, sudden change, and emotion—is hardwired, involuntary, and connected to the emotional system of the brain. Our ancient ancestors survived danger by sensing movement or change in their environment and that system still turns our heads today. Switch on any TV or video game and children's heads twist to look. For a generation of kids surrounded by screens, this reactive attention system is well developed. But Jeremy needs his focused attention to follow his second grade teacher and, according to what she told his parents, he wasn't up to the task. Jeremy's focused attention is located in his prefrontal cortex and needs to be developed.

Many of the traditional ways children increase their focused attention have disappeared. You might recall the license plate game or the alphabet game that generations of youngsters played on car trips. Whoever spotted the most out-of-state license plates by the time the family arrived at their destination was the winner. Today, many kids pass the time on the ride watching a DVD or playing a handheld video game. Important in all aspects of learning, focused attention helps children develop critical thinking skills, a key for success in today's information economy. The kids who can reflect, synthesize, and critically analyze information and ideas have a big advantage over those who can't.

Here are some suggestions to help children build attention skills.

- Give babies only a couple of toys at a time, so they learn to focus on one.
- Keep TVs off in the room where children play so their attention isn't distracted.
- Establish routines so young children know what to expect.
- Let children "figure out" a problem. Ask, "How can we fix this?" or "What do you think we should do?"

- Card and board games build focused attention skills. They require taking turns, setting a goal, and planning a strategy.
- Build a child's ability to follow a verbal one-step direction, to two-step, to three-step, as they are able.
- Have them practice following written directions from simple to more complex.
- Read a story and ask your child what it was about.
- Play chess and Scrabble, and put together puzzles as kids get older.
- Establish after-school routines. Designate a place where your child can place all school-related materials so he knows where to get them when it's time for homework or the next morning when he's heading out the door.
- Set a homework timer to help older children stay on task.

How Can I Focus? I'm Doing Five Things at Once!

My friend Austin recently shared this experience with me. He thought his ten-year-old daughter was diligently doing homework. He knocked and heard a cheery "Come on in." As he entered, his daughter was in front of her computer, with her cell phone in one hand, a text message popping up, while the latest song from her favorite group blared from her iPod. The only thing resembling homework was the math book open on the table next to the keyboard. "I thought you were doing homework," he said. She gave him a puzzled look and responded, "I am."

Some try to tell us that wired-in kids are excellent multitaskers. The typical teen today has access to a computer, TV, video game system, cell phone, iPod, or MP3 music player, and a handheld video game player, and usually all of this within the confines of his own bedroom. We'll talk more about the effects of this digital age in a later chapter, but for now, what does this multitasking do to memory and attention?

It's untrue that teens can focus on two things at once—what they're doing is shifting their attention from one task to another. In this digital age, teens wire their brains to make these shifts very quickly, but they are still, like everyone else, paying attention to one thing at a time, sequentially. Common sense tells us multitasking should increase brain activity, but Carnegie Mellon University scientists using the latest brain imaging technology find it doesn't. As a matter of fact, they discovered that multitasking actually decreases brain activity. Neither task is done as well as if each were performed individually, fractions of a second are lost every time we make a switch, and a person's interrupted task can take 50 percent longer to finish, with 50 percent more errors. Turns out the latest brain research supports the old advice "one thing at a time."

It's not that kids can't do some tasks simultaneously. But if two tasks are performed at once, one of them has to be familiar. Our brains perform a familiar task on "automatic pilot" while really paying attention to the other one. That's why insurance companies consider talking on a cell phone and driving to be as dangerous as driving while drunk—it's the driving that goes on "automatic pilot" while the conversation really holds our attention. Our kids may be living in the Information Age but our brains have not been redesigned yet. I advised Austin that the next time his kids told him they can do homework while watching TV or talking on the phone, he should say, "Sorry, one thing at a time." Decide when kids' study time should be interruption-free and you won't hear "What was I thinking about?" or "How do I do this?"

Why do we continually break our attention with cell phones and other digital interrupters, even if we know it's bad for driving or disrupts our homework task? Dr. John Ratey, a Harvard researcher and one of the authors of the book *Driven to Distraction*, gives us a clue. He believes that we have rewired our brains to crave stimulation, that digital media have hijacked our brain's ability to keep focused attention. People crave novelty. According to Ratey, people "get a quick burst of adrenaline, a 'dopamine squirt,' when they use digital devices." Dopamine is that "feel good" neurotransmitter that keeps us coming back for more. Texting, tweeting, answering the cell phone, and being connected on social networking sites are irresistible emotional jolts, even while driving or studying. Constant distraction shrinks attention spans and is a real threat to kids' success in school.

There are times, of course, when we need to make quick mental shifts. There are other times, however, when we have to be able to concentrate. Our techno-culture is giving kids plenty of practice in reacting to stimuli. We need to make sure that they can also concentrate on one problem or task.

Working Memory and the Rule of Seven

Working memory is shorter than short-term memory; it lasts a matter of seconds. That's the type of memory we use when we look up a phone number and quickly dial it before we forget it. Unless we consciously try to remember it, we won't recall it an hour later. We now know that working memory is located in the prefrontal cortex, the executive part of the brain. There is a great deal of scientific interest in working memory because that is where we "think." Some scholars believe that working memory is what we call consciousness, although there is an ongoing debate about this. While the jury is out on that philosophical question, there is no dispute about working memory's importance.

Working memory enables us to simultaneously hold incoming information for a matter of seconds while linking it to long-term memories. In one of the most cited psychology studies, Princeton University scientist George Miller identified the capacity of working memory in 1956 as seven "chunks" of information. Subsequent research has repeatedly confirmed the number seven, plus or minus two, which means that while some people can hold nine "chunks" in working memory and others only five, most of us can handle seven.

"Chunking" is our ability to link disparate bits of information together into one piece of information (or "chunk") that's held in the working memory, a grouping technique that frees up space for even more information to be chunked. For example, a third grader trying to read the word *because* for the first time might use up all her working memory space as she retrieves the sound of each letter from long-term memory. With enough practice, however, she can recognize the word by sight and instantaneously bring it from long-term memory as one chunk. Then she will still have six chunks to work with and can link the word *because* with other words in the sentence.

University of Virginia scientist Daniel Willingham provides an example of how this works. Read the following letters once, cover the list, and see how many you can remember.

X C N
N P H
D F B
I C I
A N C
A A X

You probably can't remember more than seven letters, the capacity of working memory. Now see how many you can remember from this list.

X
C N N
P H D
F B I
C I A
N C A A
X

Each list contains the same letters in the same order. The reason you were probably able to remember more from the second list is that recognizable acronyms popped out of long-term memory as "chunks," and this "chunked" information allowed you to fit a lot more data into your limited working memory space. Someone from a remote village in Papua New Guinea, for example, would probably find each list equally difficult to remember because he wouldn't have acronyms like FBI and CIA stored as chunks in long-term memory for easy retrieval. The more information we have in long-term memory, the more "chunking" we can do, and the more efficient and productive our thinking.

Critical for things like reading comprehension, mathematical calculations, and problem solving, a highly functioning working memory is tantamount to a child's success in school and life. Kids who can hold multiple chunks in their working memory without getting distracted or losing their place have a very important advantage. Even a top-notch working memory will not help if there aren't enough facts and procedures stored in long-term memory, however; we need to have something to think *about*, after all. Long-term memory contains both facts (for example, the state capitals) and procedures (for example, how to add numbers). Willingham explains that there are four requirements for effective thinking.

1. Information from the environment
2. Facts from long-term memory
3. Procedures from long-term memory
4. Adequate space in working memory

Thinking depends on all four elements, and if the long-term memory cupboard is bare, all the space in working memory will be consumed by disparate bits of information. Consider two fifth graders trying to solve a math problem involving 7 times 6. John has memorized his multiplication tables and can recall the fact "42" from long-term memory as one chunk, leaving him lots of working memory space to deal with the rest of the problem. His classmate, Jim, however, doesn't have the multiplication facts wired into long-term memory so he uses precious working memory space to apply the procedure of multiplying 7 by 6. There's no doubt that John will have a tremendous leg up on Jim in solving the rest of the problem.

The working memory limit is so important that I call it the *Rule of Seven*. It's intended to underline the implications of the limits of working memory. Since its capacity is a precious and scarce commodity:

1. I don't want to clutter it with distractions.
2. I want to furnish my long-term memory with as much information and as many procedures as possible to allow maximum chunking.

Imagine sixteen-year-old Jake getting ready to take the PSAT test. He wants to do well so he's gotten a good night's sleep and has a big supply of sharpened #2 pencils in his pocket. The trouble starts when Jake starts the reading comprehension section of the test. His cell phone vibrates in his pocket, causing him to lose his train of thought. His working memory shifts from the test to wondering about the call or text. "What was I reading?" he asks himself as he refocuses. He redirects his attention to the text, which is an essay about the American Revolution. He can read the words "Declaration of Independence," "Minutemen," and "Liberty Bell," but gets bogged down trying to figure out what they mean since he has almost no factual information about the Revolutionary War in his long-term memory. When he gets to the end of the tract, he doesn't have a sense of what the writer said. To answer the questions, he must reread every sentence. His anxiety rises and his heart starts to race because he knows he's taking too long. Jake still has dozens of questions to answer when the proctor signals that the time is up.

The Rule of Seven explains why Jake struggled with the test. Each time Jake was distracted his working memory resources were directed away from the task at hand. In addition, instead of easily chunking the Revolutionary War terms, he had to devote working memory resources to wondering what a "Minuteman" might be.

Children with attention deficit disorder come wired with brains that are easily distracted, meaning that stray thoughts intrude and take up space in working memory. We'll discuss this in more detail in chapter 14. For now let's note that it's important to talk to your child's teacher or your pediatrician if your elementary school age child has difficulty finishing school work, listening to an entire story, staying on one activity, remembering things, sitting still, or staying focused. These children often need special help to build a better-functioning working memory.

Building Long-Term Memories

A very close friend teaches English to recent immigrants. One of the reasons she enjoys her work so much is her students' eagerness to pay attention to all that is novel and to learn when, where, and how it all fits into their new world. Encoding is the first step in memory formation, but for the memory to last, the encoded information must be stored. Here's where H.M.'s experience was so enlightening. After his surgery, he lost the ability to store memories so that he could retrieve them later. The surgeon had removed a key part of H.M.'s brain—the hippocampus.

Thanks to H.M., we now know that the hippocampus is where memories of facts and events—what scientists call declarative memory—are processed and sent to storage. If the hippocampus connects the newly encoded information with other preexisting memories stored elsewhere in the brain, then the new memory trace, a short-term memory, is consolidated and linked into the existing memory structure. It now has the potential to become a long-term memory. The brain has nooks and crannies all over the outer cortex for long-term memories. They can be enlarged or changed depending on new experiences. Forgetting happens when the neural connection remains unused and unfired, causing it to decay. For example, a child learning to print letters taps into her memories of drawing lines and circles. The more she practices connecting lines and curves into letters, the stronger the new neural letter patterns become. We'll talk later in the chapter about some of the things that can interfere with this process.

It's interesting and helpful to note that short breaks help us encode and store memories. For example, if your third grader is memorizing how to spell words, she'll be more successful if she practices in intervals, giving her brain a little vacation between study times. She can try the words after school, then wait and try them again after dinner. And if she really wants them in long-term memory, she should practice them again just before bedtime. As I'll explain in chapter 8, sleep consolidates and reinforces memories. Each time she practices, she brings those words into working memory, lighting up the neural network that reaches to her hippocampus and out into the cortex where word storage bins are. Firing those networks in intervals strengthens the connections faster than if she studies in one marathon session.

Memory Retrieval

We can't use encoded and stored memories unless we retrieve them. That's the third step in what we call "remembering." We retrieve memories every time we answer questions like "Where are those keys?" or "How do you find the volume of this cube?" or "Can you read the first word?" or "What's the name of that song?"

We also depend on retrieving memories to define who we are. Our sense of self is the accumulation of all our memories of our past experiences. Not only do they define who we are but we need them to make sense of new experiences in our lives. There was a recent case of an amnesiac man who showed up at a Seattle hospital with no sense of his identity. Although he could remember how to open a door and turn on a light, he had lost his entire autobiographical memory. The local media broadcast the story and family members quickly arrived at the hospital to identify the man. He didn't recognize any of them. He found the stories about who he was very interesting in a fictional sort of way because he couldn't relate any of them to himself. Unfortunately the media lost interest in the story so I never found out if he was able to recover his lost memories.

What Do Babies Remember?

Babies come fully equipped for memory. In fact, newborn infants pay attention to their mother's voice more than any other voice in the room within minutes after birth. They clearly remember that voice after listening to it for nine months. Infants will also respond to music they heard while still in the womb, showing they recognize the familiar sounds.

Over time, their memory feats become more impressive. Scientists have shown that babies as young as seven months are good at memory games. In one study, a six-month-old infant was shown a toy and two buckets, labeled A and B. In full view of the infant the researcher hid the toy in Bucket A and then let the child reach for it. This was repeated several times, the toy always hidden in Bucket A. The researcher then changed the game and, in full view of the infant, put the toy in Bucket B. The baby at six months reached for Bucket A, showing that she remembered that's where it usually was. Her working memory was not yet capable of retaining the new information so she went with her longer-term recollection. By seven months, however, her working memory was up to the task. She reached for Bucket B even after longer and longer waiting periods.

As your child gets older, play concentration card games like this one. Buy a deck of picture cards or use two decks of playing cards (the younger the child, the fewer the cards; start by using six cards—three pairs of matches—when your child is three years old). Show your child the pictures or the playing cards, then mix them up and place them facedown on the table in rows and columns. Start by turning one card over in its place. Then turn over the card in the other row that might be its match. If the pictures match, then the child claims them and gets another turn. If the cards don't match, replace both cards facedown again and the next person takes her turn picking cards. The object of the game is to collect as many matched pairs as possible. This game really challenges a child's visual memory and stretches her working memory to hold on to more items. Kids love this game—especially if you ham it up.

What About That First Birthday Party?

Young friends of ours just celebrated their son Devin's first birthday with an open house for 140 people—both parents wanted to thank their large extended families and a host of friends for helping them successfully navigate that sometimes overwhelming first year. I hope they took pictures because Devin won't remember the party, the food, or the guests. Babies remember their mother's voice from the womb, so why can't they recall much from before the age of three later in their lives?

Scientists have struggled with this question for years, dubbing it infantile amnesia in analogy to adult amnesia victims, or positing that these experiences become part of the subconscious mind. The explanation still eludes researchers, but they have discovered some surprising facts about infant memory. Dr. Andrew Meltzoff, codirector of the University of Washington Institute for Learning & Brain Sciences, revolutionized our understanding of infants and memory. In fact the basic memory processes in babies are the same as those found in adults. The difference is maturation and experience. One of Meltzoff's early experiments with babies clearly shows the memory strength of one-year-olds. He showed a baby a box, then touched his own forehead to the box; the box immediately lit up. Imagine how exciting that is for a one-year-old. But the curious thing is, Meltzoff did not let the baby try this new and exciting way to use a box. He made him wait. Later, the baby was brought back to the room with Meltzoff and the box. Without repeating the trick, Meltzoff handed the box to the baby, who immediately touched his forehead to the box and squealed with delight as the box lit up. He found one-year-olds could remember what to do with the box up to a week later, and eighteen-month-olds up to four months.

So if babies Devin's age remember past events, why won't he remember his birthday party? Scientists think it's because a baby's retrieval system is immature. Unless his parents replicate the original birthday party cues, repeatedly firing the birthday party memory circuit, it fades. As he gets older, his retrieval system will be more robust and he'll remember parties from year to year.

Building Memory Scaffolds Is Crucial

Another reason he won't remember his first birthday party is that this early memory has nothing to attach to in his brain. He doesn't have a life story yet. Without a key to that memory, it will sit isolated and impossible to retrieve. Memories are not recorded like photographs or movies, all in one whole piece. Instead individual sensory experiences are broken into bits and pieces and stored all over the brain, but connected by neural networks. When we remember an event, we pull the memory fragments into our working memory and reassemble them into a coherent whole. The biggest factor that helps us retrieve memories is our memory "scaffolding." New memories that fit into the scaffolding are easier to retrieve.

The beauty of this is that the scaffolding is easy to build. All you need to do is have conversations with your child and expose them to experiences. Now, your conversation with your one-year-old may be a little one-sided, but babies do remember, so we need to refire those memory circuits and reinforce his memory for family members and other features of his life. Our good friend Karen provides childcare for her grandson, Nathan. It's amazing to watch her help Nathan build memories of his family with the assortment of photographs that covers her refrigerator. Her earliest conversations with Nathan went like this. "Nathan, here's mamma," Karen would say as she pointed to the picture of Nathan's mom. "Here's babba," Karen announced as she shifted attention to the photo of Nathan's dad.

Karen built Nathan's recognition memory for many everyday things in Nathan's life. She would direct Nathan's attention by pointing with a verbal cue, helping him learn to focus on a picture or object. Then she would quickly follow up with more descriptive language. "There's mamma with her red shirt on, Nathan." As she pointed to a picture of a rabbit she added, "Remember Nathan, you went to the park and saw the bunny with mamma and babba." Sitting with Nathan in the yard, she would direct his attention to everything around him, the grass, trees, plants, flowers, bugs, toys etc., describing and connecting the object to his experience. Soon after that she began to ask him to point to an object. "Show me the spoon, Nathan" or "Where's the book?" Then, "Put your ball in the box. Good job, Nathan. This is a big box. What else can we put into it?"

As Nathan learns to speak, Karen can increase her efforts to help Nathan build memory scaffolding about the people, things, and events in his life. Her conversation will be very interactive, asking Nathan not only "who" the people are, but "what, where, when" and most importantly, "why" and "how" questions. With every question Karen will invite Nathan's response, involving him in the conversation. She will take his response and elaborate on it, feeding him more information that he can tuck away into his memory, building an ever more elaborate scaffolding of basic knowledge about his world. Typically, children reach two language milestones in the preschool years that feature this scaffolding process: talking about people and objects in the here and now, and telling stories about what happened. These both create opportunities for Karen to enrich Nathan's personal memory and knowledge.

Just think of all the information Nathan will remember from his conversations with his grandmother.

"Nathan, see the ball. It's a blue ball."

"Nathan, where's the ball? Show me the ball."

"What's this, Nathan? Yes, it's a ball. Can we play catch with the ball? Roll the ball to grandma. This ball rolls on the floor because it's round."

"Remember yesterday, Nathan, when you played catch with Grandpa? What did you do with the ball? Why did the ball go up in the air? That's right, Nathan, the ball went up because you threw it. Then it came down."

"Tell me about a game we can play with the ball, Nathan. Yes, we can play baseball. You played baseball with your babba, didn't you? What else do we need to play baseball? Do you know? That's right, we need a bat. This bat is long and fat, isn't it? What do we do with our bat and ball? Wow, you hit the ball very hard with the bat and made the ball go far just like your babba did yesterday. Your smile tells me you feel happy. What do you want to do next with the bat?"

By involving Nathan in the conversation and not talking at him, he'll learn more words and he'll remember fuller pictures and thoughts about how his world works. Loyola University Chicago scientist Catherine Haden conducted a longitudinal study and found that parents and caregivers increase their children's learning potential when they talk with their children about past events. The more elaborate the scaffolding is in the preschool years—the more knowledge a child has—the more brain locations he has in the future to which he can link new memories. When it comes to memory, the rich get richer.

How Talk Can Build Children's Memories

These researchers outlined several conversation tips they found help build kids' memory and understanding:

1. Ask your child who, what, when, where, why, and how questions, as in "Why do we wear this special baseball glove?"
2. Make associations between what's happening now and what a child already knows. For instance, "You watched baseball with your babba yesterday, didn't you. How can we play baseball?"
3. Follow up on a child's interest with more questions and talk. "What else do we need to play baseball? Do you know?"
4. Give the child positive feedback on her comments or actions. "Good job."

I'll add one tip of my own. Tell your child stories and encourage them to tell you stories. Storytelling helps kids build narrative skills and retrieve memories of life events and knowledge. Kids love stories, and reminiscing and storytelling with your child builds memory skills. Here's an idea for a family story game from the article "Memory Exercises for Everyday" by Jenny Rachel Wilson: Take three objects and put them on a tray. Take turns making up a story connecting the objects to each other, with one person starting and the next person adding a sentence, and so on. At the end of the story, take the tray away and see who can remember the three objects.

Emotions Mark Memories for Easy Retrieval

Some memories are etched so clearly that we can recall them in great detail years later; we call these flashbulb memories. Just mentioning the date September 11 guarantees a cascade of crystal-clear feelings and images. The emotional impact of that event chemically tagged the memory so vividly that I even remember I was tying my tie when I heard the first report on the radio of a jet crashing into one of the World Trade Center towers.

The brain's basic job is to help us survive and thrive so especially important events are chemically tagged for quick and easy retrieval. The events can be scary and dangerous like 9/11 or especially happy like a wedding or the birth of a child. Whenever an event triggers a strong emotion, as with 9/11, the brain chemically tags the memory of that event. The stronger the emotion is, the stronger the tag. Memories of these events are much more likely to register in long-term memory; they last longer and are easier to recall.

Your brain will actually remember the emotions of the event much more clearly than the details over time. Here are some suggestions to help children manage emotional memories.

- Teach children to name their feelings to help them understand and build emotional control. Happy events are fun and easy to recall, whereas sad, scary, or angry memories can be haunting.
- Help children sort out their feelings as they build their life stories. Painful family or community memories can overwhelm children without support.
- Talk in a supportive, calm manner. "I know you are feeling angry. . . ." "It feels sad when you get . . ." Naming and understanding feelings helps parents and children build strong, close relationships and promotes emotional growth.

Emotions Can Build Powerful Connections

Every Christmas Eve I gathered my three kids in my lap and read them *The Night Before Christmas*. I started when Dan was two months old and stopped when my kids were so big that they draped over the couch. That tradition actually started with my own father and still evokes strong emotions when I think of him. What I find particularly rewarding is when my kids start talking about the traditions they would like with their own children. I am a strong believer in traditions as a way to build strong connections and values in children. Kids thrive in an environment of safety, security, warmth, and love. These emotions are powerful motivators when linked to behaviors that we want children to continue.

Another trait that I value is perseverance, sticking to a job until it's done even if it's hard. Kids build self-esteem when they build competency, the proud "I can do it" feeling.

"Dad, can you help me with this essay?" Brian asked one evening.

"What's it about?" I said.

"We read a book in class and I have to write my reactions to it and I don't know what to say," Brian responded.

"Tell me about the story—who were the main characters and what did they do?"

Brian proceeded to relate the story and in the process actually talked about how he felt. Without having said anything, I suggested he should just start writing. An hour later, Brian came in and proudly showed his finished essay. What I hope Brian will remember is his good feelings when his efforts produced a job well done. We want as many positive emotional memories as possible for our kids to take with them throughout life.

Memory Strategies—The Game Plan

I remember the day the dreaded multiplication tables came home in Dan's backpack. My own youthful experience with multiplication tables was painful, leaving me with memories of my father's frustration. I was prepared to give Dan whatever flash card help he needed even if it took forever. Expecting a struggle, I was surprised when Dan cheerfully took out his multiplication table chart. All I could see were 144 math facts that needed to be committed to memory. Dan, however, had a plan. He was already using memory strategies, such as making associations and grouping, chunking the information, which would make the task so much easier. By the time he finished explaining about x0's, x1's, x2's, x5's, x10's, and that 6 x 3 = 3 x 6, etc., which he marked off with highlighter all over his chart, he ended up with a couple dozen multiplication facts that he actually had to memorize. Now I was feeling a little left out. Not such a big deal after all.

I also remember Erin asking me to quiz her on biology terms when she was in high school. Whenever I asked her a term, she had linked it to another fact to help her remember it. These mnemonic tricks work because they create additional neural paths to the information. The technical name for this is "elaborative encoding," meaning that I want as many connections as possible, increasing the odds that one of them will fire, enabling me to retrieve the memory.

Elementary and high school kids face many memory challenges. How well they do depends a great deal on their working memory, how much basic knowledge they have, and how adept they are at using memory strategies. As kids progress through school they need ever more sophisticated tactics to support more complex thinking and calculating. Researchers David Bjorklund, Charles Dukes, and Rhonda Brown describe several techniques to enhance memory.

1. **Rehearsal:** Younger elementary kids use simple verbal rehearsal, such as repeating their ABCs or spelling words over and over again. Older kids will often modify this into a "self-test"—they will say or write the item, look away, repeat, then check to see if they are correct. This is based on the "neurons that fire together, wire together" principle.
2. **Organize into categories:** It's easier to remember information in

chunks. Younger children can put items into a category, e.g., these are animals, these are foods. Older kids can be taught to find the categories or to cluster ideas. A student studying history might be asked to find the three main reasons for the start of the Civil War.

3. **Retrieval:** Help kids develop cues that aid in memory retrieval. Younger kids might need pictures. Older kids can use mnemonic cues and outlines.
4. **Study time:** Teach children to do memory tasks in intervals. Older kids can be taught to structure study time and spend more time on harder tasks.
5. **Elaboration:** Teach older kids to associate new knowledge with what they already know, create a bigger picture, even create a crazy picture cue in their heads that will trigger an association between two things.
6. **Study techniques:** High school students need study techniques to help them memorize large amounts of material. Summarizing, underlining, and identifying main ideas helps create structure that aids memory.

Help Your Child Build a Memory Game Plan

For infants and preschoolers, the game plan is simple. Give them love and security and use conversation and experiences to help them learn about themselves and the world around them. Preschoolers don't use effective memory strategies because they're not developmentally ready. Their brains' neural networks need to grow and wire in. Play simple memory and category games and build basic knowledge with your child in the preschool and early elementary years.

Older children often come up with some memory strategies of their own. We can teach them others. The basic game plan starts with asking kids to think about what's in their memories and how memory works. Memory isn't something we usually think about; we just do it. By asking your child how she remembers, she will start to understand the importance of paying attention, naming things, grouping information, and rehearsing. Ask your child, "How did you study those terms?" and see what strategies he uses. "Did you look at the word, cover it, say it out loud or write it, and then check?" Suggest other strategies like outlining, creating associations, finding patterns, and grouping. Remember the advantage gained by engaging working memory in intervals. That gives your neural networks more chances to refire over the same network. Your child's memory will improve with practice. The more memory strategies your child can choose from, the more successful he or she will be at school.

Here are four ways to build better memory strategies:

1. Play memory games.
2. Practice putting items into categories.
3. Create multisensory memories: repeat out loud, write down, or create.
4. Build study techniques for text material, such as underlining or identifying main ideas.

How Do We Remember How to Ride a Bike?

To answer the last question from the beginning of this chapter, "Why do I remember how to ride a bike?" consider how a young child first masters this complicated task. I fell a lot so I had to pick myself up and repeat my attempts over and over, each time inching closer to balancing. What happened during these practice sessions? My brain created a neural network for riding a bike, firing with every movement and adding to the network each time I could pedal a second longer. Eventually, after a lot of practice, my muscles wired in a new skill.

My bicycle riding went from an explicit, or conscious, memory while I was learning into an unconscious, or implicit, memory once I could ride like the wind. Implicit memories are those that take a lot of time and effort to learn, like riding a bike, using a keyboard, or reading, but just happen automatically once learned. The movements or thoughts happen quickly outside of our conscious, working memory. If you remember H.M.'s story from the beginning of this chapter, he couldn't remember what he had for breakfast, but he could learn a new motor skill, like drawing—but he couldn't tell you about his new skill later. His explicit memory for details and facts was cut off in surgery, but his implicit memory system functioned. Want to get lost in your unconscious self? Practice a skill until it becomes "second nature."

DO

- ✓ Talk, sing, play, and read with your baby.
- ✓ Point your baby's attention to and talk about people and objects around her.
- ✓ Reminisce about people and past events with your preschooler. "Remember when we . . ."

- ✓ Involve your preschooler with who, what, where, when, how, and why questions.
- ✓ Build your child's basic knowledge about the world.
- ✓ Play memory games with your child.
- ✓ Help your child or teen make memory tasks multisensory.
- ✓ Make homework time distraction-free.
- ✓ Talk with your child or teen about how he remembers. What strategies does he use?
- ✓ Talk to your child's or teen's teacher about how he or she teaches memory strategies.
- ✓ Teach your children about the Rule of Seven and its implications for good thinking.

DON'T

- ✗ Don't overstimulate your baby with too many playthings.
- ✗ Don't talk at your child, instead of with your child.
- ✗ Don't forget to ask your child questions about their world.
- ✗ Don't let your child get too little sleep. Memory neurons keep firing during sleep.
- ✗ Don't encourage your child or teen to study in marathon sessions. Instead space study over time.
- ✗ Don't let digital media interfere with your child or teen developing focused attention.
- ✗ Don't miss an opportunity to build memories.

What do I want to continue?

____

____

____

What do I want to change?

____

____

____

FIVE

Brain Food: Nutrition and the Brain

It happened every morning. My mother would greet us with a smile on her face and a spoon of cod liver oil in hand. We hated the fishy smell and taste, but my mother never wavered. Who knew my mother was a neuroscientist! Today brain scientists extol the virtues of the omega-3 fatty acids found in cold-water fish—like cod—for brain health and growth. My mother would be surprised to know she was on the cutting edge of brain science and nutrition.

Everyone knows nutritious foods build strong bodies. They build healthy brains, too. Unfortunately our Western diet is full of sugary, fatty, and fast foods that don't do our brains any favors. From the moment of conception, our brains rely on the foods we eat to supply the nutrients and fuels needed for brain growth and performance. Just as a car won't run if you put sugar in the tank, our brains can't function well if we don't eat the right fuel.

Our Kids' Brains Are Growing

The food we give our children affects their brain growth in three ways: the brain's cellular structure, the wiring of neural circuits responsible for everything from heartbeats to our thoughts and feelings, and the production of myelin, which insulates the neural pathways to enable electrical impulses (information) to move faster and more securely.

Remember, a baby's brain at birth, even with complete circuits for basic survival, weighs only around a quarter of an adult-sized brain. The brain areas needed for complex thought, learning, and feeling still need to grow and wire together. This process continues through childhood right up into adolescence and young adulthood, when the prefrontal cortex, the brain's "executive center," is fully wired. The science of nutrition and the brain is fairly new. We do know that eating healthy "brain food" improves how children feel, sharpens their memory and attention, increases learning and concentration, and builds an agile, quicker-thinking brain.

PARENT TOOL KIT

Nutrition and the Brain

Children eat a lot during their growing years. With the myriad of food choices in our culture, it is easy to forget what foods the brain needs every day. Use the items in this tool kit to assess your understanding of the importance of brain-building foods.

Yes	No	
☐	☐	1. The brain needs certain nutrients to function well.
☐	☐	2. My child eats a healthy breakfast.
☐	☐	3. I know what my child eats for lunch.
☐	☐	4. I understand what my child's brain needs for a constant source of energy.
☐	☐	5. My child consumes protein from meat and/or plant sources.
☐	☐	6. I am on the lookout to eliminate "bad" fats from my child's diet.
☐	☐	7. I understand the role of "good" fats in a healthy brain.
☐	☐	8. Eating meals together as a family is important.
☐	☐	9. Snack time can be important brain-building time.
☐	☐	10. As a family we talk about healthy foods and healthy brains.

The more yeses in this tool kit the more likely your child's food will be brain building.

A child's brain works full speed every moment of the day. Besides directing all the body's activities and growing, the brain is busy making sense of all the input your child sees, hears, smells, tastes, and touches. On top of that, the brain has to encode what's important into memory and have it handy for easy retrieval. Your brain needs a lot of energy to function. Remember, although the brain accounts for only 2 percent of the body's weight, it consumes about 20 percent of the body's energy. That's why what we eat is so important.

Glucose Is the Brain's Fuel

Glucose (sugar) is the energy fuel your brain needs to function. While glucose is not listed on anyone's menu of favorite foods, carbohydrates and other foods that can be converted to glucose are. The best sources of carbohydrates are whole grains, vegetables, and fruits. These foods are converted to glucose during digestion and travel to the brain via the bloodstream. If your child's brain doesn't get a steady supply of glucose her physical and emotional energy will drop, and she'll have concentration and attention problems.

As I looked out over my second-hour class of high school students, I could tell who had eaten breakfast and who hadn't. Kids who skipped breakfast had that tired, glazed look in their eyes, their heads already drooping. The fact that half the class shared this drained demeanor did not bode well for learning French that morning. I gave my pep talk about eating a good breakfast, but my sensible advice fell on deaf ears. If I had known the current brain science on nutrition and attention at the time, I'd have been talking about complex carbohydrates. As it was, I could see that I'd motivated the kids to head straight for the vending machines for a candy bar or soda pop "pick-me-up." Glucose is sugar, so why were these sugary foods a bad idea for getting the teens primed to learn?

The refined or simple sugars found in cookies, candy, cakes, and soda do supply the brain with a quick jolt of glucose. Unfortunately the brain doesn't function well with a "jolt." It experiences a quick spike in energy followed by an even quicker drop. This drop can lead to emotional slumps, fatigue, and concentration problems. Many of the snacks students substitute for breakfast or eat to give them a pick-me-up end up backfiring. Studies show that when teens skip breakfast, their food choices throughout the rest of the day don't make up for the vitamins and nutrients they've already missed. Their classmates who do eat breakfast are much more likely to eat brain-power foods the rest of the day.

Since a child's brain needs to be powerful all day, it's a bad idea to rely on sugary, fat-filled foods for brain energy, memory, and concentration. Whole grains, nuts, fruits, and vegetables are a better choice. In fact, a third of a child's diet should be complex—not simple—carbohydrates.

Proteins: The Brain's Building Blocks

A child's brain needs protein to grow new brain cell connections. The body breaks down the protein a child eats into its building blocks: amino acids. The brain then uses these to build new neural pathways, which allow brain cells to communicate with each other. The brain also converts amino acids into the chemical messengers or neurotransmitters used to carry messages from one brain cell to another.

The body can manufacture some amino acids on its own, but there are nine that we must include in our diet. They are often called the "essential amino acids" because it is critical that we eat them. Complete protein-rich foods are eggs, meat, fish, and dairy products like milk, cheese, and yogurt. Quinoa, the grain grown high in the Andes Mountains, is the only plant source that is a complete protein food. These foods contain all the essential amino acids the brain needs. Other plant sources of protein—grain products, beans, legumes, soy, and other vegetables—are incomplete proteins. You have to be careful to eat a variety of plant protein sources so the brain gets all the amino acids it needs. A brain-healthy diet includes a variety of protein sources, whether you are a meat eater or vegetarian.

Brain building is so intense in the first three years of life that baby's food should be packed with nutrition, filled with the right amount of vitamins, minerals, fat, and protein.

I remember standing in a friend's kitchen early one morning. Karen was cooking French toast for her three-year-old daughter, Claire, who was a very fussy eater. Karen had cooked the French toast the usual way with eggs and milk. Then she did something unusual. She cracked an extra egg on top of the toast.

"I have to sneak extra protein in for Claire or she won't eat it. If I give her a separate egg, she'll leave it on the plate. But she doesn't seem to mind when it's on top of French toast." I was a new parent at the time and was impressed at Karen's cleverness. I learned too that parents need to pay attention to what their children are eating or not eating and work in clever ways to give them a nutritious diet. What kids eat does matter because their brains are constantly building new connections.

Fats: The Brain's Insulation

Low fat, high fat, good fat, bad fat—the words jump off every box on the grocery aisle. We know our adult hips and stomachs don't need more fat, but what about a child's brain? The importance of fat in a child's diet cannot be overstated because the brain is mostly made of fat—over 60 percent. Each brain cell or neuron has an outer membrane composed mainly of essential fatty acids. Healthy fats make sure these membranes remain pliable and not rigid, enabling each cell to do its job. The billions of brain cells do their jobs by "talking" to one another, sending electrical signals down a long cable or axon that makes the jump to another cell's axon with the help of neurotransmitters. Myelin, around 70 percent fat and 30 percent protein, is a protective covering that coats the outside of these cables and allows neurotransmitters to form "docking" stations at the end of each cable. Myelination of neurons is important because it keeps the electrical signal intact as it moves down the cable, enabling that signal to move at lightning speed. Without this fatty insulation, brain cells would not be able to process effectively.

Four sixth graders were huddled around a table at school. Their task was to imagine a new food product and create an ad touting its benefits. I was helping in my son's class with a unit on media advertising. I marveled at how quick these kids were. They were reading, brainstorming, writing, talking back and forth, summarizing information, and generating clever ideas. They were quick and agile thinkers, blending ideas until they had the project completed. How much did myelination contribute to their ability? Quite a bit, I think. They must have been eating quite a bit of healthy fats!

Now here's the key—relatively few neurons are myelinated at birth. That's why a baby's movements are uncoordinated, why his eyes are unfocused and why a baby is born "helpless." The brain's neurons are having a hard time talking to one another and a lot of brain building needs to happen. Myelination happens most rapidly in the first two years of life. We can see this most easily as babies gain control of their hands, arms, and legs. This process continues throughout childhood and into adolescence and early adulthood as major areas of the brain are "wired" in.

Good Fats and Bad Fats

Not all fats are created equal. By now we've all heard that unhealthy saturated and hydrogenated or trans fats clog our arteries and hearts. But do we know the effects of good fats and bad fats on the brain? Our brain cells function best when their membranes and myelin coverings are flexible. Saturated and trans fats, found in partially hydrogenated vegetable oils and shortening (think processed foods, junk food, and sweets), will stiffen a brain cell membrane and decreases that cell's ability to do its job. We literally can't think as well. Once in the membrane these bad fats also inhibit the cell's ability to process healthy nutrients.

What type of fat, then, is most healthy for a child's brain? Neuroscientists have found that the brain functions best when it's given long-chain polyunsaturated fats, especially the omega-3s my mother supplied us in her spoonfuls of cod liver oil. These fats, found in milk and other dairy products, fish, eggs, avocados, seeds, and nuts, keep the brain cell membranes and myelin flexible, allowing brain cells to do their best work.

For infants, mother's milk is the best source for these good fats. That's why the American Academy of Pediatrics advises moms to breast-feed their children for at least six months if possible, or a full year or more. Breast milk is the ultimate brain food for babies (with an added iron supplement starting around six months of age), containing the perfect balance and type of carbohydrates, proteins, fats, and other essential nutrients.

The brain growth of children is so crucial during the first two years of life that there is no reason to feed babies and toddlers low-fat foods. They need a greater proportion of fat in their diets than older children, anywhere from 34 to 54 percent of total calories. In fact, children under five need more fat in their diets than older children and adults. If your child is not lactose intolerant or milk allergic, whole milk is a good choice for children in their second year, when they are able to switch to cow's, soy, or goat's milk. Wait to introduce lower-fat 2 percent milk until after a child is two years old and save the skim milk until a child is five. There are lots of sources of good fats for your child's diet if he or she is lactose intolerant, including lactose-free or lactose-reduced milk. Talk with your pediatrician for recommendations if you are concerned about weight.

Vitamins, Minerals, and Other Micronutrients: The Brain's Guards

Vitamins are those small food nutrients with a long list of alphabet-soup names: vitamins A, B complex, C, D, E, and K. The list of minerals sounds like we're in a mining camp: iron, phosphorus, sodium, magnesium, manganese, and calcium. We know they are critical for healthy bones, skin, eyes, hair, and organs. But what do they do for the brain?

A brain without sufficient amounts of essential vitamins and minerals is a brain in trouble. Vitamins and minerals are essential for many brain functions, such as memory, cell protection, myelin production, and making sure the brain gets enough oxygen. They also are critical for converting amino acids into neurotransmitters, those chemicals that carry "messages" from one brain cell to another. If the brain handed out Academy Awards, vitamins and minerals would get the Oscars for best supporting actors. The brain uses thirty-eight of the forty-five nutrients the body uses for healthy functioning.

Fortunately a healthy, well-balanced diet will provide the vitamins, minerals, and other nutrients our children's brains need in abundance. Vitamins in a pill should never replace healthy food, but to be sure your child is getting the recommended daily allowances (RDAs) of vitamins and minerals, check with your pediatrician; they might recommend adding a vitamin supplement. In that case avoid brands that lace the vitamins with sugar. Besides harming children's teeth, the sweet, sugary varieties aren't good for the brain. Also, too much of anything, even a good thing like vitamins, isn't a good idea, so don't over-dose your child.

Pregnant women should take prenatal vitamins and supplements prescribed by their physician during pregnancy, because the baby's brain development depends on her eating healthy foods and vitamins. Following dosage directions is important, however, because mega-doses can actually be harmful. Brain health is a principal reason that nutrition programs for pregnant moms and young children are an investment in our future.

Antioxidants: The Brain's Protectors

As the brain uses glucose, oxidation occurs and unstable "free radicals" are released. These free radicals just wander around looking for something to hook on to. They want some stability. Unfortunately, when they latch on to brain cells, they oxidize and damage the cells. If you peel a banana and leave it out in the open for an hour, it will get brown and squishy. That's oxidation in action and gives you an idea of what's happening in your brain. The good news is that there are chemicals that combat the troublemaking free radicals. They're called antioxidants, and fruits (especially blueberries), green leafy vegetables, fish, nuts, oils, and vitamins C and E are loaded with them. A healthy diet with antioxidant protection minimizes free-radical damage.

There's a children's garden in our neighborhood. Each summer over a dozen preteens gather with a couple of adults and plant a large vegetable garden together. They plan, prepare the soil, plant the seeds, water, weed, and harvest. Once the produce starts coming in, they run their own miniature farmer's market outside a local café. They market the produce with posters around the neighborhood and make sure everyone going into the café knows they can buy some locally grown, great-looking veggies at a good price. The kids handle the sales, and the profits are saved for a well-earned outing. When I watch these kids I realize they are learning more than sales and marketing. They are making healthy food connections and discovering where their food comes from. I am sure that they are also enjoying some of their harvest.

The Common American Diet

We Americans as well as people in other developed countries eat more food that is highly processed, and processing means a lot of bad fats, simple sugars, and salt. You couldn't design a diet that is less healthy for the brain than the one that many American children eat. There is almost no good brain food in the popular "beige diet" that features fried chicken nuggets, French fries, pizza, and macaroni and cheese.

The food industry knows that our built-for-survival brain likes three things: sweet, which indicates that the food is safe to eat; fat, which our body wants to store to help us survive the famine; and salt, which is necessary for survival. To boost sales, therefore, they load their products with all three.

As a result, we may feed our kids a lot of food that is laced with simple sugars without even realizing it, because the industry has dozens of words for sugar. Take a look at a list of ingredients on a package in your home and see how many of the following words you find:

- ☐ Brown-rice syrup
- ☐ Corn syrup solids
- ☐ Dextrin
- ☐ Fruit juice concentrate
- ☐ Honey
- ☐ Maltodextrin
- ☐ Mannitol
- ☐ Raw sugar
- ☐ Sorbitol
- ☐ Sucrose
- ☐ Turbinado
- ☐ Corn sweetener
- ☐ Cane juice
- ☐ Dextrose
- ☐ Glucose
- ☐ Invert sugar
- ☐ Malt syrup
- ☐ Maple syrup
- ☐ Rice syrup
- ☐ Sorghum
- ☐ Syrup
- ☐ Xylose
- ☐ Corn syrup
- ☐ Dehydrated cane juice
- ☐ Fructose
- ☐ High-fructose corn syrup
- ☐ Lactose
- ☐ Maltose
- ☐ Molasses
- ☐ Saccharose
- ☐ Sorghum syrup
- ☐ Treacle
- ☐ Any word ending in *ose*

These are all disguises for simple sugars. Pay special attention when these words appear among the first three or four ingredients. That means the product is mostly sugar. The reason that pediatricians and public health advocates want soda machines out of schools is that soda pop is nothing more than liquid candy.

The bad fats can hide, too. Descriptions like these usually mean "a lot of bad fat" when you see them at a restaurant: au gratin, battered, breaded, buffalo, buttered, creamed, crispy, fried, Hollandaise, Parmigiana, scalloped, Scampi.

This type of diet is a big factor in the current obesity epidemic. In fact, there was not one state in the United States that met the *Healthy People 2010* obesity target of less than 15 percent. According to the latest Centers for Disease Control statistics, 16.9 percent of children and adolescents are obese. While the health issues associated with being overweight and obese should motivate us to change our diets, the impact of this diet on our brains is just as important—especially for our kids.

Eat a Rainbow

What does a brain-healthy diet for children look like? Renowned nutrition expert Dr. Mary Story of the University of Minnesota makes it easy. "Kids should eat a rainbow," she says. "Brain-healthy foods come in a variety of colors, so think about a variety of vegetables, fruits, whole grains, low-fat or nonfat dairy products, and lean protein, and cook with olive or vegetable oil to have a brain-healthy diet." And she isn't talking about the rainbow of color dyes that get added to children's cereals to make them look fun.

Once your family has made a commitment to eating brain-healthy foods, has discussed the connection between food and health and their brains—how well they feel, think, and learn during the day—and has made a commitment not to skip breakfast and to try to eat healthy snacks, you might be wondering what your family should eat to start their day. Here's what brain scientists and nutrition experts recommend for brain power all day long:

BREAKFAST

Whole grain cereals. Avoid the sugared brands and add your own fruit, nuts, and seeds.

Fruits—all of the berries, oranges, plums, pears, kiwi, cherries, and bananas.

Eggs wrapped up in a whole-grain tortilla.

Oatmeal. Avoid the sweetened kinds in the packets. Perk it up with fruit, especially strawberries or blueberries.

Quinoa—the only grain that contains complete protein.

Whole-grain breads or toast with jam or real peanut or almond butter.

Leftover veggies or protein from last night's dinner is great when wrapped up in a tortilla and heated.

Yogurt with fruit.

Small glass of 100 percent fruit juice.

Glass of whole milk for children under three, 2 percent for kids under five, and skim when the kids are older.

Introducing Solid Foods

As soon as I held each of my children, I knew how special each was. I also knew how much I had to learn, since babies are so different from the teenage students I was used to teaching. Monica and I relied on advice from our pediatrician, Dr. Mace Goldfarb, about infant nutrition. He told us that babies need high-fat, calorie-dense, nutrient-filled food for brain development—specifically, breast milk or infant formula for the first six months.

Introduce solid foods between five and seven months; a good plan can help make the transition smooth and the brain healthy. First of all, since babies that age actually gum more than chew, all their food should be soft or soft cooked. Here are some of the recommended brain-healthy foods for five- to seven-month-olds.

- Cereals and grains like rice, barley, or oats
- Fruits like avocado, apricots, apples, bananas, mangos, nectarines, peaches, pears, plums, prunes, or pumpkin
- Vegetables including sweet potatoes, squash, carrots, green beans, peas, and parsnips
- Proteins like chicken, turkey, or tofu
- Whole-milk yogurt for dairy

Many parents are surprised that some babies between eight and ten months become less interested in food. That's because their newly found scooting and crawling mobility makes them more eager to explore. Not to worry. The little adventurers will not starve. The solid foods still need to be soft or soft cooked since their molars won't appear for several more months. In addition to the foods listed above, you can add the following brain-healthy items to a baby's menu: blueberries, pasta, egg yolks, and cheese. Pork can be added to the list of proteins.

By the time a baby is ten to twelve months old she may start to show some definite food preferences and may be already getting tired of pureed foods. Don't be surprised if she insists on feeding herself. Although she may put more food on the floor or in her hair with those early attempts, before long she'll have mastered the hand-eye-mouth coordination needed to hit the target.

Any food can trigger an allergic reaction and there's greater risk if there's a family history. Savvy parents know the telltale signs of food allergy, including runny nose, itchy eyes, and skin rashes. The most severe and dangerous reaction—requiring immediate medical care—is anaphylaxis, with symptoms like shortness of breath, hives, or stomach cramps.

There are two strategies that can minimize food allergy problems when introducing solid foods. First, it's best to introduce new foods in the morning or early afternoon so that you're not dealing with a bad reaction after your pediatrician's office hours or at night. Second, it's smart to follow the "four-day-wait rule." Waiting four days after introducing a new food allows time to make sure there isn't an allergic reaction and makes the list of suspects a lot shorter if there is. While any food can trigger an allergy there are some common culprits. Ninety percent of food allergies are caused by milk, eggs, peanuts, tree nuts, fish, shellfish, soy, and wheat. That's why the U.S. Department of Agriculture recommends that egg yolks not be introduced until a baby is eight months old, and egg whites until twelve months. Babies shouldn't eat peanut butter or shellfish until they're two years old.

Very young children's stomachs are small. When Dan started eating cereal, we gave him enriched cereal grains so that he would not fill up before he could eat a balanced meal and saved the whole grains until he was over eighteen months old. We avoided high-fiber foods because they're difficult for young children to digest.

We also followed Goldfarb's advice to be careful of choking hazards with young children. We avoided popcorn, nuts, seeds, hard or soft candies, or chunks of raw vegetables until our kids were four years old. We were careful to cut up any food into small pieces, especially round foods such as grapes or hot dogs, chunks of cheese, or fruit pieces. We made sure that harder-to-chew foods such as meats were first mashed or cut into tiny pieces.

With older kids, their food for lunch and dinner looks a lot like what we adults should eat.

LUNCH

Raw vegetables with a dip
Fruits and fruit smoothies
Small bites of protein from last night's dinner
Whole-grain breads for sandwiches
Salads
Whole-grain pastas
Soups made with beans and legumes
Yogurt with fruit
Cheese
Milk

DINNER

Vegetables, especially green leafy vegetables like spinach, broccoli, and kale, complemented with squash, peppers, sweet potatoes, cauliflower, and tomatoes.
Salads. Have the kids make their own, adding ingredients like avocado, nuts, and seeds.
Chicken, fish, seafood, or beef. Kids love hot dogs, but most are loaded with nitrates so it's best to make them occasional treats.
Whole-grain breads and pasta.
Potatoes.
Soups. Look for low-salt options. You can chop, sauté, and add turnip greens, kale, chard, or collard greens to a store-bought soup to make it a powerhouse.
Olive and canola oils are healthy oils but try sunflower, sesame, or pumpkin oil for a different flavor.
Milk.
Fruit or fruit smoothie for dessert.

Good and Bad Fish

Fish, a great source of omega-3s, is known as a "brain food" for good reason. Unfortunately our industrialized society has released tons of mercury into the air, which eventually falls into our oceans, rivers, and lakes, where fish consume it. Mercury is a known neurotoxin and can damage developing brains. The good news is that not all fish pose a mercury hazard, but it's important especially for young kids and pregnant moms to avoid those that do—swordfish, shark, king mackerel, tilefish, and albacore-white tuna.

The fish that are the richest in omega-3s are the cold-water varieties like salmon, mackerel, herring, lake trout, and sardines. Eating several servings a week is great brain food. Other recommended fish and shellfish are canned light (yellowfin and skipjack) tuna, catfish, tilapia, pollack, shrimp, clams, scallops, crabs, and oysters.

Snacks

A lot of unhealthy brain food sneaks into this category. The best way to get your child to eat healthy snacks is to have healthy food out and available. Snacks can be a time to pack in solid nutrition if we can limit what the

Chinese call "garbage food." Teens especially are drawn to frozen and processed foods at the same time their growth spurts spike hunger pangs. Since they're conscious about how they look, making the connection between junk food and their appearance might motivate them to eat a healthier diet than sweets and soda.

Give kids alternatives to processed snacks by providing treats such as:

- Fresh fruit or smoothies
- Veggies with dip
- Whole-grain crackers with cheese or real peanut butter
- Whole-grain cereal
- Homemade snack mix with nuts, raisins, cranberries, and whole-grain cereals
- Yogurt
- Whole-grain toast with melted cheese

It's important to encourage kids to drink water between meals—a big plus for healthy brain cells. It's easy for kids to mistake thirst for hunger, so keeping them hydrated can reduce snacking on junk food. Mid-morning and mid-afternoon snacks are important to keep glucose levels in the brain constant, but we need to be careful not to ruin their appetites before a brain-healthy meal.

Avoid Food Wars

Even though it's important to provide nutritious food for our children's brain health, we don't want to go overboard. There is nothing wrong with the occasional candy bar or ice cream sundae. I remember the Saturday night when our kids decided to take over the cooking duties. They kept the menu a secret, got the food, and set the table for Monica and me, complete with candles and cloth napkins. At the designated time, five-year-old Erin escorted us to our places. After we were seated, seven-year-old waiter Brian appeared with a beret atop his head and a towel over his arm. With paper and pencil in hand he announced our dinner menu: hot dogs, macaroni and cheese, and Jell-O.

When it came down to choosing their own menu our kids had ditched the veggies, fruits, and whole grains and headed straight for the hot dogs. Monica and I smiled at each other, ate with gusto, and gave the beaming waitstaff, Brian and Erin, and chief cook Dan a round of applause at the end of the meal.

Family meals can become battlegrounds if we're not careful. Left unchecked, kids often choose unhealthy foods. From the two-year-old who realizes he can close his mouth and refuse to eat, to the teen who skips breakfast and thinks chips and soda are a balanced diet, steering kids to a healthy diet can be a challenge. So we have to do so without making it a nonstop power struggle. This is a tricky balancing act, but here are some tried-and-true tips to help us find the middle ground.

- Don't use food as a reward. There's nothing wrong with a tall glass of lemonade and some chocolate chip cookies after completing some yard work, but avoid food treats as inducements for completing tasks.
- Toddlers and young children won't always eat the same amount at every meal, so don't force them to eat. Children know when they're full. If a child does not seem hungry at the dinner table, watch to see what he's eating right before the meal. If he has a glass of milk or fills up on other snacks, then he really won't sit down at the table and chow down what you've prepared.
- Use small servings of food on a child's plate. Large servings can seem overwhelming and an invitation to play with food instead of eating. If you keep portions smaller, your child may ask for more.
- Avoid food arguments. If a child refuses to eat, just remove his plate when dinner is over. Don't cook a whole second meal catering to his taste. He will be hungry by the next meal, if you haven't let him graze in the kitchen.
- Don't use food as an emotional replacement to help them feel good. Using food often to help a child "feel better" can lead to an unhealthy relationship with food and a lifelong struggle with weight.

Strategies to Encourage Healthy Eating

In this fast-food world with kid-targeted food ads and busy schedules, how do we put healthy foods on the table and how do we encourage our kids to eat them? If you've been living in fast-food, microwave land, here are some suggestions.

1. Plan ahead. If you have healthy foods, such as a variety of fruits and vegetables and whole grains on hand, you will use them in

meals. Even better is to actually plan some meals ahead of time so you can think about how to add brain-healthy ingredients.

2. Start small. Don't change your family's whole diet all at once. If you whisk all the familiar foods away, your kids might have trouble making such a big adjustment. Just try making one change at a time. For instance, try whole-wheat spaghetti instead of the familiar white kind.
3. Cut back on buying prepackaged, overprocessed, sugar- and trans-fat-filled snacks. Have a bowl of fruit on the table and a bowl of cut-up veggies in the fridge.
4. Don't let soda and sugar fruit drinks stand in for water. Encourage your kids to drink water between meals, with milk at mealtimes. One hundred percent fruit juice should be a treat.
5. Start talking about the connection between healthy food and how you look, feel, and learn.
6. Kids will copy what *you* do. If your kids don't see you eating healthy foods, either as snacks or at mealtimes, they won't eat them, either.

Maybe you just need to have a healthy food checkup. As kids get a little older, schedules get busier and sometimes we forget how easy, tasty, and fun it is to eat healthy. Try these ideas:

- Choose a rainbow. Have the kids help you shop. Ask them to find three different colored vegetables and three different colored fruits, add a few to your basket.
- The food processor is a healthy cook's best friend. Puree or chop up vegetables and add them to pasta sauces, soups, and other dishes. This is an easy way to get brain healthy foods into the meal.
- Stock up on good choices. Plan healthy snacks.
- Frozen veggies and fruits are a good convenience food. Their nutrients can last up to a year.
- Try a new food. Getting tired of eating the same three vegetables and fruits? Try something new. Mix the colors.
- Make a family commitment to eating healthy foods.

IS YOUR CHILD A FUSSY EATER? TRY THESE IDEAS.

1. Make sure your child's portions are small. Mounds of food can look overwhelming. Pediatricians recommend that a child's

serving of each food equal "one tablespoon for each year of a child's age."

2. Raise cooks. Eating is central to everyone's life. Involve your kids in meal planning, cooking, setting the table, and cleaning up.
3. Keep trying. Many kids will reject a new food the first time it's served. It usually takes frequent servings before it looks safe to try. Be persistent, without forcing the change. Try pairing a new food with one that your child knows and likes.
4. Plant some veggies. Even a tomato in a pot will help kids see the connections between what they eat and where it comes from. It's exciting to eat veggies right from the garden.
5. Make mealtime a media-free zone. Kids will pay more attention to the TV, video game, iPod, or cell phone screen than they will to the food on their plate. Our brains are hardwired to pay attention to movement, so that's where their attention will be.

My last advice is to eat meals together as a family. Children eat healthier meals when they eat with their families; more fruits and vegetables and less soda. A University of Minnesota study also found that teens who eat with their families do better in school and have fewer high-risk behaviors such as drug abuse and sexual activity, and fewer suicide attempts, violent acts, and academic issues.

Children's brains, right up through adolescence, are wiring in social skills. They need to fire their neurons repeatedly to acquire these life skills. Chatting with each other, talking about the news of the day, practicing table manners ("Please pass the . . ."), sharing memories, and listening to your kids' stories strengthens family bonds and helps kids wire in these skills. When healthy brain food is on the table your kids are getting a double dose of protection.

DO

- ✓ Talk with your kids about the connections between healthy brains and healthy foods.
- ✓ Make sure your kids eat a healthy breakfast with protein, if possible, and servings of milk or yogurt, fruit, and whole grains.
- ✓ Avoid "food wars."
- ✓ Have family meals together.
- ✓ Avoid simple sugar treats.

- ✓ Have healthy snacks like fruits and veggies available.
- ✓ Choose food to eat, especially vegetables and fruits, in a rainbow of colors.
- ✓ Get kids involved in planning and preparing meals.
- ✓ Drink water and milk, instead of soda and fruit drinks.
- ✓ Aim for five fruit and veggie servings every day.
- ✓ Take care to wash fruits and vegetables thoroughly. Research has linked commonly used pesticides with attention deficit disorders (ADD and ADHD).
- ✓ Plan meals and buy food at the start of the week to avoid impulse, fast-food eating.
- ✓ Make one small change at a time.

DON'T

- ✗ Don't put a bottle of soda on the table at dinnertime.
- ✗ Don't skip breakfast, lunch, dinner, or snacks.
- ✗ Don't go overboard. Don't become the "food police."
- ✗ Don't let your children "graze" all day long.
- ✗ Don't forget that frozen vegetables and fruits also have high nutrient values.
- ✗ Don't get into brain energy slumps by eating sugary, processed treats.
- ✗ Don't have a list of "forbidden foods"—your child will just want them more. Any food can be eaten once in a while.

What do I want to continue?

____

____

____

What do I want to change?

____

____

____

SIX

Play Is Serious Business

"Dad, can we play on the jumping bed tonight?"

That familiar question echoed hundreds of times when my three kids were little. They christened an old queen-sized mattress Monica and I put on the floor of our semi-finished attic the "jumping bed" and spent hours rolling around and jumping on it, especially during the long, snowy Minnesota winters when outside play meant thick layers of wool and down.

Following a treasured routine, I trudged upstairs pretending to be very tired. The kids followed, barely able to contain their excitement. "Kids," I said, "I'm really tired tonight. Can you give me a couple of minutes of peace and quiet on the jumping bed? Why don't you just play quietly while I rest?"

"Okay, Dad," Brian responded, and Erin piped in with "Sure, Dad, you just rest."

Of course, I knew the pretext. No sooner was I stretched out "asleep" when a Walsh kid hurtled through the air, and mayhem commenced. Dan, Brian, and Erin either took turns jumping on me or combining forces to bring me to submission. The soft mattress provided enough cushion so I could flip them over my back as they ran full speed at me. I feigned panic with pleas for mercy while the kids erupted in shrieks of laughter. They loved these epic battles, and, as I'm sure you guessed, I did, too. We had great fun together and burned off some pent-up kid energy. What I didn't realize is that the jumping, running, rolling, and flipping also wired together a myriad of important brain circuits.

Sensory Integration and Movement

The brain's job, as master control center, is to interpret, understand, and react to the enormous amount of information streaming in through a child's senses. Everything he can see, touch, smell, taste, and hear, as well as his sense of movement and his body in space, sparks brain growth. But just building up large amounts of sensory information is only the first step. It's in play where the real business of childhood happens—where the child interprets, integrates, understands, and derives meaning from this tsunami of sensory data.

Only 17 percent of a newborn's neurons are wired together, and a baby's senses are not equally developed at birth. Touch is the furthest along, and the area around the mouth is the most sensitive. When our son Dan was an infant, like all babies he put everything in his mouth as soon he could, the best way for him to extract the most information about a toy, his hand, even his toes. In these early months he couldn't visually focus well, control his limbs, or coordinate many movements. It's not that Dan arrived completely helpless. He came prewired with, among other skills, the capacity to nurse, digest, eliminate, and signal distress with a cry. However, rolling, sitting, crawling, standing, and eventually walking were still months away. Just as the brain wires together the circuits that integrate incoming sensory data, it also coordinates thousands of large and small muscle contractions involved in eye movement or needed to grasp, hold, drop, roll, sit, stand, walk, balance, and run, to say nothing of advanced skills like running, skipping, riding a bicycle, or playing ball. While all these skills will eventually be smooth and automatic, first the brain must wire together all the neural networks needed for these complicated operations. No wonder babies spend so much time sleeping, I thought.

In chapter 1 we discussed the phenomenon of neural blossoming and pruning. Blossoming, you will recall, is the overproduction of dendrites—the branches on the ends of the brain cells. Pruning explains how experience selects which branches will be wired into networks while allowing the others to wither back and die. A child's brain engages in a myriad of dynamic blossoming and pruning episodes so she can wire the neurons that are used into networks. The basic brain principle—the neurons that fire together wire together—explains how it all happens.

At a recent social gathering of six families, fifteen-month-old Nathan held center stage. He worked the room and proceeded to charm everyone in sight. He played pat-a-cake with twenty-nine-year-old Lucy before moving on to a game of peekaboo with sixty-three-year-old Bob. Then he moved to the middle of the room and started to spin around in circles. He went faster and faster until he got so dizzy he fell into a giggling heap. As soon as he regained his balance he was up spinning and falling again.

As I watched Nathan play, it occurred to me that his games were good brain development examples. He practiced hand-eye coordination with his pat-a-cake game with Katie while simultaneously working on his sense of rhythm and cadence. His peekaboo game with Bob helped him strengthen his sense of object permanence, to know an object is still there even when he can't see or touch it. Finally, Nathan instinctively spun himself around, as all kids love to do, to wire the very complicated brain circuits behind balance. It turns out balance requires connecting three systems: the sensitive nerve endings in our inner ear (what's called the vestibular sense) connect with our sense of vision and these both connect with our "proprioceptive sense," our body awareness as we move. All three systems synchronize for good balance and fluid movement. Spinning, rocking, and rolling all build the connections that bind them together. That's why kids love to spin and play on playground equipment that goes around in circles. Neuroscientists have discovered that activities such as spinning and swinging also encourage a child's ability to focus their attention. The cerebellum, one of the brain's four major areas, is associated with movement and is also connected to the abstract thinking and mental focus areas of the brain. Nathan, with his rendition of a whirling dervish, had a great time entertaining his adult audience, but he also did some heavy-duty brain construction at the same time.

Play stimulates kids to move their bodies and build their brains. Toddlers love to be twirled and turned upside down. Preschoolers love to run and bend their bodies into different shapes. School-age kids love to climb and run. Teens sometimes risk life and limb. Play is the laboratory where a child's brain integrates sensory information to make sense of her world, coordinates muscle movement, and eventually thinks, first concretely about what she senses, then abstractly about what she imagines.

If you sense that your child does not play because he does not meet movement developmental milestones, talk to your pediatrician to evaluate for possible neurological or motor problems. Possible signs to be aware of would be a significant delay in turning over, crawling, or walking; a clumsy gait when other children have started to run easily; a significant lack of coordination; muscle rigidity; or engaging in significant repetitive behavior, such as constant spinning. Motor skill delays can keep a child from participating in activities at school and can have academic and social repercussions. Every child is unique as she grows and meets her developmental milestones. You know your child best and it's always okay to check out your concern with your pediatrician if you feel your child is out of sync with what you would expect at her age.

Move to Build a Better Brain

Kids naturally enjoy moving their bodies, so encouraging this one is easy.

- Have a box of things for outdoor games: balls, ropes, Frisbees, beanbags, etc. Let kids make up their own games and rules.
- Let your child swing and climb often, if not in a yard, then at a park.
- Watch your child explore outdoor places.
- In the summer, a sprinkler or small pool can provide great fun. There may be water fun at a local park.
- Find a large open space where your kids can run around. If you bring a ball, so much the better.
- Don't stay inside during the winter—get outside every day.
- Make sure daycare or after-school care includes time to play outside or in a gym space.
- Create a space indoors where your kids can roll and tumble on the floor.

Play, Exploration, and Brain Development

Play comes in all shapes and varieties as children grow and explore the world. A six-month-old infant waves his hands and squeals with delight with a game of peekaboo. Toddlers might take an hour to walk around the block as they stop and explore every twig, leaf, and bug. They also begin pretend play as they put their stuffed animal or doll to sleep. Preschoolers enjoy wrestling and the kind of rough-and-tumble that Dan, Brian, and Erin liked so much on the "jumping bed." Ages three to six is also the height of fantasy, pretend play as kids try to be kings and queens, fairy tale characters, or superheroes. School-age children enjoy all sorts of social play, games with their friends, storytelling, and made-up dramas or plays. Some prefer the relative quiet of board games and creative projects, while others gravitate to sports. The pretend play of childhood may channel into the arts and creative expression for teens. Scientists now know that in addition to being fun, play shapes a child's brain in ways that profoundly affect the future adult. While it may seem frivolous at times, play is actually very serious business.

The importance of the environment for brain development has been known for a long time. In the 1960s, University of California, Berkeley neuroscientist Marian Diamond compared the brains of rats raised in stimulating environments with those raised in plain surroundings. She found, for example, that maze-running rats had bigger and better brains than rats in simple cages with no mazes. Additional studies showed that rats whose cages contained play equipment had thicker cerebral cortices than bored rats with no opportunity to play. The cerebral cortex is that gray, folded, and wrinkled outermost covering of the brain where thought occurs. Memory, language, attention, perception, consciousness, problem solving, and complex thought are all key functions of the cerebral cortex. Now, here's the exciting part: scientists found that the thickness of the cerebral cortex is related to how smart a person is, or how quickly they can learn or solve a problem. Running mazes like rats will not make children smarter, but engaging in play will, because, as we've learned, play builds brains. Scientists found (again in studies of rats) that after times of rough-and-tumble play, brains have increased levels of a critical element needed for the growth and upkeep of brain cells, BDNF (brain-derived neurotrophic factor). Play is so important for brain development, the United Nations declared play a universal right of every child.

PARENT TOOL KIT

Play for a Healthy Brain

Use these questions to test your parental "play IQ," and find the connection between play and healthy brains.

Yes No

☐ ☐ 1. I understand children learn when they play.

☐ ☐ 2. I realize there are many different types of play and that children have different preferences.

☐ ☐ 3. I know how important it is for a child to have some unstructured playtime.

☐ ☐ 4. I realize how important it is for a child to have a stimulating environment.

☐ ☐ 5. I know what it means to "follow my child's lead" during playtime.

☐ ☐ 6. I am aware the best toys are not necessarily the most expensive.

☐ ☐ 7. I try to make sure my child has the chance to play outdoors.

☐ ☐ 8. I understand how rough-and-tumble play aids children's brain development.

☐ ☐ 9. I know free play can develop imagination and creativity.

☐ ☐ 10. I make sure to have time to play with my children.

The more yes answers in this tool kit, the more likely you are to keep a balance of different kinds of play in your child's life. Use the information in this chapter to give your child's brain a boost with play.

Importance of Free Play

Five-year-old Mattie converted the living room into her pretend castle. She was, of course, the princess who lived in the castle and ordered all her dolls and play animals (as well as her three-year-old sister, Tess) to do her bidding. Mattie's fantasy play was very elaborate and free flowing. She supplied ongoing chatter about the events of the day and what everyone was supposed to do. Even though Tess was bossed around, she appeared to be a willing player. Their play involved dress-up, crown making, magic wands, and feasts in ever more elaborate fantasies that went on for hours.

Meanwhile, Mattie's ten-year-old brother, Ben, was outside with his friends, playing a game they had just made up. They called it "no out-of-bounds soccer." The six boys and girls divided themselves into two teams, and the object of the game was simple: keep the ball away from the other team. A lot of chasing and running around the yard ensued. The game lasted until Ben's sitter poked her head out the door to ask if they wanted some lemonade.

The living room-turned-castle and "no out-of-bounds soccer" were both examples of unstructured, imaginative, free play where the kids made up the rules as they went along. There were no adults to organize, give directions, supervise, or explain the game's regulations.

Children learn from all play, but there seems to be a special benefit for their brains if they have the opportunity to engage in free or unstructured play, with no preset rules or adult directions. Free play lets the child test and try, make mistakes, adapt, create, problem solve, role-play, cooperate, and much more. As a bonus, free play doesn't cost parents a dime. Unfortunately it is also disappearing from the lives of too many kids.

There are at least two reasons for the decline of free play. The change in family structures is certainly one. Two working parents or an overworked single parent are often strapped for time. Their children, sensibly enrolled in structured daycare centers or after-school programs, classes, and clubs, may miss the opportunities that come with unstructured time where they can learn how to daydream, imagine, and entertain themselves.

Another factor contributing to the demise of free play is the competitive pressure to jump-start academics. Stan and Carol fretted about getting Emily into the right private pre-kindergarten program as soon as she was born. They put her name on the waiting list right away and had her in music, dance, and enrichment classes before she turned three. Carol had the latest educational software on the family computer and she and Emily spent hours on a prereading program complete with letter recognition flash cards, workbooks, and interactive computer programs.

Shortly after Emily's fourth birthday she started to complain of stomachaches, and at her fourth-year checkup, the pediatrician asked how she was doing.

"I'm okay," Emily responded. "But sometimes my stomach hurts."

"Really? Can I ask you some questions about that?"

"Okay," answered Emily.

The pediatrician asked Emily questions about how often, when, and how painful her stomachaches were. He also asked her about her appetite, how she was sleeping, and whether her head ever hurt. As soon as the nurse took Emily to another room to check her hearing and eyes, Stan asked the doctor if the stomachaches could be a symptom of something serious.

"We'll check everything out, Stan, but I wonder if Emily's stomachaches are a sign of stress."

The doctor continued: "I know from talking with Carol in past visits that Emily is involved in a lot of activities. I'm seeing more and more overscheduled kids who don't get enough downtime. I'm sure that all the activities Emily's involved in are beneficial. The questions is whether all of them together are too much." Dr. Porter added, "You know, Stan, all kids need some slow to grow. They need some free, unstructured time so they can catch their breath and make up their own fun. It's easy for good parents like you and Carol to have Emily involved in enrichment activities with the best of intentions. You just have to make sure your plans don't backfire simply because there's too much of a good thing. Anyway, you and Carol think about it. I'll let you know in a day or two if any of the lab tests turn up anything else that might explain the stomachaches."

Carol answered the phone when Dr. Porter called two days later. "All the lab tests came out fine, Carol. Emily's in good health."

"I'm glad to hear that, Dr. Porter," Carol said. "I'm also glad that you talked to Stan about how busy Emily is. We talked about what you said and we think you're right. I've put away the phonics program and we're going to cut back on some of Emily's activities. I went online and read some articles on the 'hurried child syndrome.' The description fit a little too close for comfort so Stan and I decided to take your 'slow to grow' advice."

Free Play Encourages Language Development, Imagination, Creativity, and Executive Function

In chapter 3 we saw how words are the tools of thinking. For children, play is the arena where they can use words in new and novel situations. The creativity involved in play fosters language development and thinking skills. New play scenes demand problem solving and expanded vocabulary. Whether they play alone or with others, children will have ongoing conversations. They might rehearse language they heard elsewhere, but they never just repeat. Children will use words in new and novel ways, and practice makes their sentences more complex.

Free play stimulates language and creativity in ways that workbooks, flash cards, television, and many "educational" toys can't. Yale child psychologists Dorothy and Jerome Singer studied children's play for decades and concluded "there is a strong correlation between creativity in adults and childhood creativity." They have also studied the impact of media versus free play on imagination. For example, if you read a child a story and then ask them to draw a picture, the picture will be their imaginations' creation. On the other hand, if you show a child a video and ask them to draw a picture, they tend to draw a picture of what they just saw. Someone else is doing the imagining.

Daniel Pink makes a compelling case for creativity in his book *A Whole New Mind: Why Right Brainers Will Rule the Future.* He argues the future will not belong to those who only excel in logic, calculation, or other left brain activities. He outlines six creative brain skills—design, story, symphony (the ability to connect seemingly unrelated ideas or information), empathy, play, and meaning—that he believes will also lead to success in the future. Computers and workers in lower-wage countries will take over the more rote skills and left-brain occupations like accounting and computer programming. Creativity and imagination will be more valuable in business, science, and the arts. Many economists agree with Pink that our former industrial and information economy is transforming into a creative economy, which rewards ideas, innovation, and creativity. Play nurtures a child's creative and imaginative brain.

Here are some ways to encourage the type of play that promotes creativity and imagination.

- Make sure kids have some unstructured time in which they are free to make up their own play activities.
- Don't always rush in to fill your child's time.
- Don't panic if your child complains of boredom. It's not your job to be a nonstop entertainment committee. You might say something like "I'm sure you can find something to do. See if you can think of three fun things to do and then pick the best one."
- Convert large packing boxes or blankets into forts, playhouses, shops where children can play grocers, bakers, restaurateurs, or whatever else they can dream up.
- Have an art box handy, full of paper, material scraps, glue, markers, scissors, pipe cleaners, small boxes, and stuff for kids to create their own art projects.
- Fill your child's world with different kinds of music.
- Have a dress-up box, full of old clothes.
- Take field trips around your community. Your child will re-create the trip in play.
- Don't forget the kitchen. Kids love to cook and have fun eating their creations.
- Read and tell stories to your children and ask them to make up their own.
- Let your child doodle with paper, colored pencils, or crayons.
- Provide materials that encourage your child to build and create with their hands.

Another bonus that comes with free play is its contribution to developing the brain's executive functions, such as the ability to focus attention and manage impulses. Kids with good executive function are more "in charge" of their brains. Research shows that free play helps children develop these critical skills.

Storytelling

We all love a good story. Give me information in a story form and I'll remember it more easily. Better yet, give it to me in a story with emotion and I'll remember it for sure. Anthropologists tell us that stories are a feature of every culture that they have ever studied. The reason stories are so universal is that our brains are literally built for them. As we saw in chapter 4 we organize and make sense of new information by linking it to what we already know, the stories we have created about who we are and how the world is.

Neuroscientist Michael Gazzaniga, the director of the Sage Center for the Study of Mind at the University of California, Santa Barbara, identifies this function as the brain's "interpreter" and locates it in the brain's left hemisphere. Thus storytelling is built into our brains and it turns out that telling and enjoying stories are powerful ways to develop social awareness and connections.

The power of stories to evoke emotions of sadness, fear, joy, or happiness lies in another brain structure, called mirror neurons. When an emotional scene is played out before us, these neurons enable us to feel that emotion ourselves even though we are not directly involved. A twelve-year-old can feel sad when Harry Potter's friend is killed by Voldemort, even though he's never met an evil wizard in real life. His mirror neurons make it possible. Storytelling nourishes this empathy and unleashes bountiful imagination and creativity in children's minds.

I recently had the opportunity to discuss the important link between storytelling and creativity with a professional storyteller, Michael Mann. The first thing I learned is that storytellers are needed more than ever. "It wasn't always so," Michael explained. "A generation or two ago, storytelling was common. Unfortunately today it's a real change of pace for kids." Mann does a lot of his work in elementary and high schools. "Teachers are often surprised kids are so attentive when I tell stories. They tell me how hard it is to keep students' attention these days," he added. "Many kids have trouble connecting to their imagination at first." "When I tell a story, students will ask me, 'What does it look like? What color is it?' That's because they're used to having TV or video game producers do all the imagining. But after a while they really get into it. They discover they can do it and it's fun. Kids' imaginations aren't defunct," Mann said. "They're just underused. I explain to the kids that imagination is like a muscle. The more we use it the better it gets. I also remind them that imagining isn't just fun. We use it to solve problems. If we can't imagine, we get stuck on worn-out solutions that don't work."

All kids are natural storytellers. Michael also told me how storytelling is the bridge to becoming a good writer. I give them questions to prime the pump. For example, I ask them to think about their favorite place to play. Then I get them to describe it with all their senses. 'What does it look like, smell like, sound like?' Then I get them to connect with their feelings by asking them to remember a time when they were happy, sad, or angry there."

Michael doesn't have kids write down their work right away—the next step after connecting with their feelings is "oral editing," which is a fancy term for retelling the story. He explains that every time they retell the story, it will grow and get better. They tell their stories out loud and then retell their stories to another group of their classmates. Only then do they write down their stories.

"You should see how good many of the stories are and how proud the authors become," said Michael.

Try these tips and use storytelling as a way to stimulate your kids' imagination and creativity.

- Turn off all media during mealtimes and recount events of the day in story form.
- Ask your children about their day and listen to their accounts, adding encouraging questions like "What happened next?"
- Use car trips to swap stories instead of watching DVDs.
- Encourage oral editing by asking kids to retell their stories to visiting relatives or friends. For example, "Tell grandma about that wild thunderstorm we had the other night" or "Tell Aunt Joan about your class trip to the zoo."

Toys and Technology

I recently had dinner with friends at a restaurant. A young couple dined at the next table, with their baby daughter, probably about six months old. Not surprisingly, it wasn't long before the baby started to fuss in mom's arms. As soon as the baby squirmed, the mom placed her in the stroller they'd stationed next to the table. This was no ordinary baby carriage, however. This latest high-tech version looked more like a rocket ship's cockpit than your grandmother's pram. My tablemates and I were startled when the young mother flicked a switch and the stroller's dashboard buzzed to life with multicolored blinking lights and sound effects. The baby did quiet down as she passively stared at the high-tech light show, the envy of a rock concert technician.

One of my tablemates, a thirty-something mother of preteens, was as startled as the baby. "Talk about sensory overload!" she said.

We live in a high-tech world, and electronics have taken over a lot of kids' toys. The bells and whistles can be impressive and parents can easily be sold on the notion that the fancier the gizmo, the better it is, and the more kids will like it. We need to remember that toys shouldn't be about entertainment. Electronics that turn kids into passive watchers do not stimulate creative play. As one expert said, "Toys should be 90% child and 10% toy. The child should be the play creator; the toy is only the prop."

Imagination and creativity don't just happen. Children develop these important traits the same way they build others—by practice. Simple toys help children think, adapt, and create their own worlds. They can even help children overcome fears in the process. The brain's language and thought centers light up at each new and novel turn. These new neural networks lay the foundation for more complex creative thought, and these connections are strengthened by play.

It's not that new technology cannot make for fun and creative play. The key is for kids to be the participants and creators, not observers. My daughter Erin and her friends Gretchen and Julie did exactly that when they watched the inspiring gymnastic performances of the Olympics. The next evening, the three children marched into the family room and asked if we would like to watch an "important video." For the next thirty minutes, the rest of the family sat mesmerized by what appeared on the screen. The three girls had spent the entire afternoon recording their own version of a gymnastic event and even included commentary from Olympic announcers. I can still remember the howls of laughter and the standing ovation all of us gave the girls. It was a great example of how kids can use technology in an entertaining, creative, and imaginative way.

Here are some tips for choosing toys.

- Buy young children simple toys that can be used in multiple ways such as blocks or play dough.
- Have toy animals, people, creatures such as dinosaurs, cars, planes, trains, etc. Children will use them as props to play out events from their own lives.
- Look for toys that encourage the kids to create and build. Classics like simple blocks for the younger kids and Legos or other building sets for older kids are excellent.
- Art supplies.
- Older kids enjoy creating, filming, and editing a story or mystery.
- Choose computer programs or video games that encourage kids to strategize and solve problems instead of just blowing things up.
- Look for games and toys that might stimulate an interest in a hobby, such as butterfly gardens, stamp collecting, cooking sets, airplane kits, electronics kits, and more.
- Introduce music to your children with musical toys and toy instruments.
- Don't be wowed by electronic bells and whistles.

After-School Care, Childcare, and Preschool

When you check out after-school or early childhood care, ask about play options with your provider. Hopefully they have a multitude of creative, brain-building playtimes right in the schedule. Here are some questions you can ask:

1. Does the home or school have a safe, bright play area?
2. Is the play area filled with simple but creative toys?
3. Are the toys suitable for the age of your child?
4. Do children have time for unstructured, free play? How much time?
5. Is there a safe outdoor play area?
6. How much time do children have for outdoor play?
7. Do children spend time watching TV or playing video games? How much time?
8. Do children use a computer? How much time is spent?
9. What creative activities can older children choose to do?
10. How does the provider help children negotiate problems with peers?

Play and Socialization

A caring adult is a child's first playmate. The parents or caregivers who cuddle, coo, sing, gently dance, talk, play peekaboo, and hold their infant are building that baby's first social connection of love and trust. As babies begin to explore, the adults are there to encourage and connect, talking, helping their babies begin to make sense of their world.

Play becomes the vehicle for building social connections with family members and eventually other children. Step by step, children assemble the social skills they need for friendship and social interactions as they learn to take turns, share, cooperate, solve disagreements, and read social cues.

Although we don't know exactly why, rough-and-tumble play, especially for boys, also appears to play an important part in developing children's social brains. Our kids spent much of their free time wrestling on the floor when they were young. In fact after watching young monkey wrestle on a zoo trip, Brian piped up, "Hey, Dad, those monkeys play just like us!" Play wrestling has been studied in the animal kingdom for decades. Scientists have found that when juvenile animals are prevented from wrestling with peers, they grow into overly stressed adult animals that have a hard time relating to others and handling social encounters. Perhaps early play fighting helps wire the brain networks needed for handling emotions and building trust. Whatever its function, this physical play appears to be critical for socialization.

Stuart Brown, the founder of the National Institute for Play and author of *Play: How It Shapes the Brain, Opens the Imagination, and Invigorates the Soul,* began his teaching career on August 1, 1966, the same day that Charles Whitman shot forty-six people from the University of Texas tower. His subsequent research into Whitman's background, as well as that of dozens of other murderers, revealed a common thread: they never played when they were children. That startling finding launched Brown's research career into play.

Today Brown is convinced play is critical for developing social skills. It allows children to practice and experiment, to learn to negotiate, to work in a group, to be adaptable and flexible—skills that will help them socially and academically in the future, during adolescence and adulthood. Brown's research leads him to conclude that play is at the heart of fairness, justice, and empathy and that the absence of play has dire consequences for brain development and socialization.

Here's how parents can help their kids build better social brains.

INFANTS AND BABIES:

- Hold, cuddle, talk, sing, read, play simple games like "So big" with your infant.
- Play and talk with your baby to explore simple toys and objects. Babies need to explore their world. Remember, babies will put everything into their mouths. It's their best way to learn about an object.
- Give your baby time to play on his own so he can learn how to amuse himself.
- Use everyday tasks, such as changing time, as a time to talk, sing, or play a game such as peekaboo.

PRESCHOOLERS:

- If you want to enter and support your child's creative play, get down on the floor. Observe your child and follow her lead. Let your child control the content and direction of the play. Save "showing her how to do it" until later.
- Enjoy engaging in all sorts of play, indoors and outside. Make sure your child has the opportunity for free play, not rule-based play.

- Within reason, don't overprotect your children from rough-and-tumble physical play between siblings and peers. You can get down on the floor and mix it up yourself, observing commonsense safety precautions.
- Ask your child to tell you about what they are doing, creating, building, etc. Accept and give positive comments. "Wow, you really worked hard." "You are really creating something." "What a fun place to be."
- Give your child time for fantasy play either by himself or herself or with a friend. Parents can help by supplying the objects needed. For example, a blanket over a chair or table makes a great tent and sets the scene. Help your child problem-solve if he needs something. "What do you think you should do?" "How do you want to solve this?"
- Always let the child take the lead in fantasy play. Observe and enter into their play only if asked to.
- Teach children how to wait and take turns when playing with others.

SCHOOL AGE:

- Continue to enjoy playing all sorts of games with your child. Children at this age also enjoy rule-based games, such as board games, sport games, and video and computer games.
- Give your child space and time to negotiate with friends how the game is played or what their rules will be.
- Support your child's interests. If they like planets and stars, read books, visit a planetarium, go online—visit the NASA website, supply materials for her to build a planet. Ask, "What would it look like?" Follow your child's lead. Don't overdo with buying too much or taking over.
- Turn jobs into a game. Use imagination and problem solving. For instance, make washing the car into a game.

TEENS:

- Encourage your teenager to get involved in extracurricular activities.
- Show your support by attending athletic events, plays, recitals, concerts, exhibitions, science fairs, and other events.
- Encourage your adolescent to explore a variety of activities.
- Give teens space to explore and express themselves.

Rule-Based Games and Organized Activities

I've paid a lot of attention to free and creative play, that unique childhood activity where the child makes up the rules of the game. But board games, video games, organized sports, directed play, clubs, and enrichment classes are also beneficial, helping build children's memory skills, ability to follow directions, skill building, and problem solving. Strategy games, whether offline or online, challenge a youngster's brain to think ahead, weigh alternative approaches, and calculate risk-reward ratios. Accomplishing a game's task or challenge can add to a child's sense of competency. The give-and-take and negotiation involved in playing a group game also help build social skills. While there are some very good electronic games on the market, don't overlook classics like checkers, chess, Go, Clue, Sequence, and card games.

It's important for younger children that the emphasis is on skill development and not winning. Check any team out very carefully before signing your child up. Make sure your child is emotionally ready for the level of competition involved. Support coaches who play every team member, giving everyone a chance to have fun and improve.

As a child gets older, sport teams can involve a tremendous time commitment. A few kids thrive at this skill level. For others, however, this overspecialization brings too much pressure and competition, the loss of important family time, and less space in their lives for other activities. Consider any team commitment carefully and weigh the benefits considering your child's age and overall interests.

Encourage a Range of Interests

I was familiar with athletic teams, scouts, day camps, and other organized activities from my own childhood and from my years of teaching high school and coaching. I was not prepared, however, for the request Dan made when he was ten years old. "Dad, can I join the Herpetological Society?" he asked one night at dinner.

"The what?" I asked.

"The Herpetological Society," he answered matter-of-factly. "You know, snakes, frogs, iguanas, reptiles, and things."

"Dan," I answered, "I've never even heard of herpology, let alone know whether you can join it."

"It's *herpetology,* Dad," Dan responded with a hint of exasperation. "And the name of the club is the Herpetological Society. They meet once a month at the university and it's really cool. People bring snakes and other reptiles and they discuss different 'herps.' Can I go?"

I knew Dan was fascinated with snakes, frogs, and other crawly things, but how was I to know there was a club for their fans? I did some investigation, and Dan's information was correct. The Minnesota Herpetological Society met the first Friday evening of every month at one of the University of Minnesota buildings. It looked legitimate so I promised Dan I'd take him to a meeting. A few weeks later Dan and I walked into a room full of adults and an assortment of snakes, lizards, salamanders, turtles, toads, newts, and other creepy critters. (I found out that herpetology is the "study of creeping animals.") The first person to greet us was a middle-aged man tattooed from head to toe. "Welcome," he said. "Can I help you?"

I explained that Dan was interested in coming to a meeting because he liked snakes. I asked if it would be okay if we sat in. "Absolutely," he responded. "We love to have visitors and we're always happy when a youngster shows up. I'll give you a brochure about membership and introduce you to some other members." This friendly man turned out to be the president of the club. Dan was mesmerized and talked me into coughing up the ten dollars so he could join. Dan was the youngest member of the society, and either Monica or I had to drive him to the evening meetings. He enjoyed it greatly and learned a lot. So did I.

There are all sorts of activities and options for kids' interests as they get older. Expose them to a wide range. You never know what will pique their curiosity. Who knows? You might even end up joining your local herpetological society.

Is Play Endangered?

Historically, people didn't worry about kids' play because they lived less structured lives. Today hectic family schedules and pressures to perform academically are restricting play opportunities. Play-focused nursery schools have given way to academically oriented preschools. Standardized tests are prompting schools to cut back on recess time, which may be the only free play time during a child's school day. Empty parks and playgrounds tell a tale of children who choose video games over real-world experiences.

Regular relaxed playtime alone, or with parents or friends, may be more beneficial to children than an added enrichment activity to an already overscheduled life. Playtime gives parents some of their best opportunities to connect with their children, who need the resiliency of a secure connection with their parents. Keep organized activities, including sports, in balance with family time and free play time. Even child prodigies need time to just play.

The biggest lifestyle change in children's lives over the last generation is the time spent using media. We'll talk more in a later chapter on the benefits and risks of these new media on children's brain development. For now, it's important to remember balance. The unique benefits of free, unstructured play are not found in a TV program or video game. Children create their own new and novel situations in real-world play with thoughts, language, emotions, and sensorimotor activity that build better brain networks. The challenge for today's parents is how to give this important building block a place in their kids' day.

DO

- ✓ Make space in your child's day for free play.
- ✓ Enjoy and play with your child as often as you can.
- ✓ Let children learn to play by themselves.
- ✓ Give your child "simple" toys that have a variety of play uses.
- ✓ Allow reasonable rough-and-tumble play.
- ✓ Get your child outdoors to play.
- ✓ Encourage running, jumping, climbing, etc.
- ✓ Allow your child to negotiate with friends.
- ✓ Let your child take the lead and set the rules in unstructured playtime.
- ✓ Play games that involve problem solving and strategy.
- ✓ Keep screen time in balance with other play opportunities.
- ✓ Encourage a wide range of activities.
- ✓ Praise effort more than ability as your child gets involved in sports and other organized activities.

DON'T

- ✗ Don't overmanage your child's playtime.
- ✗ Don't make competition part of young children's play. They will be afraid to try.
- ✗ Don't jump in and solve all your child's play problems. Support his or her problem-solving solutions.
- ✗ Don't overschedule your child.
- ✗ Don't jump in and resolve disagreements your child has with friends. Let them figure things out.
- ✗ Don't get fooled by bells and whistles on toys.
- ✗ Don't forget to make play areas safe.

What do I want to continue?

What do I want to change?

SEVEN

Brain Workouts: Why Exercise Is Critical

Years ago, premature infants were wrapped up very tightly after they were born so they couldn't move, since doctors wanted the infant's calories directed toward growing, not wasted on movement. Someone with good sense eventually realized that the premature infant would be turning somersaults and doing handstands if he were still in the womb, so maybe movement was good for a developing baby. Subsequent studies confirmed that gently exercised babies grew more muscle mass and stronger bones in their arms and legs. Moreover, their bodies produced more growth-stimulating hormones. Today the goal of hospital nursery staff is to simulate a womb-like environment for premature newborns, including movement, and, as a result, premature babies today both gain weight and develop faster, so their parents get to take their newborns home sooner. If we could peer inside these babies' brains, we would see neurons sprouting new branches like weeds. Brain scientists now know exercise doesn't just build strong bodies. It builds strong brains.

"Mens Sana in Corpore Sano"

If you ever find yourself walking past Columbia University Teachers College's Horace Mann Hall on 120th Street in Manhattan, look up at the inscription on the building that reads, "Mens Sana in Corpore Sano." That phrase, coined thousands of years ago by the Roman poet Juvenal, means "A sound mind in a sound body." Its permanent placement in one of America's great universities makes more sense every day. While generations interpreted the phrase to mean we should strive to have a strong body and a strong mind, in recent years scientists have discovered that a sound body *makes* a sound mind. Sandra is a living example.

Sandra is one of many students who volunteered for a study to see if exercise improved classroom performance. Along with her classmates Sandra started by taking a series of math, reading, and problem-solving tests. Then she agreed to wear a heart monitor and play highly active games with her class, such as tag and jump rope. The heart monitor helped her keep her heart rate high, and she even received rewards for doing so. After three months of these exercise sessions, she took math, reading, and "executive function" tests again. Her scores were much higher.

A lot of exciting new research links exercise and school performance. Scientists running these experiments learned that kids who exercise and play vigorously for twenty to forty minutes a day are better able to organize their schoolwork and perform better in the classroom. Using brain scans, scientists now see that kids who exercise vigorously have more brain activity in the prefrontal cortex part of their brains, where higher-order thinking and executive functions occur. While we've known for a long time that exercise builds strong muscles and a healthy heart, these neuroscientists found that moving and exercising our muscles directly builds better brains.

Animal research showed this for decades. In one study, scientists put some mice on running wheels and let them exercise away. Over in the next cage, however, their running-wheel-deprived cousins sat around and relaxed. The aerobic mice showed impressive brain growth, especially in the area of the brain related to memory and learning. Their lazy cousins got no such benefit.

It shouldn't surprise us that muscles and brains are connected. Our evolutionary ancestors were born to move and although we're not the quickest creatures on the planet, we run, walk, climb, jump, and swim quite well. Thousands of years ago, quick moves kept our forebears out of the tiger's jaws. Even better for our survival, our ability to think and plan not only kept us safe but helped us find and hunt other animals for food. Human survival depended on both our muscles *and* our brains. And new research confirms that exercise not only increases the brain's ability to focus, but also builds and strengthens brain cells involved in planning, memory, and learning.

PARENT TOOL KIT

Exercise and Your Child's Brain

Use these questions to see if your child gets enough brain-healthy exercise.

Yes No

☐ ☐ 1. My child gets age-appropriate physical activity every day.
☐ ☐ 2. I know moving muscles builds brains.
☐ ☐ 3. I realize the memory center of the brain, the hippocampus, particularly benefits from regular workouts.
☐ ☐ 4. I know exercise releases brain-boosting chemicals.
☐ ☐ 5. I understand being physically fit improves reading and math skills.
☐ ☐ 6. I know children benefit from a variety of exercises.
☐ ☐ 7. I make sure screen time is balanced with physical activity time.
☐ ☐ 8. I recognize exercise fortifies the brain's control center and helps a child focus.
☐ ☐ 9. I appreciate the fact that exercise increases the supply of brain chemicals that underlie emotional stability.
☐ ☐ 10. I understand exercise reduces stress chemicals in the brain.

Today's sedentary lifestyle robs our children of the chance to build strong bodies and healthy brains. The more yes answers, the better equipped you are to ensure your children get the exercise they need.

Exercise and the Thinking Brain

What is the connection between vigorous exercise and brain development? Two areas of the brain—the prefrontal cortex (the seat of executive functions, working memory, and planning) and the hippocampus (the seat of memory and learning)—directly benefit when a child gets out and plays hard. Here's what happens.

Maria is kicking the soccer ball across the field, and as she does so, her heart and breathing rates increase, she begins to sweat, and muscles throughout her body contract, producing and pumping into her bloodstream a protein called IGF-1. A member of the group of proteins called neurotrophins because they promote neuron growth and function, the IGF-1 is transported very quickly to her brain when her heart is beating so strongly. The protein goes right to work in her brain, sparking the production of other vital chemicals, including brain-derived neurotrophic factor, or BDNF, the most important of these chemicals. John Ratey, the author of *Spark: The Revolutionary New Science of Exercise and the Brain,* calls BDNF "Miracle-Gro for the brain." He explains that just as Miracle-Gro causes plants to thrive in our gardens, BDNF causes neurons to flourish in our brains.

As Maria continues to play soccer, the BDNF levels in her brain keep on rising. The benefit is particularly pronounced in her brain's memory and learning center, the hippocampus. You may recall from chapter 4 that it's the small structure in the center of the brain (shaped like a seahorse, after which it was named) where memories are registered. BDNF actually stimulates the production of new cells in the hippocampus, causing them to blossom and form new connections. Present at these points of communication between neurons, BDNF not only helps preserve the neurons you already have, but also strengthens and increases new connections, improving the brain's ability to take in and record new learning. Will Maria get better grades in school by exercising? Yes, if she combines it with study and homework.

Maria's exercise helps her brain in other ways as well. When Maria runs, she causes more neurons to fire in her brain's executive center, the prefrontal cortex. That's why the exercising students in the study earlier were better able to organize their schoolwork and complete projects. Maria will find she's more alert after she exercises, and she'll discover it's easier to focus and figure out problems. In short, she'll be able to "think better" because her prefrontal cortex is where her "working memory" is located. As we discussed in chapter 4, working memory is like a desktop where we connect information from long-term memory with incoming data. Imagine the benefits of "Miracle-Gro" for the millions of neurons doing the "thinking" work of the brain.

Exercise and the Feeling Brain

Maria also reports feeling better and more alert after exercising. It turns out that when her heart is strongly pumping, she's also increasing the amounts of three neurotransmitters in her brain—dopamine, serotonin, and norepinephrin—which have a positive impact on her emotional state. Dopamine is the "feel good" chemical, helping Maria feel happier, more equipped to handle problems, and better able to concentrate. The higher concentration of serotonin stabilizes her mood so Maria feels more relaxed and confident. Finally, norepinephrin boosts her energy, increases her ability to focus, and facilitates memory registration and storage. No wonder runners describe feeling "high" after a long run.

There is some new research showing that the serotonin squirt can also reduce anger and aggression. I told the former Green Bay Packers football star Darrell Thompson about the research recently and he wasn't surprised. He told me, "That's why we have all the kids in the Bolder Options mentoring program I run exercise every day as part of our routine."

Exercise and School Success

The jury has reached a verdict—exercise builds strong brains, and exercise can improve school performance in children. Dr. Charles Hillman at the University of Illinois has found that exercise has lasting cognitive benefits across one's lifetime, especially with learning that requires more effort. In his research in the Department of Kinesiology and Community Health, he focused on the benefits of exercise for preadolescent children, finding that students who walked on treadmills at 60 percent of their maximum heart rate did better on reading tasks and, even more importantly, increased their ability to focus and concentrate. Recently, many school boards have decided to scale back or eliminate recess and physical education in order to improve test scores. This is counterproductive since brain research shows that exercise during the school day improves brain functioning and raises test scores. Research like this should cause school administrators and school boards to rethink some of their decisions.

Help Kids Keep Fit

The new brain science discoveries about the importance of exercise also raise additional red flags about skyrocketing rates of childhood overweight and obesity. Almost one in three American children weighs too much. For kids ages six to eleven, that's triple the rate from three decades ago. We know that overweight children are at greater risk for type 2 diabetes, hypertension, musculoskeletal problems, elevated cholesterol, sleep apnea, early onset puberty, asthma, and other problems. Now we can add compromised school performance to the list since researchers have found that academic achievement goes down for kids who are overweight or obese.

There are a number of factors contributing to children's couch potato lifestyles, including the decrease in the amount of exercise kids get in the school today compared to previous generations. In a 2006 national survey, the School Health Policies and Programs Study, the Centers for Disease Control and Prevention found that less than 4 percent of elementary schools, 8 percent of middle schools, and 2 percent of high schools provide daily physical education or its equivalent. Even time-honored recess has disappeared from some schools. Another CDC study, the Youth Risk Behavior Survey, revealed that only 35 percent of teens got the recommended levels of physical activity.

Today's kids don't just get less exercise at school; their homes are often exercise-free as well, with screen-time the number one activity for kids today. As we'll see in chapter 13, the average K–12 student today spends over fifty hours a week in front of some sort of screen. That's the equivalent of a full-time job. Our bodies and brains were designed to move, not sit for hour after hour watching TV, playing video games, or surfing the Internet. How have we reached the point where a sedentary lifestyle is the norm for our nation's kids?

Some parents report they're afraid to let their children run around outside. The media do a great job of stoking parental fears with round-the-clock coverage of accidents, disease, and crime. The late George Gerbner wrote that one of the biggest effects of media on society is what he called the "mean-world syndrome," his term for the way media attention to catastrophes changes our outlook on our communities. I am not trying to say a fear of strangers is unfounded, but we need to balance that concern with the harm caused by lack of exercise. To get our children outside running around, we should get to know our neighbors so we can all watch out for kids in playgrounds, backyards, and other open spaces. When neighborhoods *are* too dangerous for kids to be out on the sidewalk or in the park, we need to engage schools, neighborhood groups, worship communities, and youth-serving organizations to provide safe places for kids to play.

One neighborhood I know designated every Wednesday night as family night in their neighborhood park. Families came when they could with various balls, Frisbees, jump ropes, and anything else that might be fun to play with. They played games for an hour, some sport-like, some just games, like tag, with adults and kids of all age groups. Everyone ran around and had a great time. This provides a great example for other communities to follow.

Overorganized Sports

Overorganized sports contribute to the decline of physical activity among kids. The hypercompetition eliminates all but the very talented or the privileged who can afford special coaches or clinics to hone their skills. Many times the way we organize kids' sports doesn't serve them well.

I want to be clear that I am not against organized sports. I coached during all ten years of my high school teaching career. All three of my kids played on teams including baseball, softball, basketball, soccer, cross-country skiing, and hockey. Monica and I volunteered to coach some of those teams when the kids were little, and we sat in the stands cheering when they were older. That said, I also believe we have overorganized sports even for the younger kids. Just because a child is on a team doesn't mean they are getting a lot of physical exercise. Youth sports can be very good for kids if the philosophy emphasizes overall fitness and provides children with a lot of playing time. When a team is overorganized and overcompetitive, fewer kids get a chance to play and most spend more time in the car going to practices than actually playing.

What Kind of Exercise Is Good?

The first thing to remember is that we're not talking about gym workouts for kids. Climbing StairMasters and pumping iron are not what kids need, nor will children "work out" for thirty minutes at a time. Kids get all the needed benefits when they ride a bike, skateboard, jump rope, swim, skate, play tag, ski, do martial arts, chase one another, jump, wrestle, skip, or do any of a thousand other things that kids do when they're active. In fact, experts suggest the key to increasing children's endurance, flexibility, and strength is to encourage them to move in a variety of ways. The important thing is to promote any aerobic activity that gets kids to increase their heart rate. You can tell it's aerobic if your child's heart is pumping fast and she's breathing hard.

Flexibility and balance are important, too. That's why dance and gymnastics like cartwheels and somersaults are good. Even play wrestling increases flexibility and balance. Small children enjoy rolling on large exercise balls. One winter day I came in to discover a climbing gym in our living room. Monica had joined a toy lending library, and a large wooden climber was her latest prize. "We have it for three weeks!" she exclaimed. With a slide that extended into the dining room of our small house, I could see the squealing kids were already having a lot of fun. That climber became everything from a fort to a pirate ship, and we were all sad the day we packed it up to return it so the next family could use it.

Climbing, using a chin-up bar in the doorway, or hanging from playground equipment are all great ways for kids to strengthen their muscles and build their brains. Physical work around the house is another great way for kids to get exercise. Let them carry the groceries from the car or, if they are little, at least the can of tomatoes. Washing, drying, cleaning, picking up toys, outdoor work—kids should have responsibilities and do their part for the family. They'll get fitter, too. Remember, every time your child works their muscles, they build their brains, and fit kids build better brains.

How Much Exercise?

Babies, toddlers, and preschoolers are just naturally active movers most of their waking hours. It's important to provide them with a safe space and plenty of time to crawl, run, and play. Obstacle courses with old cardboard boxes, large pillows, small boards, hoops, even small ladders laid down on their side provide physical challenges as they crawl over, around, and through objects in their path. Under the watchful eyes of adult caregivers, babies and toddlers should have playtime to explore outdoor spaces. At this age children love to move and a range of activity will build strength, flexibility, and endurance. Free play for preschoolers provides plenty of exercise, indoors or out. Also let your preschooler join family walks for short distances. Try getting them out of the stroller as much as possible.

Elementary-age children and preteens should get in at least one hour or more of physical activity every day. All types count so encourage a variety of aerobic, strengthening, balancing, and flexibility options. Team sports become an option at this age, but look for leagues and teams that emphasize fun, teamwork, and inclusion while downplaying the competitiveness. There are all sorts of exercise opportunities once we start to look for them. It's both fun and healthy to walk or bike on an errand instead of jumping in the car, or climbing stairs instead of hopping on an elevator. Weekend hikes, camping trips, canoeing, swimming, ice skating, and other pastimes are all better than whiling away hours watching TV or playing video games.

There is a disturbing new trend among teenagers in America. As kids progress from elementary school into high school, they get less and less active. Researchers at the University of California, San Diego followed more than one thousand kids for six years. They found that physical activity dropped forty minutes a day each year between the ages of nine and fifteen.

The average adolescent in the United States only spends thirty-five minutes a day exercising on weekends, when they usually have more time on their hands. It didn't make any difference what ethnic or racial group they belonged to, or whether they were boys or girls, rich or poor, urban dwellers or suburbanites. Across the board, American teenagers move less and sit more. Is it any wonder the number of overweight teenagers skyrocketed from 5 percent to 17.4 percent in the past twenty years?

There are several reasons behind the teenage slowdown. First of all, as already mentioned, many high schools have cut out or cut back physical education. Second, opportunities for high school students to participate in athletics decrease. A shrinking percentage of teens makes the junior varsity or varsity squads. Third, as we will discuss in chapter 13, media and technology have taken over many teenagers' lives. Adolescents who might have been skateboarding, biking, or in-line skating a generation ago now sit inside playing video games, updating their social networking page, or texting their friends.

Teens are in worse shape than ever so we've got to get them moving again. Don't accept the typical response, "There's nothing to do," when you tell them to turn off the TV or Xbox 360. The list of possibilities goes on and on—cycling, trampoline, rowing, Tae Bo, soccer, walking, skating, dancing, cross-country and downhill skiing, skateboarding, pickup basketball, swimming, tennis, yoga, jumping rope, martial arts, racquetball. Some might gravitate to working out with weights at the gym or using an elliptical trainer. Buy a push lawn mower and put them in charge of keeping the lawn in shape. Tell them about charity runs or biking events that raise money for a charity they believe in. Try anything to get them moving for their bodies' and brains' sake.

Pedometers are inexpensive and can serve as great motivators. Buy one for everyone in the family and keep track of your steps every day. Have friendly family contests with real prizes. Make a family chart and write down everyone's steps every day for a week. Then set a goal to increase the number of steps for the next week. See who in the family increases their steps the fastest. The goal should be to eventually reach 10,000 steps a day for adults, between 11,000 and 12,000 for girls, and 13,000 to 15,000 for boys.

Don't Go Overboard

Any good thing can be overdone, including exercise. While vigorous exercise increases the BDNF supply in the brain, constant overexercising can cause stress in the body and the brain, leading to excessive weight loss and overuse injuries. If your child is exercising to the exclusion of other social activities or exercising to the point where injury occurs, then it's time to cut back. We'll see how stress interferes with brain functioning in chapter 11. For now, let's just remember that as important as exercise is, we don't want to push our kids too hard in an activity that is either not age appropriate or beyond their abilities. That's one of the problems with hypercompetitive teams. Short practice runs under a mile for a kids' race with mom or dad can be fun for the whole family, but marathon training would push the exercise into a danger zone. Keep exercise playful and fun. Challenge and hard work are good, but too much can be counterproductive.

DO

- ✓ Make sure your child plays and exercises every day.
- ✓ Talk to your child about the connection between moving muscles and building brains.
- ✓ Encourage a variety of movement to build strength, endurance, and flexibility.
- ✓ Get started with family exercise time.
- ✓ Have fun.
- ✓ Give your child household jobs that work muscles.
- ✓ Check the amount of exercise or playtime your child gets at school and in after-school programs.
- ✓ Encourage your kids to dance to music.
- ✓ Try wearing a pedometer to increase steps each day.
- ✓ Make sure sedentary activity is balanced with exercise and movement.
- ✓ Try video games that make your child move.
- ✓ Turn electronic screens off when the weather turns warmer.
- ✓ Connect your child with the outdoors.

DON'T

- ✗ Don't make exercise a workout chore.
- ✗ Don't force a child to join a sports team.
- ✗ Don't let screen time crowd out exercise and playtime.
- ✗ Don't let your child get out of shape.
- ✗ Don't stress your child by expecting physical performance beyond their ability or age.

What do I want to continue?

____

____

____

What do I want to change?

____

____

____

EIGHT

Your Brain's at Work While You Snooze

Caitlyn could hardly remember the last time she had a full night's sleep. She still recalls her parents telling her to get as much sleep as possible when she got pregnant. "Once the baby arrives," they warned, "sleep goes out the window." That was seven years ago. Three children later, sleep for Caitlyn and her partner was still a scarce commodity, and her brain often felt "foggy." She frequently found herself yearning for just a few more hours of shuteye. What a difference that would make, she thought. Was she right? Do a few hours make a difference?

The Sleep-Brain Connection

Do you know what your child's brain does in the middle of the night? If you're lucky to have a sound sleeper, your child's brain is busy at work, sifting through the day's learning and memories, solidifying new synapses, retiring weak ones, and solving problems. Sleep and children bring parents a mixture of reactions. It's restful and rewarding to watch a baby sound asleep and fun to carry toddlers to bed after they collapse in exhaustion. There are also moments of anxiety checking on a newborn's breathing and wondering if our teenagers will ever get to sleep at a decent hour so they can function the next day.

Sleeping children seem so relaxed it's hard to imagine their brains feverishly toiling away. But a sleeping body belies a very busy brain. So what happens when your child's brain slips from its conscious awake state into slumber? The first step toward deep sleep happens as the different regions of the brain stop communicating with one another. Dr. Giulio Tononi, a scientist at the University of Wisconsin, Madison's Center for Sleep and Consciousness, believes that our conscious state depends on our thinking brain buzzing, with brain cells "talking" to one another. We slip into the deep, dreamless cycle of sleep when these regions no longer connect and our brain stops processing and integrating new information. Neurons in the brain stem, the part of the brain that connects with the spinal cord, turn off the neurotransmitters that facilitate this communication. "Sleep is the most familiar alteration of consciousness," Tononi says. "Every night, when you fall into the deep sleep cycle, your consciousness fades." What happens next is a roller-coaster ride.

Sleep Is a Roller-Coaster Ride

All of us, including children, have two sleep states: slow-wave or non-REM (rapid eye movement) sleep and REM sleep. Both of these sleep states are needed for your child's brain to consolidate memories, repair itself, and release the hormones needed for growth and development. Non-REM sleep is the body's nondreaming, deep sleep. During this time, the brain directs the repair and restoration caused by the daily wear and tear on your child's body and brain cells. My mother used to send me off to bed, answering my protests with the words, "If you don't go to bed, your body will never grow." She was right. With good nutrition and exercise, growth hormones are released throughout the day, but it's after the onset of deep sleep that a child's brain directs the strongest release of hormones to help bones and organs grow and muscles mend.

There are actually three stages of non-REM sleep and your brain cycles through the stages one after another. When your child first falls asleep, she enters stage 1, then, after a few minutes stage 2, into the deep sleep stage 3. From there she cycles back to stage 2, then into the REM sleep stage for a time, then back down to non-REM stages 2 then 3, and back up through 2 and back into REM sleep. It's confusing, but we don't need to keep track because the brain does it all automatically. The pattern continues through the entire time we are asleep. For adults this cycle follows a ninety-minute pattern, spending 20 percent of each cycle in REM sleep and 80 percent in non-REM sleep. For infants, babies, and young children, the cycle is very different. Newborns spend about fifty minutes in a cycle, with the time evenly divided between REM and non-REM sleep. By six months of age, babies spend 30 percent of their sleep time in REM sleep and by the time children are ten, their cycle in and out of REM sleep approaches that of the adult ninety minutes. This constant cycling of sleep stages leads children (and adults) through periods of light sleep and even short periods of wakefulness during the night.

Dreaming

Your child will not remember the non-REM stage, but it's a different story for REM sleep. Dreaming occurs during REM sleep, and you might notice his eyes moving from side to side, his breathing rate change, and he may even smile or frown. Dreams have always fascinated us, resulting in different theories throughout the centuries, and scientists are only now beginning to understand why we dream. In our evolutionary history, REM sleep first appeared in birds and mammals. If you own a dog you may have noticed him dreaming, complete with sound effects and movement. Brain waves recorded during REM sleep look much like they do when we're awake, spiking up and down. Dr. Robert Stickgold of Harvard University believes that dreaming in REM sleep is essential for learning how "to do things." Children's brains refire the neural networks that fired when they were actually doing things while awake. Infants' brains simulate movements and older children might refire the networks associated with playing the piano or riding a bike. This refiring constitutes a rehearsal, making complicated muscle movements easier to do the next day. In a real sense, children's brains practice while they sleep. Of course, your child doesn't actually play the piano or ride her bike at night. That's because the brain stem sends out signals that block the movement itself. Children's sleepwalking occurs when this function fails.

Stickgold and his colleagues also believe that REM sleep actually helps us solve problems by finding patterns in our memories we may have missed during the day. They asked people to detect relationships between colored shapes and most people couldn't find a pattern at first. Twelve hours later the same people could pick out 70 percent of the patterns. If, however, they slept in the interim their discovery rate shot up to 90 percent. "Sleeping on it" really does help us solve problems.

The sleep advantage really shows up when solving math problems. In an interesting German study, Ullrich Wagner, a researcher at the University of Lubeck, asked people to solve a difficult math problem using a long and complicated method that they practiced on one hundred problems. Wagner didn't tell them about a shortcut to make the problems easier and quicker to solve. During a twelve-hour break, some of the problem solvers went to sleep while the others went about their regular activities. When he reconvened the group he gave them two hundred more problems. Twenty-three percent of the nonsleepers figured out the shortcut, but 59 percent of those who had slept caught on and speeded up with the task. The sleeping brains were much more likely to find the pattern than the awake ones.

I experienced this myself when my son Brian was in middle school. He came down from his bedroom one night stumped by a math problem. "Dad, I've worked on this problem for a long time and I can't figure it out. Can you take a crack at it?"

I looked at the problem, scratched my head, thought some more, and then finally told Brian, "I'm sorry. It seems like I should know how to solve this, but I can't quite remember. I guess you're going to have to wait and ask your math teacher tomorrow."

As Brian sighed and walked away I returned to reading my book and didn't give the math conundrum another thought. Hours later, in the middle of the night, I woke out of a deep sleep with the solution as clear as a bell in my mind. I was excited to tell Brian the next morning not only that I had the solution but that it came to me while I slept. My sleeping brain clearly reworked the problem until it figured out the answer.

Emotional memories also surface in dreams during REM sleep. The brain sorts through memories, processing those emotionally tagged or important and possibly "erasing" irrelevant connections. The team at the University of Wisconsin's Center for Sleep and Consciousness studied just how the brain might accomplish this pruning. They found that during sleep, the brain "clears out" 30 to 40 percent of the proteins found at neural connections. They think this causes weak connections to get even less stable until they eventually wither away. "Much of what we learn in a day, we don't really need to remember," researcher Dr. Chiara Cirelli wrote to me during an email exchange. "If you use up all the space, you can't learn more until you clean out the junk that is filling up your brain." For the brain "spring housecleaning" happens every night.

Sleep Helps Memory

Some of the most exciting research explores the connection between sleep and memory. The brain stores memories when neurons fire and wire together. New sights, sounds, smells, touches, and tastes bombard kids every hour they're awake. Their brains work hard to integrate the new information into existing neural networks. We call this learning. Sleep gives the brain the chance to sort out and process all the neural connections built up during the day. And something happens with our memories during sleep that doesn't happen when we are awake. Researchers at the University of California, San Francisco discovered this in an experiment with kittens to see how sleep affected the way their brains coped with a visual challenge. Two groups of kittens played for six hours with one of their eyes covered, and then one group of kittens slept while the other was kept awake. Using brain imaging techniques, the researchers found that all the kittens' brains rewired their vision circuits; however, twice as much rewiring occurred in the brains of the kittens that slept. In addition, they found that the rewiring was especially intense during non-REM sleep. The sleeping kittens coped twice as well as their wide-awake playmates.

In another animal study, this time with songbirds, researchers kept track of what neurons fired as the birds sang. In order to sing, a bird has to emit sounds in a precise order, much like human language and speech. The scientists monitored these "sound" neurons as the birds slept and watched them fire over and over again in precisely the same order as when the birds were awake. While we might say that the birds were singing in their dreams, what was really happening was that their sleeping bird brains reinforced the neural connections for the sounds. It's yet another instance of the "neurons that fire together, wire together" principle. No wonder birds wake up in the morning and sing so clearly.

It makes sense, therefore, that very young babies sleep up to three times longer than adults, between sixteen and twenty hours a day. Their brains have a lot of work to do, consolidating memories and wiring all the new sensory information into more stable neural circuits. Sleep reinforces memories so the next day your baby is better able to remember all she experienced and learned the previous day. These in turn become circuits upon which additional memories can be built. Babies and toddlers continue to need more sleep than wake time to consolidate their learning. Overall, children will spend 40 percent of their time in brain-building sleep.

How Much Sleep?

When Monica and I had our first child, everything was new for me since I didn't have any experience with infants. Monica, on the other hand, had younger brothers and sisters so she had a better idea what to expect. I still remember wanting to talk to and interact with infant Dan. I couldn't figure out why all he seemed to do is sleep. "Is this normal?" I remember asking Monica. "Dan sleeps an awful lot."

"Of course it's normal, Dave," she answered. "Remember the books we read while I was pregnant?"

"I guess it just never registered with me," I answered. "I want him to be awake more so we can hang out."

Monica laughed. "Don't worry," she said, "before long I guarantee that you'll wish he would sleep more, not less."

A newborn doesn't have much of a sleep pattern because he isn't aware of any difference between day and night. He might wake up at two in the morning ready to go with his eyes wide open while yours are tiny slits. Most babies begin to settle into a regular schedule between three and six months. At that point they develop a sleep/wake cycle in tune with their circadian rhythms, which are affected by the turn of daylight and dark. Most children need more sleep than you think and more than most get. The National Sleep Foundation's Sleep in America study provides a "wake-up" call, if you'll pardon the pun.

- Babies from three to eleven months need fourteen to fifteen hours of sleep but they average only 12.7.
- Toddlers one to three years old should get twelve to fourteen hours of sleep, but most get 11.7 hours.
- Preschoolers ages three to five need eleven to thirteen hours of sleep. Yet the average for this group is 10.4 hours.
- First through fifth graders ought to have ten to eleven hours each night. American average for this age group: 9.5 hours.
- Preteens need nine hours but only average eight.
- The biggest sleep deficit is for teenagers. They average six to seven hours in spite of the fact that they should be getting between nine and ten.

Sleep needs vary from child to child, but this study underscores the fact that our kids' brains and bodies need more sleep. Some children fall asleep quickly and early while others just hate going to bed. Some kids wake up bright-eyed while others have to be dragged from underneath their covers. While sleep needs are individual, an adequate amount is critical for our kids' emotional and physical health as well as their performance in school.

PARENT TOOL KIT

Sleep for a Healthy Brain

Healthy brains need snooze time. Use this tool kit to check your child's "snooze meter."

Yes No

☐ ☐ 1. I know how much sleep my child needs for his or her age.

☐ ☐ 2. My child has a set bedtime and bedtime routine.

☐ ☐ 3. I realize that my child's brain and body both grow during sleep.

☐ ☐ 4. Neural connections get stronger while my child sleeps.
☐ ☐ 5. During sleep my child's brain "practices" what it learned during the day.
☐ ☐ 6. Sleep cycles through deep sleep and REM sleep.
☐ ☐ 7. I should make sure my child gets a good night's sleep.
☐ ☐ 8. Even missing one hour of sleep, over time, affects my child's learning.
☐ ☐ 9. Lack of sleep can make a child "hyper."
☐ ☐ 10. My child's brain refuels and repairs itself during sleep.

Knowing how important sleep is for your child's well-being at home, in school, and at play will help you give your kids enough snooze time. The more yes answers to the questions in this tool kit, the more likely you are to make sure your child gets enough brain-building sleep.

Sleepy Brains and Language Development

In chapter 3 I identified the critical periods during which a young child processes and encodes language sounds. His brain, in a period of rapid development, learns to hear, recognize, and reproduce sounds. Later he strings them together into words. What he "hears," though, can be affected by having a "sleepy brain." Just as baby birds need periods of sleep to rehearse their songs, so also children need enough good sleep so their brains can refire and strengthen the neural networks involved in language acquisition. A chronically sleepy child cannot focus on what he hears during the day nor can he consolidate those connections at night. Gaps in language awareness may result, leading to learning difficulties in reading, writing, and language comprehension later in school, since each phoneme (sound) and new word has to be wired into the neural networks in the brain's language centers. A University of Louisville study revealed that children who lose as little as one hour of sleep a night over a week's time will have gaps in their ability to identify speech sounds correctly compared to other children getting a full night's sleep.

If your child yawns frequently, it's a sure sign she's sleepy. Cranky behavior is another sure sign. Cranky kids often lead to cranky parents. The only cure is more sleep. We'll talk later in this chapter about common sleep stealers and what you can do.

A Sleepy Brain in the Classroom

Classroom teachers across the country get reports of late-night TV shows or movies they'd rather not hear. Brain science confirms their suspicions that lack of sleep hinders classroom performance. A growing mountain of evidence shows that too little sleep impacts a child's memory, attention, and mood.

Dr. Avi Sadeh studies the effects of sleep on children's development at Tel Aviv University. He wanted to know if the loss of one hour of sleep would affect kids, so he devised an experiment with a group of sixth graders. He randomly assigned the students into two groups. He asked the first group to go to bed one hour earlier than usual and requested the other group to stay up one hour later. He gave them special monitors so he could measure how much sleep each group actually got. The first group averaged thirty-five minutes more sleep than they'd gotten before and the night owls lost an extra forty-one minutes by staying up late. After just three nights, the sleepy sixth graders' performance on memory and problem-solving tasks deteriorated to a fourth grade level, while their well-rested classmates showed no decline. The gap of seventy-six minutes between the two groups made a huge difference in performance.

My friend Stacey is a fifth grade teacher who claims she can pick out the kids who aren't getting enough sleep, just by looking at the class. They're the ones nodding, yawning, or staring into space. During the day they're often touchy, jumpy, and have trouble concentrating. She keeps track and has a sleep talk with parents at the upcoming parent conferences. She also explains to her students why our brains need sleep.

In addition to sleep's effect on memory, it also affects glucose metabolism. We learned in chapter 5 that glucose is the fuel that makes our bodies work. Research now reveals that a lack of sleep cuts down on the glucose supply to the brain. To compound the problem, the part of the brain most glucose starved is the prefrontal cortex, where the executive functions like problem solving, decision making, and impulse control happen. With their brain's executive center running low on fuel, it's no wonder sleep-deprived children can't think, solve problems, concentrate, or manage their behavior as well as rested kids. They appear antsy because they need to move around to stay alert and their prefrontal cortex is less able to manage behavior.

Does Too Little Sleep Make You Hungry?

There are two hormones involved in regulating our appetite. The first is ghrelin, which I nickname "Hungry" because it's the Paul Revere that races to the brain with the message "I'm starved." The second, leptin, I call "Full" because it sends signals to the brain that we've eaten enough. When we don't get enough sleep, ghrelin increases and leptin decreases. That explains the results of a recent experiment in which men who slept four hours for just one night ate 22 percent more the next day than others who had gotten a full eight hours of sleep. Our sleep-deprivation and obesity epidemics may be related.

Newborns Sleep Sixteen to Eighteen Hours a Day

Infants sleep around the clock, and a lot of their parents wish they could do the same. In the first months, they wake up for food, diaper changes, and cuddles at all hours of the day and night. Here are some suggestions to help your baby sleep longer at night, and play and eat during daytime hours.

1. Don't play with your baby at night. Your new little one is the cutest baby on the planet, and you might be tempted to interact, especially if she's been sleeping all day. However, your baby has day and night mixed up, and she doesn't understand yet that nighttime is for sleeping. You need to help her learn this by keeping the lights low, using a soothing, quiet voice, and keeping your interactions to the minimum when you feed and change her at night. Remember, her brain is wiring in connections from experience. If she has a lot of stimulation and fun at night, she'll continue to wake up expecting you to play.

2. Put your baby in her crib when she's drowsy, letting her fall asleep in her bed. If you get into a pattern of always rocking her to sleep, nursing her to sleep, letting her fall asleep on your chest, or always walking and singing her to sleep, then she'll need rocking, walking, feeding, and your arms to fall asleep and will cry mightily if she doesn't get them. Every time she wakes up in the night, she'll need your help to fall back asleep. Remember, her brain will wire in sleep patterns based on experience. Don't wait for your baby to be sound asleep before putting her in the crib. Watch your baby for sleepy signs—she'll yawn, rub her eyes, or get fussy—so you can put her in her crib when she's tired. When she wakes up at night, if she's been fed and changed and you know there's no crisis, let her try to soothe herself to sleep for a few minutes before you rush in and pick her up.

3. Follow the American Academy of Pediatrics guidelines to prevent sudden infant death syndrome (SIDS). Place your child on his back and

remove any pillows, stuffed animals, or soft items from the crib, especially around the infant's head. These items could interfere with his breathing. Keep the room cool. If you're a smoker, don't smoke near the baby or in his room. Don't overdress the baby or make the room too warm. Researchers have not discovered the exact cause of SIDS, but studies are pointing to anomalies in the infant's brainstem that prevent the baby from rousing itself from deep sleep.

4. Make sure you give your infant awake "tummy time" during the day to help him develop muscles and motor skills, such as lifting and moving his head.

Toddlers Need Twelve to Fourteen Hours and Preschoolers Need Eleven to Thirteen

What parent hasn't heard "Please one more story" or "Daddy, I need a drink of water?" I still remember our bedtime struggles. Brian would grab on to the sides of his crib and just bounce up and down having a great time—at midnight! One of the biggest sleep challenges for young children is that they just don't want to let go—of you. Separation anxiety plays a role in bedtime problems. There were times when all three of our kids would do everything they could to delay falling asleep. Children find security in routines, so establishing one at bedtime can help them relax. The routine we finally set looked like this: wash hands and face, brush teeth, find the favorite stuffed animal and blanket, put on pajamas, have a drink of water, turn on the night light, chat for a minute, read a favorite story, and then a kiss and hug good night. We tried to stick to a regular bedtime and attempted to make the hour before bed a quiet time with no wrestling or TV. We always found that it helped to give our kids a thirty-minute and then a ten-minute warning that the bedtime routine was about to start.

After the kids were older than six months, it was hard to break the impulse to go into Dan's, Brian's, or Erin's bedroom right away if they woke up crying. We knew that they needed time to settle themselves to sleep, but a crying baby or calling child is hard to resist. Unless they were sick or clearly needed us to respond, we tried our mightiest to reinforce the message that bedtime was for sleeping.

When a child wakes up from a dream or nightmare, calm and soothe him quietly. Listen if he wants to tell you about his dream, and then when he's calm and sleepy again, tuck him in and quietly make your exit. Keep all screens out of kids' bedrooms and avoid all electronic media before bedtime.

TVs, computers, and video games make falling and staying asleep more difficult, especially if what's on the screen is scary. Electronic media are sleep thieves.

Too little sleep either causes or exacerbates a lot of childhood misbehavior and aggression. In fact, Northwestern University scientists found that preschoolers who slept less than ten hours in a twenty-four hour period were 25 percent more likely to misbehave and/or act aggressively.

School-Age Kids Need Ten to Eleven Hours and Teenagers Need at Least Nine

Bedtime routines are important for school-age children as well, so try to maintain a regular bedtime with its predictable rituals. A light bedtime snack is fine, but don't send your child to bed with a full stomach. Add a bedtime chat to the routine to give you and your child some quality alone time. Monica and I called this the "ten-minute chat," and our kids really became attached to this nightly conversation. As they got older, the "ten-minute chat" became a time where worries and concerns about school or friends surfaced. There were occasions when the ten minutes would stretch into a much longer time if the issues were sensitive or important. That quiet, calm hour before turning in is important for this age group as well. TV, the computer, video games, and cell phones rob a lot of kids of precious hours of rest. So do caffeine or sugary beverages and overheated rooms. Following these tips will ensure that your child gets the sleep he needs for an alert, active brain at school.

Sleep Log and Inventory

If you're wondering whether your kids are getting enough sleep, you might want to keep a sleep log for one week to see how much shut-eye they're actually getting. Write down the time your child falls asleep and the time he wakes up. Add nap time if appropriate. Calculate the total and compare it to the daily recommended amounts. Use the following checklist to see if you're doing what you can to make sure your child gets enough sleep to refuel and repair his brain and prime it for learning.

- ☐ I set my child's bedtime to allow for enough hours of sleep for her age.
- ☐ I have a predictable bedtime routine for my child.
- ☐ I give my child the message that bedtime is for sleeping.

- ☐ I steer my child to quieter activities during the hour before bedtime.
- ☐ I give my child thirty- and ten-minute warnings that bedtime is near.
- ☐ I make sure my child doesn't have caffeinated beverages or heavy meals before bedtime.
- ☐ I set the temperature so my child's room is cool.
- ☐ I do not include media as part of my child's bedtime routine.
- ☐ My child may have a favorite toy, blanket, book, pillow, or other comfort item.

If your child spends significant time with another parent or grandparent, try to agree on a similar bedtime routine no matter where the child sleeps. The security of a familiar routine will help her have a more restful sleep. It's also helpful to try to maintain a routine when traveling.

Sleep Problems and Disorders

Some children have more serious sleep problems beyond the normal "I don't want to go to bed" type. Let your pediatrician know if your child snores or wakes up often at night, can't get to sleep, or if you think he may not be getting enough sleep. Researchers find that children with sleep disorders are at risk for learning difficulties in reading, math, and writing. Even attention deficit symptoms, aggressive behavior, and bullying at school can often be traced to an undiagnosed sleep disorder.

SLEEP APNEA

Sleep apnea, or short breathing pauses during sleep, is not just a problem for adults. Some children can develop the disorder, especially if they are overweight or have enlarged tonsils or adenoids. A report from the Johns Hopkins University School of Medicine lists apnea symptoms including snoring and labored breathing, gasping, restless sleep, and unusual sleep positions. During the day the child may be unusually sleepy, touchy, or even hyperactive. When the scientists examined the children's brains using sophisticated imaging techniques, they discovered that children with untreated, severe sleep apnea suffered damage to the parts of their brains responsible for memory, learning, and complex thought. This explains why these children had lower scores on IQ and other learning tests.

A University of Louisville study found that among 1,500 middle school students, about 13 percent of those who ranked in the bottom quarter of their class reported loud and frequent snoring when they were children. Only 5 percent of students in the top quarter reported snoring. The researchers concluded that sleep apnea poses a serious risk for a child's school and career success and can lead to attention deficit issues, hyperactivity, and aggression. In fact, sleep apnea can be misdiagnosed as attention deficit disorder.

NIGHTMARES

Children under stress, who've experienced a big loss or change in their life, who view violent or scary images on TV or in video games, or who live under a real threat of violence often experience frightening, intense dreams. They occur in a child's REM sleep cycle, usually later in the night, and are often remembered the next day. If your child wakes crying and distressed from a nightmare, offer reassurance and comfort. If he remembers the nightmare, encourage him to talk about it to lessen its emotional power.

NIGHT TERRORS

Monica and I awoke from a sound sleep to hear our six-year-old daughter Erin screaming. We raced to her bedroom and found her sweating, shaking, and crying. Try as we might, we couldn't wake her up. In fact, we ourselves became players in whatever scary scene was playing in her brain. As I reached to hug her, Erin shrieked, "Stay away from me. Don't hurt me!" Erin was in the throes of a classic night terror, sometimes known as sleep terrors. They are different from nightmares in that the child cannot be awakened. As many as 15 percent of children experience night terrors, and they usually occur between the ages of two and eight, although people can experience them at any age. Needless to say, night terrors can be very scary for parents, especially if they don't realize what's happening.

Sleep experts are still baffled by night terrors. They know they happen during non-REM sleep but don't know what causes them. The good news for parents is that almost all children outgrow night terrors, and they rarely remember them the next day. They typically last about ten minutes, although sometimes they can go on longer. While it can be frightening to watch a child in the midst of a night terror, there is no evidence that it is a sign of a problem nor is there any evidence of harm. Night terrors just seem to be one of the brain's mechanisms that we haven't figured out yet. If your child suffers from sleep terrors, make sure her room is safe and watch over her so she doesn't hurt herself. Then tuck her in when it passes. Monica and I found that holding a cool washcloth on Erin's forehead helped.

NARCOLEPSY

Narcolepsy is a serious sleep disorder characterized by extreme daytime sleepiness. Narcoleptics will often fall asleep with little warning and at inappropriate times and places. It is quite rare, but for those who suffer from it, the onset is usually puberty. If your teen is chronically fatigued, has irregular night sleep patterns, and falls asleep during the day with little warning, you should see a pediatrician or sleep specialist for help. Most narcoleptics suffer for years because the disorder is often under- or misdiagnosed. There are medications that help but professional diagnosis and care are a must.

The Irish have a proverb, "A good laugh and a long sleep are the best cures in the doctor's book." Brain science helps us understand just how important sleep is for a healthy body and healthy mind.

Teens and Sleep

Callie was an eleventh grader who started out the year as an enthusiastic and friendly student. By November, however, she was often late for class, started missing assignments, and seemed more and more touchy. One afternoon she stopped after class to ask for an extension on a paper due the next day. I told her she could have the extension but it would result in a lower grade. Her eyes immediately filled with tears. "Callie, how are you doing?" I asked. "You seem really stressed these past few weeks."

"Mr. Walsh," she replied, "I'm really trying to keep up with everything, but there just aren't enough hours in the day to get everything done."

"What do you have on your plate?" I asked.

Callie proceeded to paint a picture of a very overscheduled, stressed-out high school student. "I take two AP classes, I'm on the soccer team, and I work ten hours a week to save money for college. On top of that I'm active with my church youth group, and I volunteer to tutor kids at the homeless shelter twice a week."

"How do you keep up with all that?" I asked.

"I can't," she moaned. "I haven't done your paper yet, and Mrs. Murray just told me I'm getting a C in Spanish. I always get A's in her class."

"Callie," I asked, "how many hours of sleep do you get at night?"

"I usually fall asleep around eleven, but I get up at five-thirty for zero-hour gym."

"So how tired are you?" I asked.

"I'm wiped," she replied. "I can hardly drag myself out of bed in the morning. I drink a lot of coffee and soda to stay charged up for the day."

"Callie," I said, "you're exhausted. There's no way your brain can operate on so little sleep." After I told Callie a bit about sleep and her brain, she looked thoughtful. "Do I really need nine hours of sleep a night or are you just making that up?" she asked.

"I'll show you the research if you want," I answered.

"I don't know anyone who gets nine hours," Callie replied.

"I know you don't," I responded. "Most kids don't get enough sleep, but you, Callie, are really pushing the lower limit. My advice to you is to cut back on some of your activities and figure out how to get more sleep. If you don't, I think you'll fall even further behind and feel even lousier."

Like many teens, Callie is under a lot of pressure to perform. Competition to get into the "right colleges" drives many to pack their schedules with Advanced Placement courses along with résumé-building activities and jobs. I'm not suggesting teens become slackers, but there is a point where an overpacked schedule puts a teen into sleep deprivation and produces diminishing returns.

Puberty brings about a big change in sleep patterns. The timing of the sleep/wake cycle shifts, so adolescents get sleepy and feel fully alert at different times than their younger brothers and sisters. What's happening is that the pineal gland, which is located within the brain and very sensitive to light, begins to secrete a hormone called melatonin when it's dark out. Melatonin makes us tired and as its levels increase, we get even more tired and eventually fall asleep. After we've had enough sleep, the brain tells the pineal gland to stop producing so much melatonin, the level of the hormone drops, and we wake up. For reasons we don't yet understand, the timing changes at puberty. Both the melatonin surges and drops occur later and later in the day, so teens are Energizer bunnies at eleven at night when their parents are dragging. On the other hand, they're still groggy the next morning when it's time to concentrate in math or Spanish class.

This happens at the same time teens' bodies and brains are going through huge changes and growth spurts. They continue to need a lot of sleep—about nine and a half hours per night for the brain to regenerate and operate at peak efficiency. Most, like Callie, don't get anywhere near that much. It's not surprising that so many teens are sleep deprived, affecting their school performance and emotional stability. Slammed doors, sudden tears, and angry outbursts are part and parcel of adolescence. Constant sleep deprivation amplifies the effects and can lead to mood swings, irritability, and depression.

The effect that too little sleep has on a younger's emotions is profound. Scientists have known for years that adequate sleep helps with emotional stability. A 2010 study led by Columbia University scientist James Gangwisch took even the sleep advocates' breath away. Gangwisch and his colleagues found that teenagers who routinely go to bed after midnight were 24 percent more likely to suffer from depression and 20 percent more likely to have suicidal thoughts than adolescents who hit the pillow at 10 P.M. or earlier.

HELP TEENS SLEEP

Although Callie had some big decisions to make about her priorities, parents also can do some simple things to help their teens try to get the sleep they need. One of the biggest sleep aids is removing sources of late-night stimulation. Many teens' bedrooms have morphed into communication and entertainment centers with video games, cell phones, TVs, and computers keeping teens connected and entertained at all hours. With their brains revved up, it's even more difficult for them to wind down when they need to. And a new discovery by scientists at Australia's Swinburne University of Technology that "pulsed microwave radiation" from cell phones causes the brain to switch to alpha waves, which are not conducive to sleep, adds to the challenge. It can take the brain twice as long to relax and fall asleep after a cell phone call. So decide on a time to turn off the cell phones and tell your teen to make any necessary late-night phone calls on the landline, which doesn't affect the brain waves, or wait until the next day.

It's also important to get teens to unplug from media and computers by nine or ten o'clock and, of course, to avoid any food or beverage containing caffeine after dinnertime. Although it takes caffeine only thirty to sixty minutes to reach peak effect, the body needs three to five hours to get rid of half the caffeine and up to fourteen hours to process all of it. All these sources of late-night stimulation only magnify the urge to stay awake. Even late-night cramming for tests is counterproductive. Reading, quiet music, and other mellow activities are good ways to help a teen transition to sleep. We saw earlier in this chapter that both deep sleep and the dreaming REM sleep are needed to organize our memories, strengthen the neural connections of new learning, and reenergize our brain to function at peak the following day. Let all your kids know, especially teenagers, that a good night's sleep before a test is more helpful than another hour of study.

SCHOOL START TIMES

High school start times often work against teens' changing sleep cycle. With classes starting at 7:15 A.M. or earlier, I remember trying to motivate semicomatose students during first period. School districts across the country are caught between the science of teen sleep and the reality of busing budgets, family schedules, and after-school activities. However, results from districts that have reset high school and even middle school start times to a later hour have found that their teens got higher grades, experienced less depression, and dropped out of school less often. School principals commonly report that the mood in the hallways and at lunchtime is much calmer, and teachers say students are more alert throughout the day.

The effect on teen driving is equally impressive. A Kansas study found that the decline in daytime sleepiness with later school start times coincided with a 16.5 percent decline in teen auto crashes. Tired teens make bad drivers. Vehicle crashes account for 35 percent of teenage deaths in the United States, with teens involved in three times as many crashes as all other drivers. Driver fatigue is a leading factor along with distractions caused by cell phone use and texting.

Banish Bedtime Sleep Thieves

Overscheduling, stress, anxiety, media, and cell phone use aren't just affecting the sleep of teenagers. Sleep thieves like these and others have snuck into younger children's bedrooms as well. Many children experience sleep difficulties. According to the National Sleep Foundation, almost 70 percent of kids ten and under have sleep problems a couple of times a week. Parents should seek help from pediatricians for kids who have difficulty falling asleep, wake up often during the night, wake up crying, or wake up too early in the morning. Sleep difficulties lead to tired, cranky kids, which in turn makes for tired, cranky parents.

DO

- ✓ Know how much sleep is recommended for your child's age.
- ✓ Establish a regular bedtime hour.
- ✓ Let a young child nap during the day, if needed. Overtired young children do not sleep as well.
- ✓ Have a bedtime routine you follow every night.
- ✓ Give your child enough time to quiet down and transition into sleep time.
- ✓ Put your baby down for sleep when she is drowsy, not fully asleep.
- ✓ Expect that your child will have restless times during the night when he needs to comfort himself back to sleep, if he is not sick or in pain.
- ✓ Keep TVs, video games, and computers out of your child's bedroom.
- ✓ Understand your teen's shifting sleep pattern.

- ✓ Help your teen understand why his brain needs adequate sleep.
- ✓ Help preteens and teens keep a bedtime routine that works for them.
- ✓ Set a "cell phone and technology curfew."
- ✓ Seek your pediatrician's help if your child snores, is very sleepy during the day, or has continued sleep issues.

DON'T

- ✗ Don't overstimulate your child right before bedtime.
- ✗ Don't let family time compete with sleep time.
- ✗ Don't let your child watch violent TV, movies, or video games that cause nightmares.
- ✗ Don't continue to respond to your child's calls once he is settled into bed, unless he is sick or there is an emergency.
- ✗ Don't give your child caffeine or a big meal right before bedtime.
- ✗ Don't let your child or teen get overscheduled.

What do I want to continue?

____

____

____

What do I want to change?

____

____

____

NINE

Self-Discipline: The Key to Success

A few days after conducting a parent workshop at Carondelet Catholic School in Minneapolis, I got a call from Frank Vascellaro, a well-known Twin Cities news anchor, with three kids at the elementary school. He and his co-anchor wife, Amelia Santaniello, had attended the workshop and were excited about a marshmallow experiment I did there—they'd repeated it with their own kids and wanted me to do it as a WCCO-TV news feature. The marshmallow experiment in question was the now-famous 1968 Stanford study done by Walter Mischel and his colleagues on delayed gratification. The four-year-olds at the Bing Nursery School who waited up to twenty minutes for a second marshmallow instead of eating the one staring at them from a table inches away turned out to be much more successful and happier later in life. The experiment is a classic in establishing the link between self-control and success.

Two weeks later, the WCCO television crew and I replicated the experiment with hidden cameras on the bare room with a table, chair, and single marshmallow. The only thing I changed was the length of time that the four-year-olds had to wait. I shortened it from twenty to fifteen minutes. Fourteen children took part with roughly half able to wait and the other half succumbing to the sweet temptation before the time was up. One little boy had the marshmallow in his mouth before Amelia and I left the room. Our favorite, however, was the boy who put the marshmallow in his mouth within the first minute—and let it sit there. As time ticked by the marshmallow began melting. The little guy remained stoically resolute in spite of the sticky mess dripping onto his chin. At the fifteen-minute mark Amelia and I reentered the room and sat smiling on either side of the young fellow. He glanced at each of us, took the oozing blob out of his mouth, and proudly announced, "I didn't bite it. Where's my second marshmallow?" What a clever lad!

The WCCO version of the marshmallow experiment did indeed spark a lot of discussions among Twin Cities parents. As Frank and Amelia predicted, it became a great teaching tool to underline the critical importance of self-discipline as a key to children's happiness and success. The research showing the importance of self-discipline for children didn't end in 1968. A 2005 University of Pennsylvania study showed, for example, that self-discipline is twice as strong a predictor of school success as is intelligence. Teachers, of course, are not surprised by the research findings. Teachers constantly tell me that they would much rather have highly motivated, hardworking students of average intelligence than very bright students who couldn't care less or who can't manage their behavior.

Discipline Deficit Disorder

A constant drumbeat of "more, fast, easy, and fun" undermines 21st-century parents' attempts to foster self-discipline in their children. Today's kids—and parents as well—are constantly told that whatever we have, we need more. Even if money is tight, there is a better model right around the corner. We are also told that everything should be quick and easy, that we shouldn't have to wait for anything. And children are taught that everything should be fun.

These cultural messages start early. Targeting babies as young as five months old, products like Baby Einstein DVDs that promise future genius are pitched to eager young parents. Their pleasant music, shapes, and colors are nice, but I advise parents to avoid these DVDs because products like these are literally wiring babies' brains not only to orient to screens before they can even crawl or utter their first word, but also to expect nonstop entertainment. When these children get to school, they'll encounter a human being for a teacher. What a bummer! Special technologies such as interactive whiteboards notwithstanding, not every concept is presented in a catchy tune and not every new lesson dances on the board. As a result some children as young as kindergartners are coming home from school complaining of boredom. Of course they're bored. They've been wired to expect nonstop entertainment.

There is nothing wrong with having nice things, convenience, or enjoyment. The problem is that popular culture overemphasizes them. When our kids overdose on "more, fast, easy, and fun," it's difficult for them to develop, and parents to foster, the key character trait for success and happiness: self-discipline.

The result is an epidemic that engulfs too many of our children. I call the epidemic discipline deficit disorder, or DDD. Here are the symptoms.

- Distraction
- Disrespect
- Impatience
- Need for instant gratification
- Sense of entitlement
- Unrealistic expectations
- Self-centeredness

The Evidence for DDD

The evidence for DDD is all around us. In 2007, the Maplewood, New Jersey, public library decided to lock its doors during after-school hours because of unruly students. The board of trustees only relented when the community committed to a multipronged strategy to restore order. One out of two new American teachers abandons the profession within five years, and the number-one reason for teacher dissatisfaction is student behavior. A young teacher at a San Francisco high school approached me after a workshop. "I'm one of the teachers you were talking about," she began. "I'm twenty-seven years old, I've been teaching social studies for five years, and I'm giving up. I just told my principal last week that I wasn't returning next year because I can't keep doing this."

Although it may be tempting to chalk up her frustration as an "inner-city problem," a month later a second-year math teacher from an upper-middle-class suburb of St. Louis with a reputation for excellent schools told me, "I think I spend more time on student behavior than I do on content."

Student behavior affects student performance in three ways. First, time spent on behavior means time *not* spent on content. Second, an undercurrent of disorder does not create a climate conducive to learning. The third impact, however, is more subtle. As student behavior becomes an issue, teachers make an unconscious and unspoken deal with students. "If you don't give me a hard time, it will boost your grade." I have shared this suspicion with teachers as I conduct workshops around the country, and I learned that this is exactly what happens. When good behavior is a given, then grades are based on scholastic performance. When classroom behavior deteriorates, then the "good students" get a good grade for simply not acting out, one of the factors behind grade inflation. Eden Prairie High School in

Minnesota eliminated naming a valedictorian in 2007 because twenty-three graduates had perfect 4.0 averages. While I'm sure these students worked hard, I think twenty-three 4.0s is evidence of the unspoken deal.

I shared my opinion about grade inflation in a University of Minnesota freshman psychology seminar and was surprised how quickly the students agreed. One coed offered this example. "In my senior year in high school I got an A for a project that I never even turned in. I know why I got the A," she added. "I was one of the good kids. My English teacher had so many kids she had to worry about acting up that I got a grade boost just for not causing her a headache." Another freshman girl quickly added, "I feel completely ripped off. I sailed through high school with good grades. When I got here at the U of M it was like getting hit by a truck. I was completely unprepared."

Concern about student achievement has grown for decades with American student performance rating as mediocre when compared with their peers in other industrialized countries. Now, after almost three decades of effort, with one program after another failing to improve students' academic performance, our standing is virtually unchanged. We placed all the responsibility for improvement on the shoulders of teachers and schools. No doubt there's room for schools to improve, but if we think we will achieve results without paying attention to the key factor of success—self-discipline—then we will continue to push a very heavy rock up a very steep hill.

Low performance will make it harder to compete with countries like China with its 1.3 billion people, boasting more honor roll students than we have kids total in the United States. And they are motivated. My wife, Monica, and I spent a month in China in late 2007, and we will long remember a scene we saw unfold late one afternoon in Dali, a town in Sichuan Province in the foothills of the Himalayas. At five o'clock in the afternoon, all the students got out of school and, like kids everywhere, they came running through the marketplace. They chased one another, yelling and screaming, burning off the pent-up energy after a long day in school. A half hour later, at about five-thirty, Monica and I looked at each other. "Do you see what I see?" she asked. "I sure do," I replied. "Take a picture because people back home won't believe this."

All over the marketplace, boys and girls sat down and started their homework. They didn't have comfortable or well-lit desks; they studied on park benches or on stools in their parents' shops. Young students stopped us numerous times to practice English, their required foreign language. Bill Gates offered this assessment of our kids' future competition in 2008: "When I compare our high schools with what I see when I'm traveling abroad, I am terrified for our work force of tomorrow."

DDD and Economic Competitiveness

Evidence of DDD surfaced outside schools in a 2006 Conference Board study of young people entering the workforce that sounded an ominous alarm. "The future workforce is here, and it is ill-prepared," concludes the report. The surprise finding is that American business leaders are as concerned about "work ethic" as they are about basic skills. Nearly three-quarters of the 430 business leaders responding to the survey cited serious work ethic deficiencies among young hires. This is alarming news in a global economy where work can quickly move to countries with a competent, motivated, and self-disciplined workforce.

On a conference call the afternoon before the Workforce Readiness Report was released, I listened to business leaders make comments like "We can teach young people the skills, but they have to be willing to work hard, delay gratification, handle frustration, and persist at difficult tasks." They listed all the ingredients of self-discipline, the trait that Mischel was testing with his marshmallows in 1968.

PARENT TOOL KIT

Self-Discipline

Parents can have a great impact on the development of a child's self-discipline skills. Use these questions to help you build a tool kit for success.

Yes No

☐ ☐ 1. I know it's important for my child to learn how to delay gratification.
☐ ☐ 2. Our family rules are clear.
☐ ☐ 3. Our family rules are consistent.
☐ ☐ 4. I know how to set and enforce limits and consequences.
☐ ☐ 5. I know how to avoid power struggles with my children.
☐ ☐ 6. I expect my child to do chores and help out around the house.
☐ ☐ 7. I model and expect respectful behavior.
☐ ☐ 8. We avoid impulse buying for our children.
☐ ☐ 9. We distinguish between needs and wants.
☐ ☐ 10. Connection builds a sense of trust for my baby and lays the foundation for discipline.

The more yeses checked off in this tool kit, the better equipped you are to help your child develop the self-discipline traits for success and happiness.

Self-Discipline and the Brain: Managing Drives and Emotions

With the downturn in the U.S. and world economies, it's never been more important or challenging for parents to foster self-discipline in children and teach our kids how to say no to themselves. Children need to manage two powerful brain forces: drives and emotions. Let's start with drives.

Recall from chapter 1 that two powerful forces determine how a child's brain develops: genetics, which I call hard wiring, and experience, or soft wiring. Most of this book is devoted to what parents can influence—the soft wiring. For the challenge of self-discipline, however, we do need to examine hardwired drives.

We are all born with certain preinstalled drives, standard brain equipment for behaviors we don't need to learn, such as the familiar flight-or-fight response. Imagine hiking down a mountain path when you spot a snake ready to spring at you. In a split second, your pulse rate soars, your blood pressure increases, and the energizer hormone, adrenaline, surges through your bloodstream so that you leap back from the menacing serpent. And consider your surprise when, from a safe distance, you realize that the deadly snake is actually a curved stick. The flight-or-flight circuits in the brain sparked a powerful reaction before the thinking brain, the cortex, even knew what all the fuss was about.

Survival is the reason our brain comes prewired with these drives, genetically encoded and exquisitely designed to keep us alive. The fight-or-flight drive is only one of our hardwired drives. Another is the drive to seek pleasure and avoid pain. That drive causes me to be very careful around the stove, where I accidentally burned myself a few days ago. Another drive, for connection with other people, is part of why we grieve the loss of a loved one.

These powerful drives also create conflict. Imagine, for example, that your friendship is very important to me. Then imagine that I do something that you find very offensive, and you emphatically say you want me to stop. I face a dilemma. If I keep doing what I want to do, following my drive to seek pleasure, I could harm or even destroy our friendship. I have to balance my need for pleasure with my need for connection and be able to say no to it. These hardwired drives are like a team of horses. Learning to handle the reins enables me to manage the team when they are at odds. Self-discipline is the balancer.

The extra 21st-century challenge is that popular culture places one of our hardwired drives—to seek pleasure—at the top of the list, increases the font size by 500 percent, bolds it, and puts a spotlight on it. The message:

"This drive is the most important of all. All the others should be subject to its demands." This environment makes it hard for children to learn "to manage the reins," which is the skill the four-year-olds at the Bing Nursery School needed as they stared at the tempting marshmallow in front of them. It was also what fifteen-year-old Roger needed on his way home from school with three of his friends.

As the four teens walked through the park, Tyler told his friends that he finally succeeded in convincing his older brother to give him some marijuana. "I smoked some last night when my parents were gone, and it's really good," he announced. "I've got enough for all of us to get high."

"Well then give me some," Evan said.

"Me, too," chimed in Sean.

Roger remained silent as Tyler began rolling a joint. "C'mon, Roger," Tyler said as he turned toward him.

"Not today," replied Roger.

"What do you mean?" asked Tyler. "What's the matter with you? This is really good stuff."

"I have to go to my aunt and uncle's house for dinner as soon as I get home, and I can't risk getting caught." As his friends started to smoke, he told them he had to go.

Roger balanced some powerful drives that afternoon. On the one hand he wanted the approval of his friends and had heard from other kids how pot made you feel good. These drives for pleasure and approval, however, were in conflict with his drive for parental approval. He remembered the promise he made not to use drugs. The fib he made up about his aunt and uncle enabled him to say no to his friends and save face. As Roger walked home he felt relieved he was able to say no this time but also worried how he would handle his friends' pressure in the future.

Managing Emotions

In addition to managing drives, children must also tame another set of powerful brain forces: emotions. The word *emotion* comes from the Latin verb *movere*, meaning to move, as Romans knew our feelings provide the energy that *motivates* us to act. Artist Vincent van Gogh called them the "captains of our lives."

Antoine de St.-Exupéry's classic novel, *The Little Prince*, has inspired an untold number of songs, drawings, poems, and plays. The most famous scene in the classic tale is when the fox shares the secret to life with the little prince. "It is only with the heart that one can see rightly; what is essential is invisible to the eye." What would life be like without emotion, the ability to see with the heart?

While emotions add richness and texture to our lives, they can also derail our plans and aspirations. That was the case with Leah, a student I knew when I was a high school counselor. Leah was very bright. She almost always knew the answers to the questions her teachers posed—but she never raised her hand. Her sharp intellect enabled her to poke holes in an argument or connect the present discussion with other information, although she never shared her insights. Since she never spoke in class and her test scores were average at best, none of her teachers knew how gifted she was. They thought she was dull, unmotivated, or both. They never suspected Leah was paralyzed by fear and anxiety. She slouched in her desk and avoided eye contact with her teachers because she was terrified they would call on her. She knew the answer, but she was convinced her mind would go blank under the spotlight of attention and she would look foolish in front of her peers. The safer route was to look bored and disinterested. On test days her heart raced and her mind froze with panic, so she seldom finished the questions.

Out of the spotlight, Leah could relax and think clearly. In fact, she wrote a term paper so good that her social studies teacher was convinced she had plagiarized it, and he asked Leah to remain after class the day he handed back all the papers but Leah's.

"Do you know why I didn't return your paper, Leah?" began Mr. Collins.

"No," answered Leah, looking at the floor.

"Leah, who helped you write this paper?" Mr. Collins asked.

"What do you mean?" Leah mumbled. "Nobody helped me. I wrote it." She could feel her face flush with embarrassment and anger.

"Leah, plagiarism is a serious offense. I don't see how you wrote this paper. It's the work of a college student, not someone who hasn't said a word all term and who barely stays awake in my class."

Leah's heart began to race uncontrollably and her eyes filled with tears. "Can I please go?" Leah asked. Before Mr. Collins could answer, Leah headed for the door. "I wrote it" were the only words she could get out.

Mr. Collins alerted me to the situation, and later that afternoon I met with Leah. "Leah, tell me what happened in Mr. Collins's class," I asked as I motioned for her to take a seat.

Leah told me about the term paper and the after-class conversation. As I listened I could feel Leah's pain and anger, and felt upset myself.

There was complete silence after Leah finished talking. A full minute later I spoke, asking Leah to come with me to talk to Mr. Collins.

"No way," responded Leah. "He's an idiot, and I don't care if he flunks me or not."

"That's not okay, Leah," I said. "We've been talking for several months about how your fear keeps you stuck. This is an opportunity for you to do something about it. If you don't start to deal with your fear, it will keep controlling you."

Leah finally agreed to go with me to talk with her teacher. Fortunately the outcome couldn't have been better. I explained how Leah's fear was the reason for her classroom silence and poor test performance. I also assured my colleague that Leah was not only perfectly capable of writing an excellent paper but I was convinced she was the sole author. Then I turned to Leah. "I'm not going to do all the talking here, Leah. It's time for you to step up. Take a deep breath and tell Mr. Collins about the research you did for the paper."

Within twenty minutes Mr. Collins apologized to Leah. Without the pressure of performing in front of her classmates, Leah gradually relaxed and described the research she did for the paper. Her answers to Mr. Collins's questions quickly revealed that Leah knew what she was talking about. "I'm really sorry," Leah's teacher said for the third time. "You always seem so indifferent in class that I couldn't imagine you would write such a good paper." Mr. Collins told me later he also assumed Leah wasn't smart enough to do such good work.

There are two kinds of fear. The healthy type keeps us alive. The unhealthy one keeps us from living. Leah's heavy dose of the second kind was a major hindrance, even interfering with her social relationships. "I'm always afraid of saying something stupid so I don't say anything," Leah confided during counseling sessions. It made her almost mute in class and in groups, so much so that Mr. Collins thought she was dimwitted and incapable of writing a lucid term paper. For Leah to have a healthy and happy life, she needed to manage her fear so it didn't imprison her. To finish the story, Leah did indeed learn to manage her fear—by the end of her senior year, she was active in class discussions, and went on to college, graduate school, and a successful career as an architect.

All of our emotions, not just fear, play very important roles in our lives. As is the case with drives, however, children need to learn how to manage them. The same anger that can motivate a girl to tell bullies to stop picking on a classmate can torpedo a relationship or career later in life if she doesn't learn how to control it. The same sadness that stings when a boy doesn't make the baseball team can prevent him from ever trying again if he doesn't learn how to bounce back.

Although other psychologists coined the term earlier, Daniel Goleman brought the term *emotional intelligence* into our modern lexicon with his 1995 book, *Emotional Intelligence: Why It Can Matter More than IQ*. One of Goleman's core features of emotional intelligence is the ability to manage emotions, a key to success in relationships and careers—and school success. A girl can be the smartest kid on the block, but unless she manages her emotions, success and happiness will be elusive. Think of all the brilliant people you know who constantly sabotage their own success because of their inability to handle their emotions.

Earlier in this chapter I compared managing hardwired drives with taming a team of powerful horses. That same analogy applies to managing our emotions. Under control, our emotional steeds bring vibrancy and energy to our lives. Out of control, however, they are like wild stallions that can drive us into a ditch. Self-discipline harnesses and manages both drives and emotions.

A Parent's First Job Is to Establish Connection

The groundwork for self-discipline is laid in the earliest months of life and the key is connection. Psychologists sometimes use the word *attachment* to describe the relationship between parent and infant. Previous generations referred to it as bonding. Whatever the term, establishing a warm, consistent, reliable, and loving relationship with infants is critically important for a child's physical, cognitive, and emotional development. In addition, a secure connection is the basis of discipline and self-discipline. A child is motivated to keep parental connection intact, so approval and disapproval mean something. Without a connection there's no reason for a child to care if a parent approves or disapproves. In the extreme, a complete lack of connection is the breeding ground for a sociopath, someone with no sense of reciprocity, someone who is only interested in pursuing his own needs and wants without regard for anyone else's.

The effectiveness of approval and disapproval, therefore, presupposes connection. Establishing that secure relationship becomes the first developmental task to help children build up their self-discipline muscles. The word *no* for children in the first eighteen months is different from the *no* a parent uses later. In this early stage a "divert and redirect" strategy is most effective. "Instead of playing with Mommy's good watch, let's play with this ball."

I met Emma at a parent meeting her daycare center sponsored. A single mom, Emma worked hard with long days as a hospital cook. Her shift began at seven in the morning so she and eleven-month-old Aubrey were on their way to the childcare center by 6:15 A.M. By the time they got home at 5 P.M. Emma was usually exhausted and yearned for some time to relax and regroup, which was not Aubrey's agenda. On most days she was ready to play with mom and explore. She crawled all over their two-bedroom apartment and it took constant vigilance just to keep track of her.

"I just love Aubrey," Emma told me. "But is she ever a handful. She's into everything. Sometimes she's so naughty. I tell her not to do something and she just does it anyway. I'm worried I already yell at her too much. She just doesn't seem to understand the word *no*. Can you give me some ideas?"

I was happy to. "First of all, Aubrey really isn't being 'naughty,'" I said. "She's being eleven months old. Now, please don't misunderstand me. I'm not saying Aubrey isn't a handful or she doesn't do things that try your patience. But 'naughty' to me means that Aubrey does things she knows she's not supposed to do. She's not doing things to deliberately bother or test you. She's not yet at the developmental stage where she knows what to do and not to do. At this age, when she 'misbehaves' it's because she's exploring, frustrated, hungry, or tired. She's not doing things *because* you don't want her to do them."

Emma wanted to know what she should be doing for Aubrey. First I asked her to make sure that she'd baby-proofed her apartment, covering up the electric sockets and removing as many safety hazards as possible so that Aubrey can explore. I also suggested she get some child gates or find ways to safely put up barriers to keep Aubrey's exploring confined to an area so that Emma can keep an eye on her. When Emma cooks dinner, for example, she can keep Aubrey in the kitchen and let her explore a safe shelf of pots and pans or plastic containers. Another tip is to avoid using the word *no*. It is much easier for babies and toddlers to understand what we do want them to do rather than what we don't want them to do. For example, rather than saying, "Don't throw your food on the floor," say "Keep your food on your tray."

"I hope I can do all that, Dr. Dave," Emma sighed.

"I know how hard and exhausting it can be, Emma. If you have relatives or friends willing to help, don't hesitate to accept their offers so you can get a break. I was glad to hear you say earlier that you don't want to get into a yelling pattern with Aubrey. Your most important work at this stage is to keep Aubrey safe and form a good, solid, loving relationship. That investment will pay off later."

The Terrible Twos Begin Before a Baby Turns Two

While it's true that Aubrey isn't doing things *because* Emma doesn't want her to, she probably will begin to deliberately test Emma's limits—and patience—nine or ten months later when she's about eighteen months old. That's when she reaches a very important, but challenging, milestone. Berkeley psychology professor Alison Gopnik and one of her then students, Betty Repacholi, devised a fascinating experiment with fourteen- and eighteen-month-old toddlers to describe this developmental stage.

The scientists placed two bowls on a table, one filled with Goldfish crackers and the other filled with small pieces of raw broccoli. Not surprisingly, all the toddlers who were part of the experiment consistently preferred the tasty Pepperidge Farm crackers to the broccoli. When Repacholi picked up a Goldfish cracker she made a disgusted face and said, "Yuck." Then she tasted a piece of broccoli and said, "Yum," with a big smile. When she asked fourteen-month-old babies to give her a treat they consistently gave her Goldfish crackers. But when she asked the eighteen-month-old toddlers, she received pieces of broccoli. The striking difference between the two age groups explains a lot. You can imagine what's going through the minds of the fourteen-month-olds. "If I like Goldfish crackers, then you must like Goldfish crackers, too." The fourteen-month-olds couldn't distinguish between their wants and those of the woman sitting on the other side of the table.

The eighteen-month-olds, on the other hand, offered Repacholi broccoli because they could figure out that people can like different things. They realized that even though they liked the crackers, Repacholi preferred broccoli for some strange reason, so that's what they gave her. At about eighteen months children begin to realize that what they like and what others like may not be the same. From that they deduce that what they want and others want can be different. Then, unfortunately for frazzled parents, they also come to the conclusion that they no longer have to *do* what they are told to do. This is the emergence of self-will.

The nickname for this stage is, of course, the terrible twos, so called because their favorite word becomes *no.* Toddlers at this age will often say no even when they don't mean it just to let their parents know they can say it. This, by the way, explains the child who intentionally heads for the china cabinet where he *knows* he's not supposed to play, defiantly looking over his shoulder at mom or dad perhaps even saying "no, no, no" as he opens the door of the out-of-bounds cupboard.

At this point, the parenting task changes. Of course, we don't want to squash a child's self-will; it is, after all, the germ of their independence.

However, we need to teach children that there are limits to their self-will. This is how they begin to learn how to say no to themselves. There are, however, two challenges. First, children do not learn this on their own. This lesson depends on parents, childcare providers, teachers, and the other adults. Second, most children do not learn how to say no to themselves in one lesson—in fact, my extensive personal and professional research into the topic leads me to the conclusion that it takes the average child 1.7 billion repetitions! We parents have to remember that it is the child's job to push against the limits, and it is our job to set them. So, for the eleven-month-old, divert and redirect is how to respond. As children get older, more tactics are needed.

Styles of Parenting

There are many different ways to respond as parents because we all have our own unique personalities, histories, and temperaments. Scientists, however, have grouped various parenting approaches into three categories and studied the effectiveness of each. One is called "permissive" because parents using this style have few rules and few consequences for misbehavior. Children seldom, if ever, hear no, and their opinions carry as much weight as their parents. This approach is based on the belief that parents do not need to teach children self-discipline because they will eventually learn through experience that they need to limit themselves and will develop self-management skills on their own. Unfortunately, research shows that most children raised in a permissive or laissez-faire atmosphere don't develop the self-discipline skills they need.

The parenting style called "authoritarian" is the 180-degree opposite of permissive, with lots of rigid rules with strict enforcement. There is no negotiation in the authoritarian household. The motto here is "I'm the parent; you're the kid. Do what I say or else." Research on this style reveals that children will comply through fear of punishment until the threat is absent. We can get children to obey through fear. Compliance, however, is not the only goal. What we really want is for our children to develop the internal controls themselves, not to conform because of external threats.

My son Dan's best friend, Ryan, had a ringside seat to see the results of authoritarian parenting once the enforcement disappears, when his college roommate partied and missed classes. My son thought he was making up for lost time, since his parents were "super strict."

Dan was right. Ryan's roommate packed up his belongings and returned home just before final exam week. "It's really too bad," Dan told us. "He was plenty smart, but he couldn't handle the freedom after being controlled for so long. He went wild as soon as his parents weren't around to crack the whip."

While permissive and authoritarian approaches fall short in teaching self-discipline, there is a method that is effective. It's what I call "balanced," where there are clear rules and consequences, with some negotiation but with the parent still in charge. The strategy of what I'll call Limits and Consequences is the key to this style.

Limits and Consequences

The "Limits and Consequences" strategy is simple to explain but difficult to implement. Here's how it works. We let our children know in advance what the expectations or limits are. We also let them know ahead of time what the consequences will be if they don't meet the expectations or follow the rules. For example, "No snack until you've washed your hands." Or, "You can't play your video game until your homework is finished." In each of these cases, you've let the child know the expectation—handwashing or finishing homework—and you've also let them know the consequences: no snack or no video games.

While it sounds simple, anyone who has done this in real life knows that the challenge comes in following through. The reason that enforcing the consequences is hard is that most kids do not happily accept the consequences. They push back. That was the case with Brandon.

Eleven-year-old Brandon loved video games. While his parents, Nicole and Chris, didn't have trouble limiting his play to games rated for his age group, the arguments about time limits were escalating, especially after Brandon's teacher sent home a note about missing homework assignments. Nicole and Chris discussed the problem, agreed on a strategy, and sat down with their son after dinner that night. Chris started the conversation. "Brandon, we're concerned that your video games are interfering with your school work. From now on—"

"What do you mean?" Brandon interrupted. "My schoolwork is fine."

Chris took a breath, looked at her son, and continued. "Mr. Peterson emailed us that you've missed a lot of homework. When we ask you, you tell us that you've done your homework. I don't like the lying and I don't like you falling behind in school. So here's the deal. From now on we want you to write down your assignments, show them to one of us, and then show us the finished assignments before you play video games."

"That's not fair!" screamed Brandon. "What are you running, a prison or something?"

Chris did not take the bait. "No video games until all your homework's done. Let me make something else clear, Brandon. We will be emailing Mr. Peterson to make sure you're doing your homework. If this plan doesn't work, then there will be no video games at all for one week."

"No way!" Brandon yelled. "If you do, I won't do any homework. Then you'll see."

Once again Chris avoided the trap. "Brandon, it's your choice. Homework before video games—no problem. No homework—no video games. You decide."

It's not easy to do what Chris and Nicole did. But it is effective.

The Eight Steps to Limits and Consequences

Here's a set of steps to effectively use the Limits and Consequences strategy.

1. Remind yourself that it's the child's job to push against the limits; it's the parents' job to set them. Some kids push harder than others, and the pushing can be more intense at different ages, like during the terrible twos and again during adolescence. All kids, however, will test limits. Some kids even seem to make it their life's work never to let a day go by without reminding their parents to question why they ever wanted children in the first place.
2. Set the expectations and limits ahead of time. For example, "Make sure you're home before dinner or you won't be able to play at Kelly's house tomorrow."
3. Let your children know what the consequences will be if they cross the limit or break the rule. For instance, "If you continue to argue about which video to watch, then you will not be allowed to watch either one."
4. When you make a rule, enforce it consistently. As in, "You chose to have friends in the house while I went to the store, so you are choosing the consequence—you will have to go with me next time when I go shopping instead of staying home."
5. Use a consequence that is appropriate. Don't choose one that is out of proportion or one that you will have a very difficult time enforcing.
6. Remind your child about the rule and consequence but avoid overexplaining, nagging, or lecturing. "If you choose to hit your sister, you will be choosing to sit in a time-out."
7. Make sure that your child knows that the consequence is his

choice. If he fails to meet the expectation or breaks the rule, then he is choosing the consequence. "If you choose to leave your toys out, then you are choosing to have them taken away for two days."

8. Enforce the consequences calmly and avoid power struggles. You might be thinking "easier said than done," so let's turn to some strategies to steer clear of power struggles.

Avoiding Power Struggles

Scott knew firsthand how easy it was to get into power struggles. He talked about his problem disciplining the youngest of his three sons, seven-year-old Cole, in my first counseling session with him. So I wasn't surprised when Scott began our next meeting with "I have to find a different way to deal with Cole. His stubbornness is going to drive me crazy. It's a struggle every time I ask him to do something.

"Since the day he started talking, I've told my friends that Cole will make a great lawyer. He needs an explanation and has a counterargument for everything. His favorite words are 'why,' 'how come,' 'later,' and 'not now.' He is incapable of taking no for an answer. The other day we were at Walmart and he wanted to go to the toy aisle. I knew how disastrous that would be so I told him we didn't have time. He whined and pleaded the entire time we were there."

"Did you give in?" I asked.

"Heck no," Scott responded. "I'm not crazy. I knew that if I gave in it would just be worse the next time."

"You're absolutely right," I said. "Good for you that you didn't give in."

"I'm pretty good at not giving in," Scott agreed. "But I am so sick of arguing with him."

I asked Scott what would happen if he didn't argue back.

Scott paused and then broke the silence after a couple of seconds. "He'd probably follow me around and badger me until I responded."

"But what do you think he'd do if you steeled yourself and were able to hold out?"

"I don't know. I guess it can't hurt to try." Then Scott looked at me. "Do you think that's been my mistake, Dr. Dave?" he asked.

"Could be," I responded. "From your description I have no doubt Cole is very strong-willed, but as much as he tries, he can't have a battle of wills if you don't join him." I added, "Don't get me wrong. I know from personal experience with my own kids how hard it can be. But I have also learned the hard way that when we want to take the wind out of our kids' sails, it's a lot smarter to take our sails out of their wind." Here are my ten tips to avoid power struggles:

1. Take three deep breaths. The increased oxygen in the brain reduces stress hormones.
2. Say to yourself, "I can stay calm." Repeat the mantra as many times as you need to.
3. Picture yourself in your mind's eye remaining calm.
4. Calmly repeat your expectation, ground rule, and consequence. Do this only once.
5. Remind your child that he is choosing the consequence if he chooses to break the rule or ignore the expectation. For example, "If you choose not to sit down and eat your lunch, you are choosing to lose your plate and have nothing to eat until dinner."
6. Do not repeat, debate, or argue.
7. Follow through on the consequences calmly and consistently.
8. If the child escalates further by throwing things, hitting, or damaging property, intervene with a secondary consequence. "I know you can control yourself. If you choose to hit me then you are choosing a time-out."
9. Have reinforcements available if possible. In extreme situations you may need to call a relative or friend to help so you can take a time-out yourself.
10. Seek support from understanding relatives and friends. You're not the only parent challenged by power struggles.

Preventing or Reversing Discipline Deficit Disorder

For the past several years I've talked about DDD with parents and teachers, and it's become clear that DDD is spreading widely. For the sake of our kids' happiness and success it's important for all of us to make an important course correction and build our kids' self-discipline.

DO

- ✓ Remember that the goal is not to say no. The goal is to teach kids how to say no for themselves.
- ✓ Get kids what they need, but not everything that they want.
- ✓ Back up teachers and schools. Our kids need us all to be on the same page.

- ✓ Set clear and high expectations.
- ✓ Expect kids to do chores and assume some age-appropriate household jobs.
- ✓ Expect kids to volunteer and be of service to others.
- ✓ Use the strategy of Limits and Consequences.
- ✓ Tell a child what *to* do, instead of what *not* to do.

DON'T

- ✗ Don't give in to the culture of "more, fast, easy, and fun." Our kids need self-discipline to be satisfied and self-reliant in the long run.
- ✗ Don't get lured into power struggles with your children.
- ✗ Don't accept disrespectful behavior or language.
- ✗ Don't give in to the temper tantrums or whining.
- ✗ Don't take misbehavior personally.
- ✗ Don't ignore misbehavior. Patterns can develop quickly.

What do I want to continue?

____

____

____

What do I want to change?

____

____

____

TEN

A Brain Under Construction: The Adolescent Years

Not long ago I received an email message from my out-of-town friend Gina asking an urgent question: "Do you think our family should see a family counselor? It appears we are incapable of doing anything right these days with our two teenagers, and I fear we might be doing permanent damage. Jerome and I are overwhelmed. Personally I need some professional advice before I completely blow a gasket."

I replied that a conversation might be more helpful than an email exchange. Gina eagerly agreed, so later that week she, my old classmate Jerome, and I were on the phone. After catching up, I asked about Aidan and Lucy, the two kids I've known for years who were now leaving their parents baffled by their behavior.

"Baffled is one way to put it. Upside down is another," Gina began. "Aidan and Lucy are still the good kids they've always been. But they both hit puberty at about the same time and Jerome and I feel like our family literally changed overnight. They fight with one another, stay holed up in their rooms for hours, don't want anything to do with us anymore, and act completely put out if we ask them to do anything."

"Lucy is obsessed with her cell phone," added Jerome. "I think she spends her entire day texting her friends and checking her social networking page."

Gina and Jerome continued to recite the litany of woes I have heard from thousands of parents over the years and remember living through myself during our kids' adolescence. I asked some questions about school and their friends and got positive reports about both categories. "Their teachers love them," Gina said, "and we like their friends." After a few more questions I presented my two friends with the same diagnosis I gave Pam and Austin in chapter 1: "adolescent brains under construction."

I explained to Gina and Jerome that most teenagers are a bundle of paradoxes. They are fun, idealistic, energetic, altruistic, and enthusiastic. They are excited about new things and often willing to try new activities. They are curious about the world and eager to interact with new people. *But*, they are also prone to angry outbursts, defiant acts, foolish risk taking, and inexplicable plummets into despair. One minute you're having a serious, informed, adult conversation and the next minute they turn into fire-breathing dragons just because you asked them to take out the garbage. They can stay out past curfew and then lie about where they were. One moment you feel connected and comfortable with your teen, and the next you wonder who replaced your child with a demon. You find yourself thinking the term *teenage brain* is an oxymoron.

Until recently we chalked all these teenage traits up to psychological factors. While there are some psychological factors at play, the real story is what's going on in their brains. Adolescence is a time of major brain changes. Their brains are a series of construction zones. When we understand those construction sites, we get better answers to the question, "Why do they act that way?"

I've always liked teenagers, which is good since they've been such a big part of my personal and professional life. My wife, Monica, and I raised three, all of whom survived into adulthood. In addition, I taught and coached high school kids for ten years, was a high school counselor after that, and then developed and managed counseling programs for teens and families for Fairview Health Services in Minnesota.

A complete tour of the adolescent brain is beyond the scope of this book, but because the preteen and teen years can be so challenging, this developmental stage merits its own chapter. Since I will only cover the "highlights," I'll refer those of you who would like or need the full tour to my book *Why Do They Act That Way? A Survival Guide to the Adolescent Brain for You and Your Teen.*

PARENT TOOL KIT

The Preteen and Teen Years

Here's a set of questions to help you think about parenting adolescents.

Yes No

☐ ☐ 1. I understand that some turmoil during adolescence is normal.

☐ ☐ 2. I know that a lot of teens' difficult behavior is because their brains are under construction.

☐ ☐ 3. I know it's important to maintain clear and consistent rules for my teenagers.

☐ ☐ 4. I'm able to avoid power struggles with my teenagers.

☐ ☐ 5. I can generally stay calm even when my teenager can't.

☐ ☐ 6. I know it's important to loosen up without letting go.

☐ ☐ 7. I model respectful behavior in the way I treat my teenager.

☐ ☐ 8. I do not accept foul or abusive language from my teen son or daughter.

☐ ☐ 9. I talk with my kids about alcohol, drugs, and sex.

☐ ☐ 10. I don't panic when my teenagers question my values because I know that's how they shape their own.

If you found yourself agreeing with the statements in the tool kit, you'll be prepared to survive the teen years yourself. Moreover, you'll be better equipped to guide your adolescents to a happy and healthy adulthood. If you found yourself answering no to some items, you may want to rethink some things.

The Teen Brain—Under Construction

Teens are known for driving parents—like my friends Gina and Jerome—nuts. No matter how mild a child is when he's very young, or how sensible a person becomes once she reaches adulthood, the chances are good that just about all kids, more than once during the teen years, will make their parents feel as if sanity hangs by a thread.

Younger and younger kids, the so-called tweens, seem to be acting a lot like their older siblings, too. It's not always because tweens copy the older kids. Puberty, which biologically launches adolescence, is beginning earlier, for some kids as young as seven. No one really knows why. Some cite nutrition or food additives. Others suspect the earlier onset of puberty is caused by the fact that today's kids are heavier. The more a child weighs the earlier puberty begins. Still others wonder if exposure to sexual images in the media is the culprit. Whatever the case, many tweens today are coping with adolescent changes.

Many of these emotional and behavioral changes can be directly attributed to what's going on in their brains. Underneath those backward-turned baseball caps and sometimes colorful hairstyles is a neurological revolution at work. From violence to sleep habits, sexuality to depression, impulsive behavior to defiance, new neuroscientific findings shed startling light on nearly every issue facing the parent of a preteen or teen. More importantly, the new research offers a crucial opportunity to help our kids through a difficult stage of life. Understanding just what goes on in their heads might give us compassion for teen struggles and suggest tactics and strategies we can best use to parent.

The Prefrontal Cortex

Whenever I speak to parents of adolescents I ask them to take their first two fingers and tap their foreheads above each eye. "Your fingers are half an inch away from the brain's prefrontal cortex, or PFC," I tell them. "I think of this important region as the CEO of the brain. It's where we think ahead, consider consequences, assess risk, and manage emotional impulses and urges."

When the prefrontal cortex is not up to the task we see distracted, risky, and impulsive behavior. There's a *Calvin and Hobbes* cartoon in which Calvin, sent to the corner for his latest crime, talks things over with Hobbes. In the last panel of the cartoon, Calvin says, "Hobbes, my problem is my lips move when I think." That's a perfect description of a prefrontal cortex not working up to par.

A big discovery in brain science is that the prefrontal cortex, the brain's CEO, is one of the last circuits of the brain to get wired. In fact, this important circuit begins its major blossoming and pruning as a boy or girl enters adolescence. This discovery makes sense to anyone who has ever lived with a teen.

I still recall the conversation that took place at our dinner table when Brian was fifteen years old. He looked across the table at Monica and me and announced, "I no longer need a curfew." I made the mistake of asking, "Why is that?" because Brian had his answer ready. He'd probably rehearsed it with his friends beforehand. "I'm a good kid," Brian said confidently. "I get good grades, and I don't get in any trouble. Don't you think it's about time you stopped treating me like a kid?"

The only answer I could muster that night was "Because we said so!" Today my answer would be different and would sound something like this: "Brian, you may think you're fully mature, but according to the latest science there are still some very important circuits that are yet to be wired. Until that's done, you've got a curfew!" In a very real way a curfew is a surrogate prefrontal cortex. The job of parent, teacher, coach, or counselor is to serve as a surrogate prefrontal cortex while the teen's is being wired.

There is an industry, by the way, that seems to know this very clearly: the automobile insurance industry. Consider some of the critical factors for good driving—good eyesight, quick reflexes, hand-eye coordination, all of which teens have in spades. You would think, therefore, that adolescents' insurance rates would be lower than anyone's! So why are their rates actually double or triple mine? It's not because State Farm knows the brain science. They don't need to. They just look at the statistics and realize that teens seek thrills and don't assess risks very well. The result is a higher accident rate, so the companies raise their premiums.

It's no coincidence that car insurance rates don't drop until the age of twenty-five. The latest brain research shows age twenty-five is when the final wiring of the prefrontal cortex is completed. Not surprisingly, it's also the age at which the accident statistics dramatically decline.

The Acceleration Center

While important, the developing prefrontal cortex is only a partial explanation for teen behavior. Things make even more sense when we see how multiple brain construction zones interact with one another. Consider how the prefrontal cortex and what I call the acceleration center work—or don't work—together.

The acceleration center is my nickname for a process in the teen brain that involves the two brain chemicals that I introduced in the first chapter: hormones and neurotransmitters. As you may recall, my nickname for hormones is "Paul Reveres," because they act as the body's messengers. At the beginning of puberty, the hypothalamus dispatches a Paul Revere to the pituitary gland with the message to start the growth spurt. We don't know exactly what triggers the starting gun in the hypothalamus, but the hypothalamus is convinced that the body is ready to become an adult and it's time to produce growth hormones. Besides all of the other changes in puberty, the average girl will grow ten inches by the end of the growth spurt, while the average boy will grow eleven inches.

Testosterone and Boys

Three growth hormones take center stage at puberty: testosterone, estrogen, and progesterone. Each is present in both boys and girls at birth, but their concentrations change dramatically at puberty. For boys, testosterone triggers the big physical changes like dramatic growth spurts and sudden voice changes. Adolescent boys can have five to seven surges of testosterone every day during adolescence, increasing its concentration by 1,000 percent. That's a lot of a powerful chemical surging through boys' bodies.

Research now reveals that there is a small part of the brain very rich in testosterone receptors. It's called the amygdala, Greek for almond because it's the size and shape of one. This brain center is almost calling out to the testosterone, "Come on in. We have a lot of empty rooms for you." What's important for parents to know is that the amygdala is the anger and alarm center of the brain, the seat of the fight-or-flight response described in chapter 1. As the testosterone surges it floods the amygdala, making boys emotional powder kegs reacting with anger to as simple a request as, "Would you please take your feet off the coffee table?"

A recent conversation brought this home clearly and poignantly. During a break in a daylong teacher's workshop about the teen brain a young man approached me and said, "Dr. Walsh. I'm really glad you explained teenage anger. It helps me make sense out of something that's bothered me for a long time." He went on to explain that during his teen years things were getting a bit rocky between him and his parents. One night his mother saw an opportunity to talk with him and share her concerns. She came into his room to say goodnight, sat down beside him on the bed and began the conversation like this. "I've been looking for a chance to talk to you because I can't figure out what's going on. Everything I say seems to be wrong, and you're often in a sour mood." She waited a second and asked, "What the matter?" He looked her right in the eye and responded, "I just don't like you." His mother's eyes filled with tears, and she left the room crying.

That conversation has bothered the young man ever since that night years ago. As he told me at that workshop, "I could never figure out why I was so mean to my mother when I was a teenager. Now I get it. It was what was going on in my brain. I think I'm going to call and apologize to her for saying something so mean that night years ago."

While teenagers can be rough on many adults they typically reserve the vintage collection for their parents. It can be rough. It's hard not to take it personally when the voice on the other side of the slammed door says, "What a jerk." While parents should not tolerate disrespectful behavior, it's a good idea to cut teens a little slack. It can help to not take things personally when we realize what's going on in their brains.

Estrogen, Progesterone, and Girls

For girls, there are two important growth hormones: estrogen and progesterone. As their production ramps up at puberty they begin an ebb-and-flow pattern. As the level of one goes up the other goes down and vice versa. This pattern repeats itself on average every twenty-eight days. Scientists have known about the menstrual cycle for many years, but more recent knowledge about how the rise and fall of estrogen and progesterone affects the neurotransmitter serotonin, which I nickname the mood stabilizer, sheds light on the behavior of teen girls. When serotonin levels are adequate a person's mood is stable. When serotonin levels start to drop there can be quick and dramatic mood changes.

As the estrogen and progesterone ebb and flow in the young adolescent girl's brain, her serotonin levels dip and rise, and her mood can change on a dime. What does that look like in real life? It's not unusual for an adolescent girl to be on top of the world at 9 A.M., in the pits at 10, euphoric at 11, and homicidal by noon. It's what's going on in her brain. To make it even more challenging, when serotonin levels dip her emotional reactions become amplified.

This explains what happened one morning in our house when our daughter Erin was fourteen years old. She came down one morning before heading off to school and decided to have cereal for breakfast. She got out the spoon, poured herself a bowl of cereal, and then walked over to the refrigerator to get out the milk. When she opened the refrigerator door, however, she discovered there was no milk. At that point she collapsed on the floor and started sobbing, "I hate my life."

Monica and I raced into the kitchen to find out what tragedy had befallen our dear daughter. Between sobs she was able to explain, "We're out of milk!" Any of us, of course, might be frustrated without milk for our cereal. But most would agree that "I hate my life" is a bit extreme.

Not long ago I was conducting an all-day workshop in Fort Wayne, Indiana, on the teenage brain. During a break a woman handed me her BlackBerry and said, "Please read this." During the session her teenage daughter had texted her. It read, "I can't find my black pants. I hate my life!" Perfect timing.

We can help our adolescent daughters deal with these emotional fluctuations by explaining the brain chemistry that makes their moods go haywire. This knowledge won't stop the emotional roller coaster, but some perspective will make it a bit easier to manage the ups and downs.

Pedal to the Metal with Brakes under Construction

We'll explore the differences in girls' brains and boys' brains further in the next chapter, but puberty for boys and for girls has a key similarity. In both sexes, hormonal fluctuation puts adolescents at the mercy of strong emotions that they are not always capable of controlling. For boys, this impulsive behavior can be aggressive and angry. For girls, it can show up as amplification of a wide range of emotions. For many boys and girls, the intensity of their feelings—of the impulses firing in their brains, whether angry, sad, sexual, or territorial, is often surprising. Many of them had not felt such strong impulses during childhood.

Adolescence is a heck of a time for the impulse control center—the prefrontal cortex—to be under construction. Just when adolescents need it most, the PFC's ability to act rationally and think through problems and challenges breaks down. Even though the teen PFC is much closer to being mature, it's no match for overwhelming hormone-driven impulses.

Adolescent brains are like a car that gets gas before the brakes. Puberty gives adolescents a body that looks like an adult's and a brain that is prone to wild fluctuations and powerful surges. The brain's gas pedal is ready for a NASCAR-paced adulthood. But, because the PFC is not up to snuff, the brain's brakes are a Model T's.

Loosen but Don't Let Go

A dad waited till other parents had left to ask his question following a recent seminar. "Dr. Walsh," the man began, "I'd like your opinion about something." I asked him to go on. "The issue we're having is with our fifteen-year-old daughter and her cell phone. She refuses to turn it off at night. It sits on her bed stand pinging with messages all night long. It has to be disturbing her sleep, and it's driving me crazy. I think I have a solution. I would like to institute a family-wide technology curfew. Every night at nine o'clock we all bring our cell phones to the kitchen, where we can recharge them overnight. What do you think of that idea?"

"It sounds pretty good to me" was my honest response.

"Would you please tell my partner that," he asked.

I turned to his partner, who had joined us, and said, "This strikes me as a pretty good idea. What's your objection to it?"

"If we did that," he replied, "our daughter would have a never-ending fit. I am not willing to put up with that. It's just not worth it."

After a second I looked at him and said, "With all due respect, I think you need to decide who's in charge in your house. It sounds to me like your fifteen-year-old daughter is calling the shots."

Because teens can drive a perfectly sane person to the brink of madness, many parents take the path this dad chose, finding it easier to retreat from the battle. This is not entirely surprising given that parenting a teenager can feel like a constant struggle without a clear goal.

Many teenagers will push parents to drop curfews, allow unchaperoned spring break trips, and permit overnight coed parties, just to name a few. In spite of what teens say, however, they need limits and consequences just like their younger brothers and sisters. Parenting teenagers is all about balance. We shouldn't treat adolescents the same as their younger siblings, maintaining all of the same rules of their childhood. Adolescents are eager to experience the world outside their parents' home, to try out new ideas and experiences. We don't want to hold them back from learning to figure things out for themselves, but they also need our guidance along the way. While they may ask for a divorce, they still need our connection. While they might fight many of our rules, they still need them. And, of course, they also need our love. In the end, parenting, teaching, or mentoring teenagers is a balancing act. It requires us to loosen the reins without letting go.

Here are some tips for striking that balance.

- Set clear rules and expectations for behavior. For example, instead of saying, "We expect respectful behavior," say, "You cannot swear, call us names, or use put-downs."
- Have conversations about limits and consequences when things are calm and everyone can think more clearly. For example, if your son breaks curfew and you're very upset, let him know that you're angry and that you'll discuss the consequence in the morning when you're less agitated. Of course, you need to make sure that you follow up as promised.
- Spell out consequences for noncompliance. For example, "If you cannot limit your video games to two hours a night, then you will not be allowed to play video games for a week. It's your choice."
- Choose consequences that fit, and follow through.
- Don't let your teen get his or her way by yelling or other objectionable behavior. That can reinforce a dangerous pattern.

"What We've Got Here Is a Failure to Communicate"

This famous line, spoken by Strother Martin's character in the classic 1967 movie *Cool Hand Luke,* also describes common scenes in homes where teenagers live. I can still remember episodes with my son Dan as a teenager when he would stop me in the middle of a conversation with, "Dad, why are you yelling at me?" This always baffled me because, as far as I could tell, I wasn't yelling. Sometimes I even had a good witness: Monica. After Dan would storm off, I'd check with her to make sure I hadn't gotten worked up without noticing. "Was I yelling?" I'd ask. "Not that I heard" was her usual reply.

I suspected that Dan was taken over by hormones, trying to change the topic, get out of something, or developing an "attitude." Now I know from the latest brain research that my suspicions were wrong. Like all adolescents, Dan was using a different part of his brain. The teen brain doesn't process nonverbal cues like adult brains do. The adult brain processes these cues in the prefrontal cortex, the site of reflection and judgment. The adolescent brain, on the other hand, processes nonverbal cues in the amygdala, of all places. As a result they are prone to misinterpret facial expressions, gestures, or tone of voice. However, their mistakes are not random. They consistently err in the direction of anger and aggression. That's why Dan thought I was yelling when I wasn't.

There are no strategies guaranteed to eliminate all parent-teen miscommunication. But these suggestions may improve the odds.

- Begin statements with "I" rather than "you." Starting with "you" triggers defensiveness.
- Focus on behavior. Instead of saying, "You're really rude," say, "I'm angry that you walked out of the room while I was talking with you."
- Avoid generalizations. As soon as an adolescent hears one, her mind starts to search for the exception to refute you. Instead of saying, "You never clear the table," say, "You forgot to clear the table this evening."
- Be as specific as possible when asking for something to eliminate confusion. Instead of saying, "Don't forget to take out the garbage," say, "Please take out the garbage before you go to school."
- Stick to one topic at a time. Avoid this kind of sentence: "I want to talk to you about your report card. By the way, I don't like the way you treated your brother last night." Instead say, "I would like to talk to you about your report card. When would be a good time to do that?"
- When there is tension between you and your teenager, avoid attacking. Remember these three steps.
    1. Name your feeling.
    2. State the reason for your feeling.
    3. State what you would like.

  Here's an example. Don't say, "You're so inconsiderate. You knew I'd be worried when you weren't on time for dinner." Instead say,

"I'm angry because you were late for dinner. I'd like you to call to let me know you're going to be late so I don't worry."

- Listening is more important than talking. Research shows that listening attentively communicates respect. That automatically sets a more positive tone and lowers the defenses. When your teenager is talking with you try to remember to
    1. Establish eye contact but don't stare.
    2. Don't interrupt.
    3. Use short phrases like "Uh-huh" or "I see." They encourage your teen to keep talking.
    4. Keep an open posture and don't cross your arms.
    5. Ask clarifying questions like "I don't quite understand what you mean. Could you explain that again?"
    6. Check to make sure you're understanding correctly. For example, you might say, "If I'm hearing you correctly, you're angry with me because you feel like I put you down last night."

Romance, Sex, and the Teen Brain

Our human brains evolved to provide us with an amazingly wide array of abilities. They are especially hardwired to help us survive and to reproduce so that the human race will continue. The fight-or-flight response is but one of many survival circuits hardwired into our brains from birth. The sexual drive is another. It guarantees that a generation will replace us, and this drive springs to life with great intensity at puberty.

Sexual awakening is a bit different for boys and girls. You may recall that the hypothalamus is the master control for the hormone or endocrine system. It has a small section known as the INAH-3 (the third interstitial nucleus of the anterior hypothalamus), which grows larger in the male brain at puberty. This is the source of the intense interest in the physical aspects of sex. The larger INAH-3, along with surges of testosterone, creates both an intense sexual interest and drive. So adolescent boys' preoccupation with sexual thoughts and fantasies is more than just hormones. It's triggered by anatomical brain changes. It's important that sensitive and knowledgeable adults talk to boys about this change so they can understand what's happening, that it's normal, and that it's not sinful. The conversation should also stress how important it is to manage this powerful drive in healthy and responsible ways.

Girls' sexual awakening is not driven by anatomical changes in the hypothalamus; it's principally powered by hormones. The two main players are testosterone and oxytocin. Testosterone, of course, is the male growth hormone. Although girls don't have as much as boys do, they have their share and it accounts for girls' interest in the physical dimensions of sex. Oxytocin, on the other hand, is unique to girls and is often nicknamed the "cuddle" hormone since it prompts the adolescent girl to want to be physically close. Oxytocin is probably the reason teen girls will walk around school in groups, arm in arm with their friends. You won't see boys doing that, probably because they don't have oxytocin flowing through their bodies.

If a girl is attracted to a boy the oxytocin will motivate her to be physically close—to hold hands, hug, or cuddle. That may not be what's going on in his brain, however. He may take this as a cue that she's interested in sex, so he may make a sexual advance. Her brain, on the other hand, may translate this into "Oh, he really likes me." There are two dimensions to this powerful hardwired drive: physical and relational. For boys it's capital *P* Physical and lowercase *r* relational whereas for girls it's just the reverse. Both dimensions are there, but their male and female brains stress each differently.

Just as communication about sex with our sons is important, so too is it critical for our daughters. Unfortunately we American parents get a failing grade when it comes to communicating with our adolescents about sex. Only 17 percent of American teens report they have good communication about sex with a trusted adult. That means that the other 83 percent are getting their information from their friends and from the media. I don't think any of us wants to trust the kids at school or Hollywood with sex education.

Here are some tips for talking with teens about sex.

1. Get motivated. Some parents don't talk with their teens about sex because they are afraid that it will spark their curiosity or give them ideas, thereby causing their kids to engage in early sex. The reality is just the opposite. Kids who have good communication with their parents delay sexual activity and are more responsible and safe.
2. Get educated. There are good books that provide solid information as well as tips for talking with teens about sex.
3. Get comfortable. Most parents feel uncomfortable discussing sex with their kids. Even if you can't overcome your discomfort, don't hesitate to share that with your kids. It might help to say something like "You know, it's hard for me to talk with you about sex

because my parents never discussed it when I was growing up. But it's a really important topic so I'm going to do the best I can." Your kids will appreciate your candor and your interest.

4. Make it an ongoing conversation. Don't approach discussions about sex as the "Big Talk." Look for opportunities to have many shorter conversations that begin in preteen years and continue throughout adolescence. Sexual topics come up regularly in the media or in the daily newspaper. Use these to start up short discussions. For example, "Did you see that article in the paper today about how many teens are engaging in oral sex? What did you think of that? Do you think it was realistic based on what's going on in your peer group?"
5. Don't try to cover too much in any one discussion.
6. Choose appropriate times when you and your teen have some privacy and are not rushed. You'll both be more comfortable.
7. Discuss sexuality, not just sex. While it is important for kids to have accurate biological information, they also need to know that a healthy sexual relationship entails respect, caring, and responsibility. You might say something like "One of the things I try to remember is that sex is just one part of a good relationship. If I'm just out for my own pleasure then I'm using the other person."
8. Discuss dating. For example, you might say something like "It really bothers me the way the media portray dating. On TV, couples who go out usually end up in bed together. Dating should be a time to get to know someone else and have fun together."
9. Don't preach. Teens hate long, drawn-out lectures. Say what you want to say and then let it go. The odds are a lot better that your kids will listen.
10. Make it a dialogue. Ask questions and then listen. Try to understand your teen's concerns, questions, and opinions. Don't cut off your adolescent with a statement like "I don't care what you think, I'm your parent, and I know a lot more about this than you do." Teens who hear such comments learn to keep their thoughts to themselves.
11. Multiple messages are okay. We can tell our kids why we think it is important to delay sexual relations until they are adults or married while also making sure they have accurate information about safe sex, birth control, HIV/AIDS, and STDs.
12. Share your values. We need to teach our kids that healthy, satisfying relationships include respect and responsibility. We need to

teach our sons and daughters that while the changes in their brains increase their interest in sex, we don't want them to rush into sexual behavior. If they work on developing communication and relationship skills they will be better prepared for the adventure that love brings and the joys that healthy relationships bring.

Windows of Opportunity

Chapter 1 discussed how important experiences are during the brain's growth spurts. As we've just seen, the adolescent brain is in the midst of important changes, so once again the window of opportunity is wide open—for better or worse. The growth spurt in the prefrontal cortex leaves teen brains very sensitive to the experiences they have during adolescence. This may feel terrifying to parents, realizing the role the PFC plays in decision making, long-term planning, and impulse control. But there is also incredible opportunity here to help our children "hardwire" these skills so that they can use them for the rest of their adult life. Learning how to deal with anger, manage sexual urges appropriately, and communicate effectively during the teen years enables the brain to wire the appropriate circuits. On the opposite side, never learning to be accountable and responsible has a greater negative impact. The same window, open for opportunities to wire the brain for good habits, is open for whatever happens, good or bad.

The take-home lesson brain science reveals is not to sit around and "wait it out" until adolescence is over. Remember, "What the brain does a lot of is what the brain gets good at."

DO

- ✓ Learn about normal adolescent behavior so you know what to expect. Read *Why Do They Act That Way? A Survival Guide to the Adolescent Brain for You and Your Teen* for the full tour.
- ✓ Set clear rules and expectations for behavior. For example, instead of saying, "I want you to help out around the house," say, "I want you to have the lawn mowed by Saturday evening."
- ✓ Spell out consequences for noncompliance. Consequences for teenagers usually involve the loss of privileges. "If you choose not to limit your texting to one hour before nine P.M., then you are choosing not to have your phone after dinner."
- ✓ Loosen but don't let go. For example, even though the curfews will get later as teens grow older, they should still have them.

✓ Have a zero-tolerance policy for tobacco, alcohol, and drugs. As we'll see in another chapter, these can have devastating effects on the adolescent brain.

✓ Make sure that teenagers have household chores so they don't become rent-free boarders.

✓ Have the courage to communicate with your teens about the tough topics: sex, alcohol, and drugs. Communication does not mean lecturing. It means listening and expressing clearly your values.

DON'T

✗ While patience is essential, don't become a doormat for disrespectful behavior.

✗ Don't get dragged into power struggles. Calmly state your expectation and consequences. Let your teen know that you expect him to comply, but that if he chooses not to, then he will have to accept the consequences.

✗ Don't ever attempt to outshout your teen. Say, "We don't seem to be able to discuss this right now. When you're ready to talk about this without yelling, we'll finish." Then make sure to come back and finish the talk. They should not be allowed to go on to the next activity until the discussion has been completed.

✗ Don't ever put your teenager down or call them names. They damage the parent-teen connection, which is the lifeline through these years.

What do I want to continue?

____

____

____

What do I want to change?

____

____

____

ELEVEN

Boy and Girl Brains: What's the Difference?

I have two sons and a daughter. We raised Dan, Brian, and Erin during the era when many experts believed any differences between boy and girl brains were purely the result of socialization, not hardwired or innate differences. Nurture, not nature, was the explanation for any gender-specific behaviors. Many parents raising both sexes, however, probably experience what Monica and I did. Try as we might, we could not ignore apparent inborn distinctions.

New brain science helps us, as well as millions of other parents and teachers, to solve the puzzle. There *are* differences between boy and girl brains. I say this with such conviction because the new brain imaging technology *shows* the differences. For example, some brain areas light up when girls speak but remain dark when boys do. So, why did we spend years denying the difference? The reasons were power and prejudice.

Historically, to maintain power in families and society, men fostered the illusion they were smarter than women. They even used brain science to make the case and measuring brain size was their first attempt. When pioneering brain scientist Paul Broca discovered in 1861 that the average male brain was 10 percent larger than the female's, men immediately seized upon this as "scientific proof" that men were more intelligent than women, and thus women shouldn't be allowed to vote or hold positions of responsibility. But, of course, brain size does not determine intellect. If it did, then whales would rule the world!

The notion that brain science proves men's superiority may seem silly now, but it was anything but silly to the billions of women who were (and continue to be) the victims of ignorant prejudice. Because brain science was used to make the case for male dominance, its role was suspect in the fight for equality and the case for nurture took over. Personality and behavior tendencies were all learned, the new thinking went. Once we raised boys and girls as equals, the distinctions would evaporate.

Though brain science tells us there are differences, talk about distinctions between male and female brains still invokes emotions stemming from the century and a half of misuse. Lawrence Summers discovered this the hard way as president of Harvard in 2005 when he suggested in a speech that there weren't more women in top academic tiers because of "different availability of aptitude at the high end." His statement sounded enough like an ignorant interpretation of brain science from the past that it cost him his job.

Proceed with Caution

While it is important to understand the differences between girl and boy brains, it is critical to do so without repeating the mistakes from the past. There are three errors to avoid.

First, different does not mean good or bad, better or worse. Distinctions do not imply a hierarchy or superiority.

Second, no two brains are alike. When I discuss differences I mean group averages, not individuals. The distinctions are true for many boys and girls, but not for all. We should not stereotype gender and should not extrapolate from the general to the individual. For example, when I describe the advantage the female brain has for language, we can all think of many individual examples that contradict the generalization. After all, didn't William Shakespeare's brain make him a gifted master of the English language? Many boys excel at theater and the arts, and many girls in science and sports. Each individual finds him or herself along a continuum of brain traits.

The third caveat is that biology does not mean destiny. As we know, experience plays a big role in how the brain is wired. When you recall the "neurons that fire together wire together" principle, you won't be surprised to learn that experience can change hormone levels and brain structures. Violinists, for instance, have more neurons assigned to control the left hand than the right. So my male brain might predispose me to certain behaviors or ways of thinking and feeling, but I could get better at others through practice. Whenever we spend more time and energy developing a skill, the more neurons are recruited to pitch in. That many skill differences between the sexes shrank during the past two generations is proof that how we raise our daughters and sons does affect how their brains get wired.

PARENT TOOL KIT

Understanding Boys' and Girls' Brains

The questions in this kit are designed to help you pay attention to the ways that boys' and girls' brains are different.

Yes No

☐ ☐ 1. I understand there are biologically based differences between girls' and boys' brains.

☐ ☐ 2. I realize it is important to keep brain-based differences in mind.

☐ ☐ 3. I know how important experience is in developing a wide repertoire of skills, abilities, and behaviors regardless of the sex of my child.

☐ ☐ 4. I know better than to limit my son or daughter based on brain information.

☐ ☐ 5. While it is important to promote good communication skills with all children, I need to pay special attention to helping boys.

☐ ☐ 6. I realize that the dramatic hormone changes at puberty affect girls and boys differently.

☐ ☐ 7. I am aware that girls' greater success in school may be because schools reward their behavior.

☐ ☐ 8. I know that boys and girls are equally aggressive but express it differently.

☐ ☐ 9. I am aware that girls are rewarded for acting like boys but not vice versa.

☐ ☐ 10. I know that girls and boys are equal in overall intelligence.

The more yes answers to the questions in this tool kit, the better equipped you are to use brain science to help you raise boys and girls to their full potential.

Books have been written on the differences between boy and girl brains but I will concentrate on the most important areas for parents to know and pay attention to. First, it's important to remember that girls mature faster than boys. Girls talk earlier, potty train a half year sooner, and reach puberty two years ahead of their brothers. The same pattern holds true for their brains. Girls leave boys in the dust in the race to brain developmental milestones. For example, myelination (insulating the neuron cables) proceeds faster for girls than it does for boys. Also, the wiring of girls' prefrontal cortex occurs sooner than for boys, probably a reason why teenage girls have lower car insurance rates, since that part of the brain assesses risk. Remember, guys do catch up by early adulthood.

The difference in maturity puts a lot of boys at a disadvantage in school. We group all children into grades by age regardless of gender. If groupings were based on brain development, a girl might be a grade ahead of her twin brother. While I'm not suggesting we reorganize grade levels, I do think it's important to recalibrate some of our expectations and adapt some of our teaching methods based on brain differences. I'll go into that more in the chapter on the implications of brain science on daycare centers and schools.

The Language Brain

With our friends' kids, Tony was almost two years older than his sister Angelina, but she started to speak when she was months younger than the age at which he did. I still remember being startled by her preschool vocabulary. Reading and writing came easily to her while Tony experienced some frustration on his way to mastering the same skills. During elementary school Angelina devoured books while Tony showed little interest in reading for fun. As a teenager, Angelina talked on her cell phone for hours with her friends whereas you could measure Tony's conversations in minutes, if not seconds. While both are now friendly, charming young adults, conversations with each are quite different. Angelina can still have a lively chat with anyone, while Tony remains more quiet and reserved. Although they are a small sample, Tony and Angelina certainly showcase our knowledge about the different language brains.

Language is often one of the clearest brain differences between the sexes. Girls talk earlier than boys, have larger preschool vocabularies, and use more complex sentence structures. Once in school, girls are one to one and a half years ahead of boys in reading and writing. Boys are twice as likely to have a language or reading problem and three to four times more likely to stutter. Girls do better on tests of verbal memory, spelling, and verbal fluency. On average, girls utter two to three times more words per day than boys and even speak faster—twice as many words per minute. The list goes on and on, with the differences persisting throughout life. Among elderly stroke victims, for example, women recover their speech much more quickly than men.

A growing body of research on these differences points us to a girl brain built with a head start for language. During infancy, the left hemisphere, the brain's language center for most people, develops before the right for little girls, whereas the order is reversed for boys. Even more convincing, females have at least 20 percent more neurons than males in the Broca area, where we produce language, and they have as much as 18 percent more volume in the Wernicke's area, where we interpret language.

Further, the corpus callosum, the bridge of nerve tissue connecting the brain's left and right hemispheres, is denser in the female brain. Many scientists believe this facilitates communication across the two hemispheres, enabling girls to link the language centers in the left hemisphere with the more intuitive right brain. Finally, girls use both sides of their brains when engaged in language while boys use only the left hemisphere.

In addition to personality differences between Angelina and her brother Tony, her built-for-language female brain probably explains why she talked earlier and still reads and writes more than he does. During my years of teaching high school I was well aware how girls joined class discussions more readily. I always chalked the boys' reticence up to social pressure. Now I think it was probably the differences in their brains. Knowing the brain science should motivate us to pay special attention to develop our sons' language abilities while also not taking our daughters' language facility for granted.

Chapter 3 gives more depth about the importance of language and how to foster good verbal skills. Parents and teachers of boys might want to pay special attention to that chapter.

The difference in verbal expression is particularly apparent at puberty. That's when girls' natural propensity for conversation is boosted by additional hormones and the result is hundreds of daily text messages, hours talking on the phone, multiple social networking site updates, and all-night talk-fests. Teenage boys' brains, on the other hand, receive their own, different "boost," making them more ornery, competitive, and solitary. Girls tend to nourish relationships with conversation while often their brothers build friendships by doing things together.

Talk About Feelings

This dramatic language difference between girls and boys also may affect how they talk about their feelings. One of the most painful experiences of my high school teaching and counseling career brings this into stark relief when Todd, a bright, popular boy, committed suicide after his relationship ended. We had all missed the signs as he didn't talk about his grief with anyone.

Youth suicide is certainly one of a parent's greatest fears. The risk rises dramatically after puberty, making it the third leading cause of death among adolescents, according to the Centers for Disease Control and Prevention. In 2007 more than one out of seven U.S. high school students reported suicidal thoughts. Half of these kids actually made an attempt to kill themselves. Todd, however, was a tragic example of a gender-based disparity within those statistics. Although girls are much more likely to talk about and attempt suicide, boys are four times more likely to actually kill themselves. All talk of suicide should definitely be taken seriously, but when a suicide, like Todd's, seems to come out of the blue with little or no advance warning, it is usually a boy. I believe one of the reasons for this dramatic and scary difference is that girls' brains help them talk about their feelings whereas boys' brains don't always lead them in that direction.

Still, while girls verbalize their moods more easily, that can bring a price. Research shows that when girls talk too much about problems, they run the risk of digging themselves into a deeper emotional hole. The psychologists who study this phenomenon call it "co-rumination." In a survey of more than six hundred boys and girls, they found girls were much more likely to share their feelings and form more close friendships than boys. The downside was girls became more anxious and depressed, not less, when they talked about their problems with friends. It appears overtalking can blow things out of proportion. Pretty soon teen girls lose perspective, everything starts to look grim, and all hope vanishes.

We parents, therefore, need to help our sons share their feelings so they get support and encouragement. We need to listen to our daughters when they are troubled and we should encourage them to work toward solutions, not sink into a spiral of sadness. Here's an example of how a parent can help his daughter avoid the co-rumination trap.

"I know how disappointed you are that you didn't get invited to Jen's party. I'd be sad, too. Are all your friends going?"

"Some are. Some aren't."

"Well, why don't you invite your friends who aren't going either to come over for an overnight? I'd be willing to spring for pizza and a good video."

"Oh, I don't know, Dad."

"Listen, you don't have to decide tonight. Check with some of your friends tomorrow, and we can talk about it again when you get home from school."

The Thinking Brain

The controversy about overall intelligence between the genders is over: there is no evidence men are smarter than women or that women are smarter than men. Gender differences do show up in several cognitive domains, however. Just as there is a lot of evidence that girls' brains give them a verbal advantage, likewise there is data showing that boys' brains favor spatial skills that make it easier for them to visualize three-dimensional objects from different angles.

Siblings Samantha and Ben are flesh-and-blood illustrations. Samantha excelled in all things verbal. She joined the debate team in high school and loved small seminars in college. She went on to law school, became an attorney, and eventually made a successful run for political office. Ben had good verbal skills but his specialty was taking things apart and putting them back together. As a preschooler he loved Tinker Toys, Erector sets, and Legos. By the time he was in middle school his parents relied on him to operate the DVD player and other electronic gizmos around the house. He was first in line to join when his high school started a robotics club; he majored in mechanical engineering in college and works for a manufacturing company today.

Research shows that boys' advantage in spatial skills exists in elementary school and even widens once they reach puberty. You can imagine that these skills come in very handy for engineers, architects, physicists, and mechanics. Ninety-two percent of American engineers are male, and the question is whether this career fact is based on brain or social factors. While experience always plays an important role, a boy's brain may give him an advantage. Recall that baby boys' right hemispheres mature before the left, the opposite order of girls. The circuits underlying spatial skills are on the right side of the brain. Even more convincing is the research on the role of hormones. Marcia Collaer and Melissa Hines studied girls whose mothers had a high level of testosterone, the principal male sex hormone, during pregnancy. It turned out these daughters were better at spatial reasoning than other girls.

There is a strong correlation between spatial reasoning and mathematics, so for a long time many researchers thought boys had an advantage there, too. Is it true? It depends. Girls actually do better than boys in computation skills and get better math grades throughout elementary and high school. On the other hand, boys do better in mathematical problem solving and have scored 10 percent higher than girls on the math portion of the SAT for the past thirty years. Then again, boys and girls score just about exactly the same on other standardized math tests. The results are pretty inconclusive.

To make things even fuzzier, expectations make a big difference. In one experiment, men and women were told that males always did better on the math test they were about to take. Sure enough, the men scored higher. However, when the next group was informed that the test was gender fair, then men and women scored the same. The takeaway for us parents is to think about the messages we send our sons and daughters and not close a door before your child has a chance to walk through it.

BRAIN TIPS

- Don't lock your kids into stereotyped expectations.
- Help your child explore all the possibilities for their interests.
- Encourage boys to develop reading, writing, and verbal skills.
- Encourage girls to explore opportunities in math and science. Find programs tailored to girls' interests.
- Get outside and play catch, kick a soccer ball, or play hoops with all your kids. Experience makes a difference.

Emotions

In addition to the billions of brain cells and who-knows-how-many circuits, two important groups of chemicals—hormones and neurotransmitters—play leading roles in our brains and in our emotional lives. The differences between girls' and boys' brain chemistry help us understand the differences in their emotional brains. We'll start by examining the role of hormones and include neurotransmitters a bit later.

Our body produces more than sixty hormones in glands located throughout the body. As we saw in previous chapters, hormones function as messengers racing through the body dispensing essential information for the smooth operation of all its functions. While the glands that produce hormones are distributed all over the body, the master control center, the hypothalamus, is located in the brain.

BOYS' EMOTIONAL BRAINS

One of the clearest differences between boys' and girls' brains is the contrasting levels of the three sex hormones: testosterone for boys and the estrogen/progesterone combination for girls. It's interesting to note that all fetuses start out female. The genetic fork in the road happens at about the eighth week, when a fetus destined to be male starts to produce testosterone, which will influence the development and function of his body and brain for the rest of his life. Testosterone develops his sex organs, makes his bones denser, and creates more muscle mass, making his body bigger and stronger. At puberty testosterone will trigger what are called the secondary sex characteristics, including beard growth and a deepening voice, changing a boy soprano into a teenage tenor or bass. While both males and females produce testosterone, males produce a lot more—twenty to forty times more.

In addition to testosterone's physical effects, we saw in chapter 10 how testosterone influences a boy's emotional life, especially fueling a quickness to anger. Testosterone also fuels a boy's propensity to seek excitement and thrills. A high school social worker referred fourteen-year-old Reggie and his family to me for counseling after he almost got kicked out of his high school for setting off a large firecracker in a boys' bathroom toilet. "He's a good kid, Dr. Walsh," the social worker told me. "If he weren't so charming and friendly he probably would be expelled. He's not malicious, but he's always getting into trouble."

I liked Reggie from the first moment I met him. He was friendly, outgoing, and had a great sense of humor. I think he inherited these personality traits from his extroverted parents, who accompanied him to the first session. His mother, Ellen, reported that Reggie was high energy from the time he could walk. When I asked her what she meant, she told me how he loved rough-and-tumble play, wrestling, and adventure. "One of our family's favorite vacations was a ski trip to Colorado," Ellen said. "Reggie was off on his own, heading for the steepest double-black-diamond runs before he was seven years old. He was fearless. The more dangerous it was, the more exciting he found it."

"We were regular visitors to the urgent care center and emergency room, weren't we, Reggie?" his father, Ken, added. "Remember the time you fell out of the tree in the backyard and broke your arm? I joked with the doctor that we should get a frequent visitor discount."

Ellen quickly reminded her husband the doctor hadn't found his joke very amusing. "Yes, and remember how he told you if we did a better job supervising, then maybe Reg wouldn't get hurt so often."

Ken smiled. "That doctor had no sense of humor." Then he looked at Reggie. "Your mother and I thought there was probably a file on us at the child welfare office with two broken arms before kindergarten and who knows how many trips for stitches."

"See, it's all your fault," Reggie joked. "If you and Mom had supervised me better I wouldn't have fallen out of that tree or had those other accidents."

I was impressed by the comfortable back-and-forth between Reggie and his parents. So many teenagers I counseled hardly spoke with their parents. Yet here was Reggie joking with his mom and dad about his history of misadventures and mishaps. I have no way to know what Reggie's testosterone level was, but his adventure-seeking, risk-taking behavior and impulsivity were manifestations that it probably flowed at a pretty good clip.

Reggie was not a deeply troubled kid, but he had the same challenges that many boys did. I concentrated my counseling to help him learn to consider consequences before he acted and to channel his risk taking in more positive directions. He got quite good at remembering my "Stop, Think, Rethink, and Act" mantra, which I had him repeat over and over again. By the time he was in the eleventh grade he was one of the top players on both the football and baseball teams, where he found a better outlet for his brain-based competitiveness and desire for adventure. Years later, reading the morning newspaper, an article in the business section caught my eye. Beneath a smiling photo of Reggie was an article about a massive commercial real estate deal he just masterminded. I thought to myself, Reggie's still a risk taker.

The adult Reggie, by the way, is not alone. Recent research reveals that adult males with high testosterone levels are more prone to make risky financial decisions, the adult version of climbing tall trees and skateboarding down wrought-iron railings.

GIRLS' EMOTIONAL BRAINS

"Girls are relationship experts while boys orient more to objects and achievement": Is this a biased stereotype with no basis in fact? If there's some truth, is the orientation the result of socialization or is it brain based? It seems this general statement is not just our imagination, and though much behavior is the result of social expectations or upbringing, some is brain based. Here's what we are finding.

A girl begins to key into others as soon as she's born. Psychologist Erin McClure Tone found newborn girls respond to another baby's crying much more than boys within the first twenty-four hours. Parents often claim it seems easier to establish eye contact with an infant girl than a boy within months after coming home from the hospital, and psychologist Rebecca Leeb wanted to know if this was fantasy or fact. She designed a carefully controlled study and discovered that infant girls increase the frequency of eye contact and mutual gazing 400 percent between birth and three months, while an infant boy's eye contact frequency remains at a lower rate.

A University of Texas study also revealed a dramatic difference between one-year-olds. Researchers videotaped mothers who brought their children into a room one by one with instructions not to let their girls or boys touch an object. The little girls were much less likely to touch the object than the boys and the way girls succeeded in not touching the object was by looking at their mothers ten to twenty times more frequently than did the boys. They read every glance and expression on their mothers' faces as cues. The mothers didn't even have to tell the girls not to touch the object. The boys, on the other hand, barely looked at their mothers and touched the forbidden object even when their mothers told them not to.

Girls' social orientation also surfaces in their choice of toys. The stereotype is that boys prefer balls, trucks, and action figures while girls gravitate to dolls. To test if these choices come from social and cultural forces, researchers Melissa Hines and Gerianne Alexander turned to vervet monkeys from southern and east Africa. They gave a group of monkeys an assortment of toys to play with, including trucks, dolls, and picture books. The male monkeys wanted the trucks while the female monkeys went straight to the dolls. Both the males and females showed equal interest in the gender-neutral books. Unless our human socialization rubbed off on the monkeys, this is more evidence that female brains are wired toward people.

Two hormones, estrogen and oxytocin, enhance the priority that girls give to relationships. Estrogen helps a girl feel good when she plays with her friends or snuggles on the couch in her pajamas listening to a bedtime story. It's not that the estrogen itself causes warm, comfortable feelings; it's that estrogen has an effect on other chemicals in our brains, the neurotransmitters.

Scientists still discover new neurotransmitters (at last count they've identified at least a hundred) whose job it is to relay electrical impulses across the tiny gaps, called synapses, that separate the branches of neurons. In addition to their electrical transmission duties these chemicals, especially dopamine and serotonin, play a critical role in our emotional life. Dopamine has numerous functions in the brain, but one role gives it the "happy neurotransmitter" nickname. When the dopamine flows, we feel good. When it floods, we feel *really* good. I call serotonin the "stabilizer" because when it bathes the synapses, we feel comfortable and relaxed. When serotonin levels drop, however, our mood goes with it, making us edgy, cranky, and out of sorts. Estrogen interacts with dopamine and serotonin, heightening the good feelings of close relationships.

Estrogen gets a further boost at puberty when the hormone oxytocin kicks in. It is sometimes called the "cuddle hormone" because it motivates closeness. The estrogen-oxytocin combination makes relationships even more important to girls and it's why their radar is tuned to notice and interpret all sorts of social cues boys miss. Adolescent girls take great pleasure in being together and experience acute sadness when they are left out.

The girl-boy difference also shows up in how each expresses anger. For a long time, scientists thought boys were by nature more aggressive. After all, they pushed, hit, and shoved a lot more than girls. More careful research, however, shows that girls and boys are equally aggressive, but their brain-based expression looks a lot different. A boy might strike a playmate whereas a girl is more apt to make another girl pay socially, what scientists call relational aggression, with talk behind her back. For example, a girl in anger might say, "We don't want you to eat lunch with us. We don't like you anymore." In our Internet age, this can play out with the push of a button with even more devastating effects that I will explore more in the chapter on digital parenting.

When it comes to expressing sadness, girls and boys cry with about the same frequency until puberty. From that point on, for the rest of their lives, girls cry five times more frequently than boys. Another hormone explains the difference, as girls produce 60 percent more prolactin than boys, a hormone that lowers the crying threshold.

A Reminder

While I highlight all the brain-based differences between girls and boys, it's important to remember the warnings at the start of this chapter. Every girl and boy is an individual. While brain science helps us better understand and guide our daughters and sons, we should make sure we don't turn generalizations into straitjackets.

We need to remember the role that experience and plasticity play in brain wiring. Each child falls somewhere along a continuum of possible brain traits and the experiences he or she has in childhood often point to interests and skills they will pursue as an adults. Brain science gives us insights as parents of daughters and sons and should not blind us to all their possibilities.

DO

- ✓ Encourage your sons and daughters to get involved in a wide range of activities.
- ✓ Foster children's language skills, with special attention to your sons.
- ✓ Name emotions for your son, helping him to interpret social cues.
- ✓ Teach both your sons and daughters to deal with anger and aggression in constructive and appropriate ways.
- ✓ Encourage your daughters to find solutions when they are sad.

- ✓ Give your daughter toys to build with. Encourage her by creating a story about what you build. Give her experiences with tools.
- ✓ Connect your sons' interests to further reading whether in books or on the Internet.
- ✓ Encourage your sons to name and talk about their feelings. Model emotional literacy for them with remarks like "I'm feeling disappointed that our picnic was canceled because of the rain."
- ✓ Get outside and practice athletic skills with all your kids.

DON'T

- ✗ Don't let brain-based expectations limit how you see each child.
- ✗ Don't communicate brain-based biases. For example, don't say, "Girls just aren't that good at science."
- ✗ Don't expect a boy (or girl) to sit still for a long period of time.
- ✗ Don't be surprised when teenagers get surly. Cut them some slack but don't tolerate abusive language or behavior. Be clear about what's out of bounds. You might say, for example, "I understand that you're angry, but you don't get to call me names."

What do I want to continue?

____

____

____

What do I want to change?

____

____

____

TWELVE

Stress and the Brain

Five-year-old Jessica talked for months about how excited she was to start kindergarten. "I'm going to the big girl school soon," she told her grandparents during their Christmas visit, nine months before she would board the yellow bus for the first time. She and her mother, Maryalyce, started to mark the days off once the calendar flipped from May to June. As summer progressed, however, Jessica no longer got out the Magic Marker every morning before breakfast to X out another date. In early August she began to wake her parents up during the night and complain she couldn't sleep. "Can I sleep with you?" she asked one night. "Come on, Jess, I'll come tuck you in again," her stepdad, Richard, said as he climbed out of bed. He carried her back, read her a short story, turned the light out, and sat with her until she fell asleep.

Maryalyce was still awake fifteen minutes later when he got back. "What's the matter with Jessica?" Richard asked as he rearranged his pillow. "That's the third time this week she's been awake. She hasn't asked to sleep with us in ages."

"She's scared, Richard," Maryalyce answered. "That's why she's started to bite her fingernails again and complained about a stomachache yesterday."

"What's she scared of?" asked Richard.

"Richard," Maryalyce replied, "she starts kindergarten in less than a month. What do you think she's scared of?"

"But I thought she was excited about starting school."

"She is, but it's also stressful. Haven't you ever been excited and scared at the same time?" Maryalyce asked. "There was just an article in the paper the other day about how stressful starting school can be for kindergartners."

Even though Jessica had been in daycare for over three years, kindergarten was going to be a big change, riding a bus with older kids to get to a school with over five hundred students and a new, unfamiliar teacher. Richard wondered if talking about it with Jessica would help, and Maryalyce said, "That's a start, but we need to be extra patient for the next couple of months. Don't be surprised if she's in here every night. We can also put a little plan into place. We need to schedule a school visit so she can see her classroom. We also need to set up an appointment with the teacher as soon as we know who she'll have, and go school shopping together so we can help her feel prepared."

Jessica's parents talked some more that night and agreed on some ways to help her deal with the stress of starting school. The next morning Maryalyce sat down with her daughter at the breakfast table while Richard scrambled some eggs. "You know, Jessica," she said, putting her arm around her daughter, "I don't know about you, but I remember being really scared when I started kindergarten. It's a pretty big deal."

Jessica looked at her mother. "You were scared?" she asked.

"Sure I was. I think most kids are scared when they start school."

That was all Jessica needed to hear before she was sobbing in her mother's lap, asking if her mother thought her teacher would be mean, whether she would make any friends, if she would miss her bus stop or forget her lunch, and voicing a dozen other worries that loomed large as the first day of school drew closer.

Maryalyce and Richard told their daughter her fears made sense but also reassured her she could handle all the challenges of kindergarten. Her parents also started their middle-of-the-night strategy plan. Like millions of children before her, Jessica made a successful—but stressful—transition from daycare to kindergarten. Four months later, as she packed for their annual Thanksgiving trip to visit her grandparents, Jessica made sure to include some of her school projects she described during their phone calls. "Grandma really wants to see these," she told her mother as she closed her suitcase. "She's so happy I really like school."

The Lifelong Quest to Manage Stress

Let's start at the beginning with the experience of a fetus that we'll call Betty. For months Betty was accustomed to a secure, tranquil environment where she hadn't a worry in the world.

Then came birth. After a rather traumatic, hours-long trip down the birth canal Betty enters a world of bright lights, loud sounds, gravity, and changing temperatures. Adding insult to injury, strangers prod, poke, and even stick her with something sharp in the sole of her foot. And for the first time in her life she's hungry. Who can blame Betty for checking out in a semicoma for a week or so? As she emerges from her coma-like sleep she discovers that it wasn't a bad dream. This is now her world and she must learn to live in it for the rest of her life.

Betty's brain interprets the dramatic change from her perfectly balanced homeostatic environment to a world of hunger, gas pains, and wet diapers as stressful. She protests in the way human infants have been doing for millennia—by crying. The smartest thing for a sensitive and caring parent to do is to try to re-create the environment Betty associates with safety. While in the womb Betty's brain had wired in an association of safety and comfort with rhythms—swaying back and forth as mom moved, the sound of a beating heart, and the swoosh-swoosh of fluids. No wonder we intuitively rock an infant back and forth as we shift from one foot to the other. We're "reminding" her of the swaying she was used to when life was better. When we whisper "shhh, shhh," we're re-creating the sound of the swishing amniotic fluid. When we hold the infant close she can hear the familiar sound of a beating heart. Nature has equipped us to instinctively re-create the rhythms that brains like Betty's associate with safety and security.

Infants cannot calm themselves. They cannot regulate their own stress reactions. They outsource stress regulation to their human caregivers, who calm them by re-creating the rhythms they're used to. As time goes by they internalize the ability to calm themselves and do it on their own. But it's a long, multiyear process. A tired and hungry two-year-old can have a full meltdown at the shopping mall, but he'll end up in jail if he does the same thing at the age of eighteen. We expect better stress regulation by then.

Stress regulation is one of the brain's "executive functions," centered in the prefrontal cortex. As we learned in chapter 10, a teenager's prefrontal cortex—the brain's executive center—is under construction, which is why he sometimes acts like a toddler.

Babies, Separation, and Stress

Stress happens to all of us, adults and children alike. Babies experience separation anxiety when they're six or seven months old and toddlers show unmistakable signs of distress between twelve and eighteen months whenever mom or dad disappears. While it can be upsetting for parents when their baby melts down every time a stranger approaches or a babysitter shows up, this type of stress is normal, and babies eventually outgrow it. Here are some steps parents can take to minimize the stress of separation anxiety.

- Invite your babysitter or caregiver over for a trial run so the two of them can get acquainted.
- When you leave your baby with someone else try to spend a little time together before you leave.
- Don't forget to say goodbye and tell your baby where you're going and when you expect to return.
- Be cheerful and optimistic. Babies have great radar. If they sense you're as troubled by the separation as they are, they will be even more stressed.
- Don't go back. Steel yourself and keep going even if you hear your baby scream in the background. Repeat exits make it harder for everyone.

Children and Stress

As children get older there are all sorts of stress hurdles to clear. I can still remember crying during my first haircut, so I'm sure that was stressful. Some stressors are common, such as tiffs with playmates, lost security blankets or toys, loud thunder, or things that go bump in the night. Others are unique because stress is often in the eye of the beholder. For example, I was very afraid of water as a little boy because I fell into the deep end of a pool before I could swim. My own kids, on the other hand, were comfortable around water because they learned to swim when they were preschoolers.

Sometimes kids tell us when they're stressed. There was no mystery, for example, about my stress reaction at the barbershop. As soon as he came at me with the buzzing electric shears, everyone in the shop heard my reaction. Other times it's an observant parent who connects a child's behavior to stress. These cues include headaches, stomachaches, hair pulling, rocking, thumb sucking, fingernail biting, toilet accidents, sleep problems, nightmares, excessive shyness, clinginess, hypervigilance, excessive worry, or angry outbursts.

Helping Children Cope with Stress

We parents must strike a balance. We don't want to ignore our children's stress signals and leave them to cope completely on their own. On the other hand we need to avoid the "helicopter parent" syndrome, meaning a parent who swoops in to solve all of their child's problems. As my school superintendent friend Phil Ledermann liked to tell parents, "Your job is not to smooth out all the bumps in the road for your kids. It's your responsibility to equip your children with good shock absorbers so they learn to handle the bumps themselves."

Here are steps to help children cope with everyday stress:

- Provide structure and clear expectations. Stress increases with unpredictability and loss of control.
- Talk with your children about their worries. As psychiatrist and bestselling author Ned Hallowell advises, "Never worry alone."
- Convey optimism. Let your child know he or she can handle the situation. "I know it's scary but you'll be able to ride the school bus."
- Solve problems with your child and encourage him to think of solutions. This will increase his sense of control. "What can you do to make this seem less scary?"
- Use humor appropriately. Don't make fun of your child's concerns but see if you can get them to laugh. It increases dopamine, the happy neurotransmitter, and decreases the stress hormones.
- Teach them to breathe when they're stressed. The increased flow of oxygen to their brains is another way to reduce stress hormones.

PARENT TOOL KIT

Helping Children Cope with Stress

The questions in this kit are designed to help you learn about the effects of stress on children's brains and what you can do to help children cope.

Yes No

☐ ☐ 1. I understand some stress is unavoidable and my job is to teach my children coping skills.

☐ ☐ 2. I know stress affects how the brain functions.

☐ ☐ 3. I realize stress can affect attention, memory, and learning.

☐ ☐ 4. I know there is a difference in how the brain deals with acute versus chronic stress.

☐ ☐ 5. I know severe stress can cause "brain damage" in young babies.

☐ ☐ 6. I realize unmonitored media can be a source of stress in children.

☐ ☐ 7. I know how important it is to avoid always rescuing my children.

☐ ☐ 8. I understand that unpredictability, lack of control, and inconsistency increase stress.

☐ ☐ 9. I realize how important it is to help children cope with severe stressors like disaster, family breakup, serious illness, or death.

☐ ☐ 10. I know breathing, humor, adequate sleep, healthy eating, exercise, and relationships are all critical for managing stress.

The more yes answers to the questions in this tool kit, the better equipped you are to raise resilient children who can cope with stress.

Stress and the Brain

Two variables determine how stress affects the brain: severity and duration. Mild stress, such as the deadline for a school assignment, can actually help focus attention and increase motivation. Our brains handle mild stress easily. Severe stress is a different story. I've mentioned several times that our brain's most basic job is to keep us alive. That's why our brains come equipped with early warning detection systems to alert us to anything perceived as dangerous and beyond our ability to cope. Within a fraction of a second the brain can trigger a fight-or-flight response sending three hormones (the body's chemical messengers) into action. First, the hypothalamus releases the hormone CRF, corticotopin factor, which in turn stimulates the release of the energizer hormone adrenaline. Adrenaline speeds up the heart so it pumps more blood to the muscles, preparing them for action. The third hormone, cortisol, alters the blood sugar level, providing a quick burst of energy; lowers pain sensitivity; tamps down inflammation; and boosts the immune system. How these hormones affect the brain depends on how long the stress lasts.

The brain reacts differently to acute and chronic stress. Noted Stanford neuroscientist Robert Sapolsky talks about stress in his fascinating book *Why Zebras Don't Get Ulcers.* He believes our body's response was originally designed for the kind of short-term stress a zebra faces when chased by a lion. If the lion caught the zebra, that was the end of the story. In the event he escaped, his flight-or-fight response would fade as soon as he was out of harm's way, so the time between activation and reset of the stress response could be measured in minutes or hours. In the 21st century, however, stress can go on for days, weeks, months, or years. Jessica's worry about the fate that awaited her in kindergarten lasted weeks. A child growing up in a war-torn country might deal with danger for years at a time.

Chronic, severe stress—whether physical, social, or imaginary—wreaks havoc on the body and its control center, the brain. While cortisol initially boosts immunity, prolonged elevation weakens it, leaving the body more susceptible to infection. It also increases fat storage, leading to weight gain. Upstairs in the brain, cortisol hangs around much longer than adrenaline and eventually damages the hippocampus, the brain's memory center. The reason we become forgetful under stress is not just that we're distracted but that the memory retrieval system is compromised. The CRF hormone adds to the damage that cortisol does in the hippocampus and, in addition, harms other brain circuits. On top of that, the brain produces less "brain derived neurotophic factor," or BDNF, when stressed. As you might recall from chapter 7, BDNF is a tonic for the neurons promoting both cellular growth and vitality. The combination of neuron damage and BDNF deficiency reduces the brain cells' ability to produce enough dopamine, serotonin, and other chemicals to maintain cognitive efficiency and emotional stability. Attention and memory suffer. Depression and anxiety follow. We don't always recognize these symptoms of chronic severe stress as the reason for behavior changes, sleep difficulties, acting out, concentration problems, social withdrawal, headaches, or stomachaches, but we should.

Emotional Memories

Three-year-old Crispin was walking with his parents on a beautiful summer evening when he was scared by a barking, snarling German shepherd.

The entire episode lasted less than a minute, and Crispin suffered no physical harm. The psychological scars were another matter. The three-year-old had recurring nightmares for weeks, and in the following months Crispin would panic at the mere sight of a dog. His fear of dogs lasted for years.

How do we explain what happened to Crispin given what I said earlier about cortisol's interference with memory registration and retrieval? Crispin's cortisol levels during the attack were undoubtedly off the charts, so why would he remember that event so long afterward? This apparent contradiction has puzzled neuroscientists studying post-traumatic stress disorder for a long time. If cortisol impedes memory, how come we all remember frightening events with great clarity years later? Scientists at Duke University found that there are special memory mechanisms to record emotional memories—positive as well as negative. It makes sense that the brain can quickly remember important emotional events if its primary job is survival. We now know emotionally charged experiences are chemically tagged for quick and easy retrieval. What appears to be a contradiction turns out to be another example of our sophisticated brains. Even though we have trouble remembering under prolonged stress, our brains are able to recall events that are important to our survival quickly and easily, and for a very long time.

The Vicious Stress Loop

Three second graders bullied Randy during his very first week on the school bus. The older kids hadn't physically hurt the first grader, but the name-calling, put-downs, and threats terrified him. His parents were pleased with the principal's decision to immediately call a meeting with the three boys and their parents. She made it very clear there was a zero-tolerance policy for any bullying and harassment, and that any further incidents would bring serious consequences.

While the school principal brought the school bus bullying to a stop, Randy was a wreck. For weeks afterward his stomach ached every morning and he often cried before going to school. He relived images of the mean boys repeatedly and worried constantly that the bullying would happen again. His parents worried this reaction was ruining the start of his school career.

Their concern was justified because scientists now know how anyone—kids or adults—can become trapped in a never-ending stress loop. Prolonged stress rewires the brain into a vicious cycle of perseveration. Portuguese neuroscientist Nuno Sousa demonstrated that protracted stress deactivates the problem-solving part of the brain, the prefrontal cortex, while it activates the sensorimotor striatum, the part of the brain where automatic habitual behavior originates. Although he did his research with rats, Stanford neuroscientist Robert Sapolsky believes the same change happens in the human brain and explains why our brain gets stuck like a broken record when we're worried about something. "This is a great model for understanding why we end up in a rut, and then dig ourselves deeper and deeper into that rut," Sapolsky says.

So what can Randy's parents do? The good news is that we can "unstick" the brain by very deliberately changing the scenery, routine, and anything else we can think of to "get our mind off" the problem. I encouraged Randy's parents to think how they could arrange a real break from routine. They asked Randy to help them plan a fun weekend that ended up including a Friday night sleepover with his friends followed by a Saturday hike and overnight camping adventure at a state park. By the time they returned home, Randy was more relaxed. Fortunately the older boys continued to leave him alone, and gradually he was able to leave for school without a stomachache or tears.

Raising Stress-Resistant Kids

While we all hope our kids never experience traumatic events, it's impossible to avoid pressure completely. In fact, we don't want our kids to be completely sheltered. After all, they'll run into challenging situations at many points in their lives. How will they handle them if they never get any practice? Kids must eventually stand on their own two feet, handle setbacks, get through life's tough times, and handle the difficulties that life inevitably brings. When parents shield their kids from all stress, they deny them the psychological muscles they need. We don't want our kids to be emotionally flabby and lack resiliency, the quality that enables kids to handle stress. Because it is frequently studied, we now have a good idea how to foster resiliency in our sons and daughters.

SUPPORT AND CONNECTION

The first ingredients needed to raise stress-resistant kids are support and connection. When kids are surrounded by people who encourage and support them, they're more able to handle life's challenges. There's a big difference, however, between support and overprotection. It's not always easy to judge where that line is, so here are some guidelines.

- Confront your own fears and ask yourself if they are realistic. Ask yourself this: "What is the worst that can happen if I don't step in, and is this realistic?"
- Talk with other parents and get their perspective. You don't have to agree with them but they may have a helpful point of view.
- If your child is anxious or afraid, help him or her find ways to cope rather than rush in to solve problems.
- Let your child wrestle with a challenge. For example, homework help does not mean doing it for them. Suggest strategies, which is much better than providing answers.
- Allow your child to make mistakes, experience rejection, and endure defeat. These are learning opportunities, too.
- Have your children accept responsibility for their decisions and choices.

REASONABLE BUT HIGH EXPECTATIONS

Resilient kids have adults in their lives who believe in their ability to succeed and who set reasonable but high expectations. We do our kids a disservice when we expect too little or too much. Kristin's parents coddled her by arguing with teachers over low grades and amount of homework. On the other hand, Valerie's parents always pushed her to do more and better. Michael Thompson's book *The Pressured Child* describes parents like Valerie's who are obsessed with getting straight A's, being the best on the team, being in the "right" group of friends, and eventually attending the "best" college. Unrelenting pressure makes kids stressed out, not stress resistant.

COMPASSION

Resilient kids are not all wrapped up in themselves. My niece and nephew Meaghan and Philip always looked for ways to earn money during high school. But they weren't doing so to buy clothes or the latest music. They saved it to help pay for their part of a volunteer project in El Salvador. Their summer trips enabled them to help another community, make new friends, improve their Spanish, and get a new perspective on the world. It also changed their view of stress. As Philip told me, "It's kind of silly to worry about a math test when my friends in El Salvador have to worry whether there will be enough food for a meal."

AUTONOMY AND RESOURCEFULNESS

Resilient kids act independently and don't ask others for what they can do themselves. Parents foster autonomy when we support and encourage but avoid taking over. We can start early with comments like "Jack, thanks for hanging your coat up." They get more substantive with "Jack, I really like the way you struggled with that math problem until you figured it out."

I wish I could say I always practice what I preach. Unfortunately that wasn't the case with my daughter Erin's Saturday job. Monica and I believe kids need to have responsibilities in order to be responsible, so ours always had household jobs. I still remember the Saturday morning I came down to see how eight-year-old Erin was doing with her job cleaning the bathroom—and found she was doing an eight-year-old version of cleaning the bathroom. I said to Erin, "Here, let me show you." I said, "show," but that's not what I did. I started to clean the bathroom myself because it was easier and quicker. It didn't take Erin long to figure out that this was a good deal. "Great, Dad's doing my job so I'm out of here." Erin quickly disappeared as I continued to scrub the sink. Unfortunately for me, Monica saw the entire scene unfold. A few seconds later Monica appeared in the doorway of the bathroom. "Dave, what are you doing?" she asked. You can imagine how defensive I felt as I responded, "What does it look like? I'm cleaning the bathroom."

"I thought that was Erin's job," Monica said.

"It was, but she couldn't do it very well," I replied, not looking up.

Monica hit the nail on the head when she said, "Dave, you're going to have to decide. Do you want a clean bathroom or a competent daughter?" She was absolutely right. There is nothing magic about cleaning a bathroom or washing dishes but making sure our kids step up to their responsibilities gives them micro-boosts in autonomy and enables them to handle normal stress challenges in stride.

OPTIMISM

A sense of optimism increases resiliency and inoculates children against stress. Psychologist Martin Seligman studied optimism and pessimism for years. His research shows that optimists don't give up as easily as pessimists, and moreover, he found that optimistic children experience less stress because they believe things will eventually turn out okay. The good news is we can help our kids develop an optimistic outlook on life by encouraging them to focus on strengths rather than weaknesses and to search for the silver lining even when things go wrong. Here are some suggestions to build children's optimism.

- Pay attention to the messages you send to your children. Do you focus on what's wrong or what's right?
- Acknowledge a child's feelings of disappointment but prevent them from going into a downward spiral. Seligman's research reveals that pessimistic children lose perspective very quickly. For example, a pessimistic child might respond to a poor grade on a third grade spelling test by first blaming himself ("I didn't do well in the spelling test because I'm *stupid*"). Second, he'd generalize, "I can't do *anything* right in school," and then he'd see the dire situation as permanent. "I'll *never* learn how to spell." Intervene if you catch your daughter or son falling into the three pessimism traps (personalize, pervasive, and permanent). A simple statement like "What can you do to get a better score next time?" can begin to change their mindset.

Helping Children Cope with Major Life Stressors

Helping children cope with stressors like entering kindergarten, spelling tests, and scary dogs is one thing. Sometimes, however, life's stressors are much bigger, such as unemployment, natural disasters like floods and hurricanes, serious accidents, financial setbacks, major illness, divorce, and death.

How can we help our kids through crises that bring them into uncharted territory, especially when there is no clear resolution in the immediate future? Here are some suggestions.

ADJUST YOUR EXPECTATIONS

- It is natural and normal for children to have a full range of intense emotions after a traumatic event.
- Intense feelings ebb and flow. Don't expect the emotional roller coaster to end quickly.
- Stress and anxiety increase in direct proportion to lack of control.
- Feeling helpless can lead to childhood depression. Be on the lookout for warning signs like ongoing sleep disturbances and expressions of hopelessness and despair.
- Uncertainty increases stress. Children will feel more anxious if the future is very uncertain.
- Expect problems with sleeping, concentration, and memory. They are normal reactions to intense stress.
- Children may experience intense anger and look for someone to blame. They may take things out on other family members.
- Because reserves are low, minor irritations may be magnified so molehills quickly turn into mountains.
- Prolonged stress suppresses the immune system and leads to greater susceptibility to illness.
- Appetites may change; some kids eat less while others overeat.

COPING STRATEGIES FOR ALL—PARENTS AS WELL AS KIDS

- In the event of a community crisis, pay attention to media that help you understand what's happening and avoid media that simply exploit your emotions. Accurate knowledge provides some measure of control.
- Do something. The best antidote for feelings of helplessness is to find something constructive to do.
- Talk. A grief shared is half a grief.
- Stay connected with others. This is not the time to isolate.
- Watch what you eat. Stress eating does not help. We end up feeling bad about ourselves and fluctuating sugar levels can make us feel even more off-kilter.
- Exercise. It's a good stress reducer.

- Avoid blame.
- Don't be afraid to do something fun.
- Try to maintain a daily routine.
- Be patient with yourself and your children.
- Religion and spirituality can bring tremendous support and help during difficult times. Take time to reflect, meditate, read, and pray according to your religious tradition. Spiritual rituals and discussions can be very important activities to do as a family and as a community.

TIPS FOR PARENTS TO HELP CHILDREN COPE WITH CRISIS

- One of the greatest challenges for parents is to cope with their own feelings while at the same time helping children do the same. Make sure you take some time for yourself. Spend time with other adult family members and friends to get support.
- Make sure you continue to pay attention to events and rituals that are important in your children's lives even though current events may be weighing heavily on your minds.
- Spend extra time with your children. They need the reassurance your presence provides.
- Don't add to the stress by overscheduling. Cut back on some things so you have more time with your kids.
- Help children with their feelings. Remember to do two things simultaneously: acknowledge their feelings and reassure them.
- Don't try to talk children out of their feelings.
- Make sure they know it is okay to ask questions and answer their questions directly, but do not give them more information than they need.
- It is okay to share your feelings with your children (depending on their ages), but do not look to them for support. We should get our support from other adults, not our kids.
- Try to avoid extreme language when describing your own reactions.
- Make sure they get plenty of exercise and sleep.
- Talk to them about constructive ways to handle their anger.
- Provide lots of physical reassurance in the form of hugs and touches.

SPECIFIC TIPS FOR DIFFERENT AGES

EARLY CHILDHOOD

Even though very young babies and toddlers may not know what's happening, they pick up a parent's worry and anxiety with their "sixth sense."

- Try to stay calm around babies and toddlers.
- Maintain normal routines as much as possible. Routines are reassuring for babies.

PRESCHOOLERS

Preschoolers are more tuned in to what is happening. They may have lots of questions.

- Security is a primary concern for this age group. Reassure them that adults are in charge and will take care of them.
- Let them know your whereabouts and plans. Keep your commitments to them.
- In the event of a disaster, preschoolers are not always able to distinguish fantasy and reality. Limit their media exposure.
- Bedtimes are very important. Stories, books, and tuck-ins are crucial.
- Try to maintain your children's normal routines.
- Give them lots of hugs and physical reassurance.

ELEMENTARY SCHOOL

School-age children are more aware of a crisis. They may talk about it with their friends.

- Children this age are also concerned about their own security. Try to spend extra time together. This provides extra reassurance.
- Ask them if they have any questions. If they do, tell them what you know without exaggerating or overreacting.
- Don't be surprised if they are more irritable and touchy. Be extra patient.
- Try to continue normal routines, especially at bedtime.

MIDDLE SCHOOL

Children this age are very aware of what is going on. Most likely they will discuss the crisis with their friends.

- Talk to your middle school children and answer any questions. This will help you determine how much they know and may help you correct any misinformation they might have.
- Acknowledge any feelings of fear and sadness.

- Provide comfort and reassurance.
- Children this age are more interested in what might happen in the future. Share what you know without exaggeration. Don't burden them with your fears.
- Some children may act out scary feelings through misbehavior. Others may become more withdrawn. Pay attention to these cues and ask them to tell you about their feelings.

HIGH SCHOOL

High school students will talk a lot with their friends.

- They might have very legitimate fears about what the crisis means for their immediate future. It is important to discuss these topics with them.
- Acknowledge any fear, sadness, or anger.
- Some teens may want to block out the whole thing. It may appear they do not care. This often masks real fears and feelings of being overwhelmed.
- Some teens may make jokes. Humor can be a way to help them cope with overwhelming feelings, but discourage them from humor at the expense of others.

Stress happens and is part of life. Sometimes the stressors are predictable and manageable. Other times they are overwhelming and disorienting. Since our brains are designed to be very sensitive to stress, severe, prolonged bouts can do real damage, so it's important we teach our kids good coping skills and help our kids through the really tough stretches.

What do I want to continue?

____

____

____

What do I want to change?

____

____

____

THIRTEEN

Cyber Brains: Parenting in an Online World

Not long ago, two blog and website hosts called me to schedule an interview about my work. I do a lot of interviews every week, but this one was unusual. Instead of a political pundit or reporter on a parenting beat, the two on the other end of the phone were twelve-year-old Shennendoah and her nine-year-old brother, Bo. Shennendoah and Bo wanted to talk to me because they started their own website, called NeuroKids, all about "kids teaching kids about their brains." Turns out these two young people have a passion for all things brain-related, and share their findings on their website. Both write their own blogs, upload videos, and post interviews with authors, neuroscientists, and other "NeuroKids." The website they've created is a kid-friendly, quirky mix of research and kid-generated commentary, hosting everything from fun Internet games designed to "keep your brain sharp" to tutorials on how the nervous system functions.

Shennendoah, Bo, and I share a similar passion for understanding how the three-pound wonder perched on top of our shoulder works. Yet these young people share their interest using digital technologies I couldn't have dreamed of when I was their age. These brainiacs are 21st-century, multimedia, multichannel communicators, combining social networking, YouTube, and blogging with the aim of engaging other kids in an exciting area of research usually left to grown-ups. As I got off the phone with Bo and Shennendoah, I was struck not only by their maturity, but also by their excitement for learning and sharing ideas in myriad ways. At a young age, these two understand their unique opportunity to explore a world of information at their fingertips. Young people a generation ago with similar passions spent hours studying and perhaps sharing their thoughts with a few friends. Shennendoah and Bo, on the other hand, are engaged in a dynamic interchange with experts as well as kids from across the world, translating ideas into multimedia digital content that makes neuroscience come alive on the Web. What a wonderful example of the benefits of growing up in the digital age.

Unfortunately not all kids have the same positive media experience as Bo and Shennendoah. Just a month after I did the interview, a professional acquaintance, Maria, got in touch. As I would learn over coffee with her and her husband, Jack, the next day, her experience with digital technologies was far different than that of the neurokids. "You've met our daughter, Meaghan," Maria began. "Overall, beyond the usual twelve-year-old drama, she is a really good kid. We've been lucky she's excited about sports, excels in school, and has a great group of friends."

"Yes, Meaghan is a great kid!" I added, wondering where this was going.

"Well, things have gotten out of control in our house lately. Meaghan started begging for a cell phone about nine months ago. She said all of her friends had one, and we wanted to keep in better touch with her anyway, so we got her one."

"I am not surprised," I responded. "More and more, kids as young as eight or nine beg for cell phones."

"Yes, but since then the cell phone has become a total battleground in our family. Even our sixteen-year-old son says he barely recognizes his sister anymore!"

"What do you mean?" I asked.

"She's connected to her cell phone at all times. Things got out of control really quickly and we found out she was sending and receiving nearly a thousand text messages a day!"

I knew that one in three teens send 100 text messages a day and how they manage such thumb-intensive communication is a wonder, but 1,000 is almost incomprehensible. "Do you mean one thousand a week?" I asked.

"No," said Jack. "One thousand every day! Obviously we've tried to curb her cell phone use but it's been a minefield. She didn't comply with any rules we set so about a month ago we took the phone away."

"How did she take it?" I asked.

"She didn't. She ran away! In a panic we found her before the end of the day. But within a few weeks as we tried to reestablish ground rules and reintroduce the phone, it escalated all over again. Last week we confiscated the phone and she took off the same day."

"That must be terrifying. You are right, things certainly sound serious."

"Honestly," Maria went on, "we got her the phone thinking it would be an easy way to stay in touch. We had no idea. To top it all off, some of the texts she writes are really inappropriate! We are at the end of our rope and don't know what to do."

This conversation began a much longer dialogue with Maria and Jack about how to address Meaghan's cell phone use. I gave them several strategies, which included collaborating with friends, teachers, and school administrators to consistently enforce agreed-upon boundaries and limits regarding cell phone use. We also discussed telling their daughter they would use tracking software to monitor the language in her texts. Finally, and most importantly, I recommended they find a good counselor to work more closely with their daughter and the family to address these issues.

These two divergent stories represent the new questions and challenges parents must navigate in the 21st century. The proliferation of electronic screens and digital technologies in our kids' lives, including video games, TV, cell phones, and the Internet, presents both opportunity as well as risk for our kids. Shennendoah and Bo found ways to maximize the benefits of these digital technologies (no doubt receiving a fair amount of guidance and help from adults in their lives), while Meaghan's 24/7 digital connectivity was creating anxiety, obsessive behavior, and lots of conflict. All these kids are good kids, with parents who care about them. But raising kids in the digital age sometimes feels like navigating without a map, in a landscape filled with both treasure and trash.

PARENT TOOL KIT

Digital Parenting

Parents help children form their media and technology habits they carry into adulthood. Use these questions to help you build a tool kit for success.

Yes No

☐ ☐ 1. We have family rules limiting how much our kids use media and Internet technology.

☐ ☐ 2. We set rules and consequences around screen time *before* we introduce new technologies into our family life.

☐ ☐ 3. We keep electronic screens out of kids' bedrooms.

☐ ☐ 4. We have "technology-free" mealtimes.

☐ ☐ 5. We support our children's school cell phone policy.

☐ ☐ 6. We keep up with technology changes so we know what is popular with kids.

☐ ☐ 7. Our kids understand responsible online "netiquette" and know not to give out personal information online.

☐ ☐ 8. We encourage digital literacy but guide our kids towards safe, age-appropriate media activities.

☐ ☐ 9. We couple digital activities with activities in the "real world."

☐ ☐ 10. We understand and pay attention to media ratings.

The more yes answers to the questions in this tool kit, the better equipped you are to help your child take advantage of digital opportunities while avoiding the pitfalls.

Digital Natives and Digital Immigrants

The increase in screen time is the biggest lifestyle change for children and youth in the past generation. Today the average American school-age child spends more than fifty-three hours a week watching television, playing video games, or using the computer. The *only* thing the average American school-age child does more than consume media is sleep.

Twenty-first-century kids are sometimes called "Digital Natives" who have never known a world without Internet access and texting. They grow up in a media-rich environment that shapes the way they live and learn. They flock to online worlds to care for virtual penguins, generate videos, and upload them to YouTube. They use motion-control sensors to play virtual basketball and dance the night away, and access this entertainment around the clock. These activities differ dramatically from Digital Immigrants: adults, who grew up with face-to-face social interaction as the norm and arguments about using the phone during adolescence.

Increasingly, parents speak of a divide between Digital Natives and Digital Immigrants. After a speaking engagement, a mother told me how frustrating it was to navigate this divide with her son. "I wasn't raised using phrases like LOL and POS to communicate with my friends," she said, exasperated. "It's like he speaks a different language and I can't keep up!" (For those readers without text-messaging teens, LOL means laughing out loud and POS means parent over shoulder.)

While the terms *Digital Immigrants* and *Digital Natives* are appropriate in a lot of cases, many adults enjoy crossing the divide. Hilarie, a young graduate student at the University of Minnesota, was delighted to tell me that her eighty-two-year-old grandmother outplayed her on the game Guitar Hero for two years running at family reunions. So whether it's virtual rock and roll or other new technologies, many adults have fun finding ways to connect with, and in some cases outpace, the Digital Natives in their lives. In addition, for the first time in history, children are growing up with parents who themselves grew up immersed in digital media.

The Pace of the Revolution

Whether a tech-savvy parent or a Digital Immigrant, the job of navigating the revolution is challenging because technologies advance at lightning speeds. If you blink, it will change—this is the lesson of the digital revolution. No sooner do we buy the latest cell phone than there's another smartphone model with more computing power for Internet surfing, music, and application downloads; a higher-pixel camera and video; and a composition of better, lighter materials. The rate of change will only accelerate. I traveled to Seoul, South Korea, to represent the United States in the first International Conference on Youth Protection and Empowerment in Cyberspace. At the conference I joined delegates from other countries to identify emerging opportunities and issues related to Internet use and children. The conference itself was a great opportunity to collaborate with leaders across international boundaries. In addition, in informal conversations with the conference hosts and other participants, I learned about the digital revolution outside the United States. What I saw was a glimpse into our future since South Korea is years ahead of the United States technologically speaking, being dubbed by many "the most wired place on earth."

Much that I saw there is exciting. As technology continues to advance, American kids will also eagerly take advantage of each new device. But I also saw the darker side. In the United States, video game addiction is a newly emerging problem. The American Medical Association has called for more research to determine whether it should be included as an official diagnosable disorder. In contrast, South Korea is struggling to contain a full-blown video game addiction epidemic. Online gambling is also a big problem, as are online predators. While the scope of these challenges felt daunting, my trip to Seoul helped me see solutions, too. South Korea, for example, has more than two hundred government-sponsored treatment programs and has trained over a thousand video game and Internet addiction counselors. First and second graders in South Korean schools learn proper netiquette alongside reading and math; with leaders willing to invest in these creative solutions, they work to ensure children can maximize the benefits of living in the most wired place on earth.

Whoever Tells the Stories Defines the Culture

Electronic screens are only going to multiply and many parents recognize that kids today have information at their fingertips, can learn with engaging, interactive technologies, and can connect with family and friends all over the world with the touch of a button, but also have concerns how technology is shaping their children's health and development. Research findings on media and children's health and development sends a mixed message, touting the educational benefits while raising the alarm about screen time's contribution to the obesity epidemic, cyberbullying, sexting, addiction, and chronic distraction.

This chapter will not resolve the debate between "good" and "bad" because this dichotomy represents a false choice. Quibbling about whether digital technologies are a brain-rotting waste of time or a panacea for the world's problems misses the point. It all boils down to *how* kids use the technology. As the world changes, every generation of parents has to redefine how to care for kids. For 21st-century parents, caring for children includes paying attention to the role of digital media in their lives. Digital media, aside from being everywhere and always available, are *powerful*, but not inherently good or bad. Whether technology has positive or negative effects depends on how we use it.

One way to think about the power of media in our society is through the phrase "Whoever tells the stories defines the culture." Humans pass stories down from one generation to the next to transmit values, cultural norms, a sense of right and wrong, and an appreciation of place and history. This isn't new. It's been true for thousands of years. What is new is that today's storytellers are mass media. Some media take this art to new heights, while others specialize in dishing out heaping servings of violence, mayhem, and disrespect. A mountain of research shows that media influence our attitudes, values, and behaviors—for better and for worse.

This research shows, for example, that video games are excellent teachers. Games present clear objectives, individualized instruction, and continuous achievable challenges; they encourage active learning through practice and feedback loops, and take place in endless virtual worlds that reduce boredom. But video games teach wildly different lessons, with recent research showing that certain video games can teach prosocial behaviors to kids, including cooperation and empathy, while violent video games can also teach aggressive and violent behaviors. These findings reinforce the same message: video games are powerful teachers and storytellers, and whether they have a positive or negative impact on our kids' health and development depends upon the games and how we use them.

The iBrain

The digital revolution has changed and will continue to transform the world in which our children are growing up. It is also altering the way their brains are wired. As you know from earlier chapters, children and youth are busy laying the neural connections they will bring into their adult lives. Daily digital technology use strengthens some neural pathways while neglected ones weaken, meaning that children's brains evolve alongside technological changes.

For example, a recent study used functional MRI technology to scan neural activity patterns while subjects searched the Internet with Google. On the first day of the experiment, the researchers found that Internet-savvy subjects used a different part of their brain during the Google search than Internet-naïve subjects. Internet-savvy subjects used the working memory area of the brain, with its ability to integrate complex information as well as sensations and thoughts. After only five days of the experiment, however, both groups lit up the same Internet-savvy neural activity areas while searching with Google. In other words, Internet-naïve subjects rewired their brains in only five days to become more effective Internet searchers. The question that occurred to me after reading about this experiment: "If our brains can forge new neural pathways after less than a week of digital activity, what happens to young brains exposed to over fifty hours week after week?"

Research shows that people who spend a lot of time with activities like video games and Internet searching react more quickly to visual stimuli, have improved peripheral vision, and are better able to sift through massive amounts of information very quickly. As our brains adapt to the daily torrent of messages, images, and information, we get better at processing this information in efficient ways. For example, a researcher in the United Kingdom found that Web surfers took only two seconds on any given website before deciding to move on to another and that the sites where surfers lingered were ones most relevant to the search terms. In other words, our brains get better and better at synthesizing and evaluating information at lightning speeds, allowing us to sift through the "white noise" and focus our attention more judiciously.

While Digital Natives may be wiring incredible capacities to take in vast amounts of information and make split-second decisions, the neural pathways for human interaction and one-on-one interpersonal skills are often woefully neglected. A colleague of mine, Hussein, told me about his family's summer road trip. "The first morning of our trip to Montana was totally calm and quiet. There wasn't a peep out of the girls in the backseat. At first it was really nice because my wife and I were able to enjoy the scenery without the usual bickering about whose stuff was on which side of the car," Hussein said.

"Sounds nice," I responded, trying hard to remember if Monica and I ever enjoyed even an hour like that on a family road trip with our three kids.

"It was nice, at first," Hussein said. "But it started to get a little eerie when we realized the reason they weren't talking was because they were glued to their cell phones. Apparently they were texting their friends, and even each other!"

"During lunch we declared the car a technology-free zone for the rest of the trip. A few times we almost rescinded our rule when shouting matches erupted between them. The girls resisted at first but overall they had a great time and I think some serious bonding happened on the road trip."

Hussein has a legitimate concern that his daughters were missing something important while immersed in their cell phone conversations. More and more of us engage in digital communication at the expense of real-life social interaction. A Stanford University study found that for every hour we spend on our computers, face-to-face interaction time drops by nearly thirty minutes. On a similar note, a recent poll from the Annenberg School at the University of Southern California's Center for the Digital Future found a 40 percent increase in family members feeling ignored because of other family members' Internet use.

While many people may add dozens of friends to their online life, they run the risk of ignoring the real people around them in their families. According to the report, shared family time fell 30 percent from twenty-six hours a month to under eighteen hours from 2006 to 2008. According to the 2010 Pew Internet & American Life Project, face-to-face communication fell behind texting as teens' favorite way to communicate with friends. Unfortunately, trends like these mean young people talk to each other less and their brains are not wiring networks for communication skills, empathetic listening, and the ability to interpret and respond to nonverbal cues.

Recent discoveries in neuroscience indicate there are specific, critical brain pathways needed to develop interpersonal skills, empathetic behavior, and intuitive instincts. We aren't born knowing exactly how to make a newcomer feel more comfortable or navigate social conflicts; we train ourselves to do this through years of face-to-face social interactions. So while Hussein's daughters may have resented the car's "technology-free zone" rule, this parenting strategy helped combat the social distancing that comes with overimmersion in digital technologies.

Distraction and Multitasking

Many kids use social networking to complement more traditional communication like talking on the phone and spending time together in person. They see social networking and other forms of digital communication as ways to strengthen real-life relationships by extending them into the online world. Research from the University of California's Digital Youth Project shows that kids hang out online with friends they already know in the "real world" through sports, clubs, theater, school, and religious groups.

However, just because kids find new and exciting ways to connect with one another online doesn't mean more is always better. It's more important than ever to pay attention to the clock. These super-communicators can overextend their relationships in the online world, giving their brains little time to rest. Dr. Gary Small, in his book *iBrain*, argues that the digital revolution keeps us in a state of continuous "partial attention," meaning we continuously stay busy and connected without ever truly focusing on one task. Many kids constantly scan for new text messages, chat updates, or other status updates from their online friends.

You will recall from chapter 4 that our thinking—working memory—capacity is seven chunks of information. A seventh grader constantly checking text messages or monitoring her social networking page while doing her math homework is continually pushing "math chunks" to the side as she responds to a friend's message. Frequent interruptions scatter our thoughts and take a big toll on effective thinking. The more complex the thinking needs to be—like math homework—the greater the toll that distractions take. It's even hard for adults to avoid online distractions. Studies show that adults who use computers as part of their work stop what they're doing to check email between thirty and forty times every hour.

I asked a group of high school seniors recently how many of them multitasked. Not surprisingly, all twenty-five students raised their hands. When I asked for examples I heard statements like "When I'm doing my homework I check and send texts, check my social site, and look stuff up on the Web." They also assured me that they could do all these things without skipping a beat. "People your age may not be able to multitask, Dr. Walsh," one girl explained, "but we can because we've grown up with it. Our brains are wired for it."

Like those high school seniors, almost all the young people I ask tell me that they can effectively multitask. They're all wrong. The research is conclusive that when any of us try to multitask we lose speed, accuracy, and efficiency.

It's possible that some kids become dependent on the perpetual connectivity because it feeds their ego and sense of worth. MIT professor of social studies and technology Sherry Turkle argues that teens suffer from anxiety, sleep, and relationship problems from what she calls "always-on technology." Just at the time teenagers need to define boundaries and develop autonomy, always-on technology enables young people to constantly seek validation from other people rather than use their own judgments or feel their own feelings.

KARE 11, the local NBC news station in Minneapolis, recently challenged a group of teenagers to go without their cell phones for five days. Most of the teens participating in the challenge sent about fifty to eighty text messages a day prior to the experiment. One young teen, Mario, commented about the loss of his cell phone: "I feel like I just got a chunk ripped out of me." Interestingly, during the challenge, parents commented that despite the emotional duress, these teens were more focused and attentive without their mobile lifelines. One teenager started drawing again, an activity he'd pretty much abandoned. Another teen's boss commented, "Her ability to concentrate is so much better, I mean, she was unable to associate with people when she has her phone." Not surprisingly, despite these benefits, after the challenge was over all of the teens were thrilled to charge up their phones again and link back into their social lives. Mario said it best: "I feel like I just got my heart and soul back in me."

Kids may not want to log out of their digital lives, but always being connected has created what Lee Rainie, director of the Pew Internet & American Life Project, calls "chronic distraction." Distraction doesn't just take a toll on homework and relationships. It is having a big impact on classroom performance, as I learned firsthand. I had the opportunity to talk with groups of high school students about the teen brain at two different high schools within weeks of one another. At the first school the students were paying attention, engaged, responding and challenging me with good questions. There wasn't a cell phone in sight. It wasn't difficult to understand why, because there were large banners in several corridors, "See it, hear it, lose it!" I found out later that all the teachers enforced the school's strict cell phone policy.

Two weeks later, I had a similar meeting with a group of students at another high school. Midway through the fifty-minute session I realized that more than half the students were paying more attention to their cell phones than to me or one another. There was little engagement and no questions. Besides feeling ignored, I couldn't help but wonder how their cell phone use affected their regular classroom performance, so I decided to check with the teachers after the students had left. "I noticed a lot of the kids were more interested in their cell phones than brain science. Was I boring or is that normal?"

"They were actually more engaged than usual," one of the teachers responded. "It's hard for any of us to keep their attention."

"Isn't there a school-wide cell phone policy?" I asked.

"Sure there is," the same teacher said. "But no one enforces it. If we confiscate phones the students and their parents complain. It's too much hassle so we've all just given up."

Even though most kids have them, cell phones don't belong in the classroom. Parents need to get behind schools' efforts to promote a good learning environment. Here are some suggestions.

1. Before you buy them a cell phone, decide if your child is ready to use it responsibly. "All the other kids have one" is not a good enough reason.
2. Sit down and talk to your child or teen ahead of time. Set the rules for cell phone use. Tell your child that since you are paying the bill, you own the cell phone. Let your child use the phone for a trial period to see if they can follow the rules. Enforce cell-phone-free time.
3. If you do allow Internet access on phones, set limits for online time and online purchasing. If you allow texting, set limits and let your kids know you will monitor their use of texts.
4. Encourage your school to adopt the "See it, hear it, lose it" policy and support its enforcement.

"Butterfly Learning"

As I write this section of the book, I am watching a butterfly through my kitchen window as it lights from flower to flower in the garden. The thought occurs to me that unless we're careful, the Internet will promote "butterfly learning," acquiring knowledge that may be a mile wide but only an inch deep. Although he doesn't use that term, this is the warning Nicholas Carr issues in his provocative book, *The Shallows: What the Internet Is Doing to Our Brains*. Like many parents, Carr argues that it is critical for our children to be able to think deeply and critically and to be able to reflect. Carr cites a growing body of research showing that the constant surfing, browsing, and switching between screens is taking a toll on the quality of our thinking. He reports, for example, new research showing that Web pages are viewed for ten seconds or less. He describes the studies that reveal that hypertexts don't enhance deeper learning as promised and how "power browsing" has replaced thorough reading. Carr opines, "What the Net seems to be doing is chipping away my capacity for concentration and contemplation."

The research on digital technologies' impact on children's brains and learning is still emerging. It is clear, however, that we cannot afford to blindly accept the promises that the giant digital corporations make about the limitless benefits computers and the Internet will bestow on our children. We need to make sure that our kids acquire *all* the skills they need to grow into successful, happy, intelligent adults.

Digital Possibilities

While there are certainly pitfalls like chronic distraction and butterfly learning that parents must guard against, it is also true that the digital revolution provides today's kids with tremendous opportunities. Not only do kids go online to connect with friends and upload their latest videos or photos, but they also explore their interests and find information.

Researchers with the University of California's Digital Youth Project differentiate between "friendship-driven" and "interest-driven" practices. Friendship-driven practices are the many ways young people extend real-world friendships into the online world by texting, connecting through social networking sites, and sharing videos and photos. Interest-driven practices are the ways that young people connect with others who share the same interests and engage in peer-based, self-directed learning, finding resources that may not be available in their communities. Even while "hanging out" online, the Berkeley researchers argue, many young people are picking up critical social and technological skills. When used properly, digital technology can help today's kids gain critical-thinking, problem-solving, and collaboration skills that will serve them well in the global economy.

There are a significant number of promising games and applications that leverage technological advances to create fun, engaging learning experiences for young people. For example, a group of Harvard researchers recently created an interactive computer simulation called River City. Created for middle school, the game is designed to help students learn about disease transmission and the scientific method. The simulation plays like a video game but contains content developed from the National Science Education Standards, the National Educational Technology Standards, and the Partnership for 21st Century Skills. The researchers found that students who played River City showed greater motivation and had higher post-test scores than their peers in the control group. Other games have been designed to help teach literacy skills, math and science, ecology, and problem solving. Video games are not the only medium conducive to learning. Researchers at the University of Minnesota are gathering data from an application called Hot Dish, available on a popular social networking site, which encourages students to share news, read, write, and connect with one another around environmental science issues.

There is also emerging research suggesting that digital technologies can offer unique ways to encourage health and fitness. A whole host of games encourage kids to get up and get active. Some of these "exergames," like Dance Dance Revolution (players must perform dance steps according to onscreen cues) and Wii Fit (players stand on a Wii balance board and engage in various exercises and mini-games to attain personal health goals), have even been incorporated into public schools' physical education programs.

Exergames are considered part of a genre called "health e-games," designed to promote healthy behaviors and lifestyles. Playing new health e-games, kids are encouraged to distinguish between healthy foods and less healthy foods, learn good hygiene, or even gain practice managing chronic diseases.

Unfortunately, while the technology exists to create engaging, interactive digital learning experiences, these aren't necessarily the blockbusters of the year. I was recently discussing some of the educational benefits of video games when a parent raised his hand, exasperated. "Dr. Walsh, I get that video games can teach educational content, but I'm not seeing these games in Target. All my son and his friends want to play are shoot-'em-up games. There don't seem to be many options for those of us who want our kids to learn digital skills without all the blood and violence!"

For parents who are struggling to monitor the content in their kids' video games and are looking for alternatives to popular first-person-shooter games, it can be frustrating that there aren't more options available. Many of the most promising games and applications are academic projects designed to test the teaching capabilities of digital technologies. While these projects can and should be used to spark mass-market games, few of them hit mainstream shopping malls. But these learning games and websites are a growing part of the booming entertainment industry. More and more researchers, parents, and policy makers are committed to finding and promoting games that encourage attainment of 21st-century skills and healthy development.

Too Much Screen Time, Too Much Kid

More and more often, I meet kids who regularly do amazing things. On any old Saturday they might fly a plane, win a championship soccer game, or climb to the top of an ancient pyramid. Then they'll have some lunch. After that, who knows? Maybe they'll race a car on one of the world's most demanding racetracks, single-handedly build an amusement park, or, if there's time, somehow save the universe by jumping across a series of bottomless chasms. And yet many of the very kids who have such grueling Saturdays are overweight and not getting enough exercise, because it's their digital personas out exploring fantastical worlds. And all too often, the real world, in their own backyards, goes unexplored. The average American kid's weekly media diet is over fifty hours a week, while physical activity plummets. And as a recent North Carolina study linking obesity and overweight rates with lack of exercise shows, less physical activity leads to more body fat. It's simple logic. If kids are spending time equivalent to a full-time job sitting in front of screens, they're not outside getting the exercise they need.

We now know that there is a direct connection between screen time and youth obesity. A study from Tufts University shows that children in families watching TV during meals eat fewer fruits and vegetables and consume more snack food. Another team of scientists found that preschool children watching more than two hours of TV a day were more likely to be overweight than children with limits on media use. Research conducted at Baylor College of Medicine in Houston revealed that overweight kids eat half of all their meals in front of the tube. Young couch potatoes don't get the exercise they need to burn off those calories and see a lot of junk food commercials. It also appears that families with TV on during meals tend to buy into TV's message that food preparation should be quick and easy. Pizza and junk foods fit the bill.

Despite this wealth of research and the Centers for Disease Control's declaration that obesity constitutes a "public health emergency," childhood obesity rates in the United States continue to rise. A disturbing report released by the Trust for America's Health and the Robert Wood Johnson Foundation in 2009 found that even after a decade of government action and policies, very little has improved—and in fact, in many cases, things have gotten worse. All fifty states have overweight and obesity rates for children that exceed 20 percent; thirty states have rates over 30 percent, rates double what they were just twenty years ago. This should get our attention, because 80 percent of overweight kids become overweight adults, greatly increasing their risk for heart disease, diabetes, high blood pressure, and other ailments.

The good news is that simply changing the media diet helps reduce the waistline. Stanford University scientists wanted to see what would happen to kids' weight if the only thing they changed was the number of hours they spent watching TV—no additional exercise or diet plan—and found that a reduction of just one hour a day made a difference. When parents ask me what they can do to tame the tube, one of the first things I suggest is to turn off the TV during meals. Doing that increases family communication and prevents couch potatoes from becoming couch melons.

The explosion of exergames and other healthy games, while promising, is unproven as a real solution. Exergames may encourage more physical activity than sitting on the couch watching TV, but they are not a good substitute for the real thing. One group of researchers discovered that children playing Wii Sports expended significantly less energy than children playing "real-life" sports. Ultimately, they found that even exergame play was not intense enough to contribute meaningfully to the recommended daily amount of exercise for children. This doesn't mean that Wii Sports aren't a great alternative to less active video games or TV. It just means that digital solutions aren't a healthy substitute for getting kids outside, involved in sports, running, jumping, and playing. So if it's a rainy day and you are choosing between passive television viewing and Dance Dance Revolution, tell your kids to put on their dancing shoes. But let's not lose focus on what really helps our kids achieve fitness:

1. Get active: with at least one hour of physical activity every day.
2. Eat fruits and vegetables: the best path to good nutrition.
3. Reduce screen time. Balance screen time with an active life and real-world learning.

Cyberbullying

I asked a middle school social worker in Minneapolis, Juan, about his greatest challenge working with students in recent years. "You know, it's like there is an entire hidden world of social drama and trauma that is partially hidden from all the school staff. It's becoming increasingly difficult to manage!"

"What do you mean?" I asked.

"Unfortunately bullying has always been a part of middle school. But it used to happen in the cafeteria or in the hallways, where teachers or hall monitors could intervene quickly. The Internet has made it totally different.

Last week I worked with a young woman whose reputation was trashed overnight. She doesn't even want to come to school.

"A group of girls somehow got a hold of her social networking username and password and changed her entire site around. They put her face on a picture of a pig and put mean language and rumors all over the page. Within about one hour, practically the entire school had seen her new page. She was totally devastated."

Cyberbullying means just what it sounds like. Cyberbullies are kids who act just like bullies from past generations. They pick on other kids and try to humiliate and intimidate them. But instead of waiting around by the door after school, cyberbullies do their damage via text messages, instant messages, and emails from a remote location. Cyberbullies send insults and threats electronically, often many of them. They circulate humiliating pictures or post demeaning descriptions on websites. Unlike the bullies of yesteryear, cyberbullies access their target's private space. Victims are often taunted on home computers or cell phones and feel there is no escape from their torturer. In addition, a cyberbully's damage can spread far and wide at the speed of light. In the old days, a teacher might have been able to intercept a demeaning or hurtful note before it got passed around a class. Now, with a click of a button, cruel messages or damaging pictures make their way around the world and back again before teachers and parents have even caught wind of it.

These aren't isolated cases. Studies show that as many as 34 percent of students have been harassed via the Internet or a cell phone. In some cases, I suspect kids don't understand how poorly they are behaving. Research at the University of California, Davis, explains why. When we're face-to-face with people, a part of our brain called the orbitofrontal cortex constantly assesses "emotional signs and social cues" that help us interact appropriately. It helps control the amygdala, which, you may remember, the brain's "anger center." When we're communicating online, cyberbullying gets out of hand because the orbitofrontal cortex is not involved. We need this brain area to catch the tiny clues that others' facial expressions give us in order to be civil and appropriate.

We need to take cyberbullying just as seriously as we would real-world bullying. Young people tend to act first and think about the consequences later. Many think the Internet offers them anonymity that will protect them from suffering any consequence. Talking about cyberbullying and responsible netiquette online will go a long way toward breaking this sense of anonymity and hold cyberbullies responsible for their actions.

Here are my suggestions for dealing with cyberbullying and netiquette.

1. Tell kids to stop and think twice before posting anything online.
2. Let kids know there is zero tolerance for electronic bullying.
3. Make sure kids understand they should never forward harmful messages or photos.
4. Tell your child that if they are victims, they should not respond, and instead should tell an adult right away.
5. Help kids learn how to apologize and work out conflict with others face-to-face.
6. Monitor what your child sends and receives online, and in texts on cell phones.
7. Make sure your child's school has a policy for cyberbullying. Bring this topic up at a parent meeting and review steps that parents and teachers should take.
8. Make sure kids understand that they should treat people online just like they would like to be treated in real life.

Sexting

Cell phone photo and video cameras present parents with new challenges involving inappropriate content. Sending a text containing sexually explicit language or photos (sexting) is a surprisingly common practice among young people. It's important for young people to know that they lose control once they hit "send." These words and photos travel at the speed of light to people and places unknown, and once on the Internet the pictures are there forever. Recent data shows that one in five youth sext despite the risks for serious long-term consequences, including criminal charges, college admissions rejections, and damaged reputations. With no federal child pornography law on the books, kids committing the same act in different states are finding themselves facing drastically different, sometimes life-altering, punishments. As parents, we need to take responsibility to monitor our children's technology use. Know what text messages your kids send and receive and whom they communicate with online. Talk to your kids about sexting and make sure they realize the consequences, even if they do not get "caught." Sexual photos are rarely only viewed by the original recipient. According to a recent survey, one-third of teen boys said they have seen nude or seminude photos originally meant for someone else.

Most importantly, parents need to talk with their kids about sexuality. Sexy videos and shows on TV, movies, and racy sites on the Internet tell kids sex is no big deal. If we want kids to grow up to be happy, healthy adults we need to give them guidance, values, and clear standards.

Here are some tips to deal with sexting:

1. Make sure your children understand that they lose all control of messages or photos once they hit the "send" button.
2. Remind teens that potential employers or college admissions officers could end up seeing sexting messages or photos.
3. Let your kids know the rules and consequences for sexting.
4. Use cell phone incidents as an opportunity to communicate with your teen about healthy sexuality and relationships.

Cells Phones and Driving

According to the Centers for Disease Control, motor vehicle crashes are the leading cause of death for teens in the United States, responsible for more than one in three teen deaths. In 2005, twelve teens died every day from injuries sustained in an accident. Speeding, alcohol and drug use, and riding without a seat belt have long been contributing factors to teen traffic fatalities. The newest risk, however, is the cell phone. Research shows that talking on a cell phone doubles the accident risk, and texting while driving increases the risk twenty-three fold. That last statistic is very alarming when we combine it with another study in which 86 percent of sixteen- to nineteen-year-old drivers admitted to driving while distracted behind the wheel.

Brain research explains why cell phones and driving don't go together. As I discussed in chapter 4, the brain's attention system is limited to one complex task at a time. Driving involves the visual (occipital lobe) and spatial processing (parietal lobe) parts of the brain. Talking on a cell phone activates the auditory cortex (temporal lobe) and deactivates the visual and spatial. In other words, the brain's attention units are shifted away from driving to conversing. Texting is even more dangerous because it diverts even more of the brain's attention resources. The results include decreased reaction time, missing critical cues like stop signs, slowing down, and wandering between lanes.

Young drivers might counter with statements like "What's the difference between cell phones and talking with a passenger or listening to the radio?" Tell them research shows that drivers adjust conversation with passengers to road conditions and tune out the radio when they need to. Also let them know that there are no gender differences and that using a "hands-free" device doesn't help at all.

Here are my suggestions for talking with teen drivers about cell phones.

1. Make sure your teen understands he or she is not to use a cell phone while driving.
2. If you or someone else calls while he is driving, ask him to either pull over to talk or let it go to voice mail.
3. If applicable, back up your family rules by reminding your teen of your state laws.
4. Be clear there are consequences for DWT (driving while texting), including loss of cell phone or car privileges for a period of time.
5. Talk with your kids about why DWT is not okay. Nurturing a culture shift where DWT is viewed as uncool and dangerous will go a long way toward creating safer roads.
6. If she breaks the rule, no cell phone and no car. It's your teen's life at stake.

Video Game and Internet Addiction

My phone rang about a month ago with a very worried mother on the other end of the line who'd heard me speak about video game and Internet addiction.

"I'm at the end of my rope, and I didn't know who else to call," she said. "I think my fourteen-year-old son, James, is addicted to video games. It all started innocently enough," she said, "playing video games in the basement with his friends. Now he plays all the time, his grades are slipping in school, he's losing sleep, and he's replaced his buddies with online friends. He won't listen if I try to talk to him, and he flies into a rage if I threaten to take the console away. I'm a single parent, and, although I hate to admit this, I'm scared of him."

"How many hours a week do you think your son plays games?" I asked.

"Forty-three," she answered immediately. "I kept track last week."

Millions of kids love video games, especially boys. For most kids and families, video games are a fun part of a healthy media diet. For others, video game play can start to replace or erode important activities like spending time with friends, doing homework, sleeping, and, in some cases, even eating. A growing number of parents are worried that their kids are "addicted" to video games. At first I was reluctant to use this word. As a psychologist, I am sensitive to flippant references to serious clinical disorders. However, as I field more phone calls like the one I just described and talk to more parents, counselors, social workers, and psychologists across the country, it is clear that for some kids, game addiction is becoming a serious problem.

A true addiction means more than doing something a lot. An emerging body of research on video game play and youth helps us understand the scope of the issue. My friend and colleague Douglas Gentile, an Iowa State University researcher, has taken the lead in conducting research on video game and Internet addiction. He likes to use the term *pathological* gaming to describe behavior patterns like the following:

1. Gaming dominates a child's life.
2. Gaming provides a great deal of pleasure.
3. The amount of time playing increases to get the same amount of pleasure.
4. The player experiences negative feelings when he tries to quit.
5. The amount of time playing causes conflict with other people or obligations.
6. The player is unsuccessful in attempts to cut down or quit.

According to his study, one in twelve young gamers exhibit these behavior patterns. He also found that compared with other gamers, they spend twice as much time playing, are more likely to have video game systems in their bedrooms, have trouble paying attention and receive lower grades at school, have more health problems, and are more likely to feel "addicted." Gentile's research gives the medical community and parents alike a better idea of the scope of the problem. There is no question that pathological game play has real-world impact on families everywhere.

Parent-child arguments about video and computer games are part of 21st-century America. So don't panic if you have your share of those, but also don't ignore signs of a real problem with compulsive playing. Here are some tips to make sure computer and video game playing remains a positive part of your children's lives.

1. Set clear ground rules about when, where, how much, and what kind of game play is allowed.
2. Limit game-playing time.
3. Require that homework and other chores be completed first.
4. Keep video and computer games out of kids' bedrooms.
5. Consistently enforce the rules. If your child refuses to cooperate, restrict access for a period of time.
6. If nothing else works, get rid of the games and seek professional help.

21st-Century Parenting

It's easy to become so entranced by our new digital wonders that we forget to have the important conversations about how we want to use technology. While technology expands the world for many, it can trap some into an addiction. Twenty-first-century parents must consciously decide how to use digital technologies as *one* of many tools in our tool kit for raising successful, healthy kids.

DO

- ✓ Have clear and consistent family rules about screen time.
- ✓ Limit the amount of entertainment screen time. I recommend none for babies and toddlers, one hour a day for preschoolers, and two hours for school-age kids. Computer time for research and homework is separate and not included in the two hours.
- ✓ Cross the digital divide! Keep up with the technology so you know what your kids are doing.
- ✓ Follow movie, TV, and video game ratings.
- ✓ Install Internet filtering software for children and Internet tracking software for teens and preteens. Tell your children beforehand that you will be paying attention to their Internet activities.
- ✓ Connect your kids' online world to real-world activities.
- ✓ Encourage your kids' interests with resources on the Web. Guide them toward safe and appropriate digital activities that foster 21st-century skill building.
- ✓ Explore websites with your teen that link kids into social service projects. Help them see they can make a difference.

DON'T

- ✗ Don't have TV, video games, cell phones, or other media on during meals.
- ✗ Don't allow TVs, video games, or computers in the kids' bedrooms.
- ✗ Don't let media time crowd out all the other activities that are important for kids and adolescents.
- ✗ Don't let children play or watch age-inappropriate content.
- ✗ Don't allow kids to meet Internet friends without adult supervision.

- ✗ Don't tolerate cyberbullying, sexting, or driving while cell phoning or texting.
- ✗ Don't ignore red-flag behavior or patterns regarding pathological video game play.

What do I want to continue?

____

____

____

What do I want to change?

____

____

____

FOURTEEN

Wired Differently: Special Needs Brains, Mental Illness, and Chemical Use

The complexity of the human brain is mind-boggling, with 100 billion neurons with the potential for one quadrillion unique connections, more than five dozen hormones, and more than one hundred neurotransmitters. These building blocks operate in a delicate balance, which also presents ample opportunity for brains to malfunction. This chapter examines brains that are wired differently, child and adolescent mental illness, and how alcohol and drugs can cause serious damage to the growing brain.

Since it is beyond our scope to cover everything in depth, I will focus on the most common challenges. There are many books and websites dedicated to providing information for interested or concerned parents who wish to seek additional resources.

Science in Its Infancy

It's important to realize that we are still early in the science of diagnosing brain differences. Frustrated parents can feel like they're getting the run-around as their child receives one diagnosis after another from various specialists. We wish that individual kids fit neatly into the couple dozen diagnostic categories found in the official psychiatric manual known as the *Diagnostic and Statistical Manual of Mental Disorders* (DSM), but that's rarely the case. (The current DSM edition is the fourth, with the fifth, DSM V, due out in 2013.)

As a psychologist with decades of experience counseling children and teens, I can tell you that diagnosis and treatment of mental disorders is still more art than science. Medications are often prescribed on a trial-and-error basis. One boy will respond very well to one medicine while the same prescription will send the next boy into a tailspin even though he presented the same symptoms. The good news is that brain science is helping us make some real progress, and soon our present methods may look rather primitive. As neuroscientist Aditi Shankardass says, "Diagnosing a brain disorder without actually looking at the brain is analogous to treating a patient with a heart problem based on their physical symptoms, without even doing an ECG or chest X-ray to look at the heart. To diagnose and treat a brain disorder accurately, it would be necessary to look at the brain directly."

Pioneer scientists like Shankardass aren't just talking science fiction. She is already using the new imaging technologies to help diagnose brain disorders. For example, she describes the case of Justin Senigar, a seven-year-old patient referred to her clinic with a diagnosis of severe autism. Doctors had given Justin's parents the devastating news that Justin would never communicate normally and might never develop any functional language. However, when Shankardass examined Justin with new brain mapping technology she discovered that he wasn't autistic at all. He was suffering constant brain seizures, which were previously undetectable. After taking seizure medication his vocabulary skyrocketed from three words to three hundred in just two months. Soon he enrolled in a regular classroom and started karate, winning championships. Shankardass believes that as many as half of the developmental disabilities are misdiagnoses.

What's a Parent to Do?

As technology helps us examine the brain directly we will reduce the guesswork. In the meantime, however, we do the best we can with the tools we have. So what should a concerned parent do if her child has a brain that is wired differently or is showing signs of a brain disease?

The first challenge is to distinguish normal from abnormal behavior. This is not as easy as it sounds, because kids are always going through growth spurts and transitioning to new developmental stages. Children and teens grow through predictable stages, but there is no precise path that they all follow in lockstep. As parents, we can err in one of two directions. We can overreact to the normal ups and downs, thereby creating unnecessary pain and anguish. Or, on the other hand, we can miss telling signs of serious issues, unwittingly depriving our kids of the help they might desperately need. The key to striking a balance between these two extremes is knowledge.

Reading warning signs is a matter of recognizing patterns. In the course of this chapter I will list symptoms to look for. Many will find something on the list that will be true for their child. Don't panic. It is not until you see *clusters* of behaviors that persist over time that you should be concerned. If you do become concerned that your son or daughter might be dealing with something more serious than the normal ups and downs of growing up, you should share your concerns with someone familiar with your child who knows a lot about normal development. Second opinions are always a good idea so you get more than one perspective. A good place to start is your child's school or daycare center, since teachers and administrators see your child every day and also deal with a wide range of other kids. If you have a relationship or regular contact with coaches, Scout leaders, or others, they might also give you valuable feedback on your son or daughter. Check out your concerns with your child's pediatrician or family doctor.

If these conversations about your child's behaviors still leave you with questions, you may decide it would be wise to talk with other professionals who work with children. Find professionals with a wide scope of experience with children and youth. There's an old saying, "If the only tool you have is a hammer, everything looks like a nail." Ask the doctor, psychologist, social worker, or nurse if they work with a range of kids with different diagnoses and if they are flexible enough to try different approaches. A school counselor recently asked me if she should be worried if 90 percent of the children referred to a certain child psychiatrist in her town were all diagnosed with bipolar disorder. "Absolutely," I answered. "That's unheard-of."

You need to be a patient but persistent advocate for your child. The mental health system for children and youth in our country is broken. There is a shortage of professionals, and insurance companies are often more interested in controlling costs than in providing adequate care. To make matters worse, funding cutbacks have shuttered a lot of programs and clinics.

Get support. Ask your doctor or school social worker, or go online to find support groups. Other parents with special needs kids will share information and tips and let you know that you are not alone. Avoid any well-meaning friend who feels they know all the answers. They can send you down the wrong path and leave you questioning yourself when their "guaranteed" techniques don't work for you. Parenting a child with a special needs brain can be exhausting. Seek out relatives and friends who will help so you can get a break.

Pay attention to your relationship with your partner and your other children. Separation and divorce rates are higher for the parents of special needs children. Take time for yourselves and avoid taking out your frustrations on one another. Special needs children demand a lot of energy and attention, leaving siblings feeling lost in the chaos. Do what you can to make sure each child gets her needs met even if you have to bring in some friend and family reinforcements to give you time alone with each child. In some instances siblings need protection from an aggressive or assaultive special needs brother or sister.

PARENT TOOL KIT

Wired Differently

This kit can help you determine if you understand the signs of differently wired brains or brain problems.

Yes No

☐ ☐ 1. Because many mental illnesses have a genetic component, I know the mental health histories of both sides of our extended family.

☐ ☐ 2. I know that a pattern of symptoms that lasts for months is more indicative of a problem than any one behavior.

☐ ☐ 3. I know the signs (found throughout this chapter) of the most common brain problems for children and adolescents.

☐ ☐ 4. I know where to get good professional advice if I become worried that my son or daughter might have a serious emotional problem.

☐ ☐ 5. I know what my insurance benefits are for professional mental health services if I ever need them.

☐ ☐ 6. I know that it's important to intervene early for a special needs child.

☐ ☐ 7. Adults in our family model appropriate use of alcohol.

☐ ☐ 8. There are consequences in our family if a child or teen uses alcohol or drugs.

☐ ☐ 9. We have a zero-tolerance policy for tobacco, alcohol, and drug use.

Challenging brains can be found in any family. Being prepared will not prevent a brain disease from striking, but it will enable you to intervene early to get your child or adolescent the help he or she needs.

Attention Deficit Disorders

Some children are born with brains that are a little bit different from most of their peers'. In past centuries they often found a niche that was a good match for their brains. The high-energy boy, for example, might have joined the village hunters at an earlier age and excelled at bringing home food for the family. That same child today, however, might be identified as a "problem child" because we expect all kids to be able to fit neatly into highly structured and organized classrooms where compliance and quiet are prized. This presents real challenges to kids whose brains aren't a natural fit for 21st-century structures, and to their parents.

That was the case for Jeremiah and his parents. A smart ten-year-old who scored at the top of his class on all the standardized tests, Jeremiah was chronically late for class. He also frequently forgot assignments, talked out of turn, blurted out answers, repeatedly misplaced or lost his books and school supplies, and often slipped into conflicts with his teachers. Eventually a thorough evaluation by the family's pediatrician led Jeremiah and his parents to discover that he did not have an attitude problem, nor did he just need to "settle down and pay attention," but instead had attention deficit hyperactivity disorder, better known by its acronym, ADHD. (Attention deficit without the pattern of agitation or hyperactivity is known as attention deficit disorder, or ADD.) That diagnosis did not solve Jeremiah's problems, of course, but it did help him, his parents, and his teachers figure out how best to help him learn in school.

ADD and ADHD are the most common and most controversial mental health diagnoses for today's children and adolescents. They are not new disorders. Educational psychologists and researchers identified the pattern of symptoms more than one hundred years ago. About 5 percent of children have a brain wired this way, and boys are six times as likely to be diagnosed with a type of ADD than girls. Most brains focus on one thing or activity and then shift to another at an appropriate time—the capacity "attention." Kids with ADD or ADHD either cannot make the shift, or their attention is constantly shifting to whatever stimuli come along. Scientists are not sure what causes some brains to have trouble measuring out appropriate attention, but the best research suggests that the disorders are linked to a problem with neurotransmitters. Their malfunction appears to have a genetic component, since parents with ADD and ADHD are five times more likely to have children with attention disorders than are parents who have normal attention spans.

Parents or teachers may consider the possibility of ADD or ADHD for a child who displays the following pattern:

- Has trouble paying attention.
- Makes careless mistakes.
- Is easily distracted.
- Loses things frequently.
- Tends to be impatient.
- Fidgets or squirms.
- Interrupts others.
- Cannot sit quietly.

A thorough evaluation is the key to an accurate diagnosis. A child should never be diagnosed or put on a drug without a comprehensive evaluation that includes a complete medical and family history; a physical examination; interviews with parents, teachers, and the child; completion of specialized behavior rating scales; and observation of the child in a real-life setting.

Medications have proven to be an effective treatment for children who have ADD or ADHD. Drugs like Ritalin, Dexedrine, and Cylert are stimulants that affect the brain's neurotransmitters. These medications help regulate attention and impulsivity and can make a profoundly positive impact in the lives of kids who suffer from an attention disorder. In the most successful cases, however, drugs are not the only means of treatment. Effective treatment should always include:

- Education for the child and the family about attention disorders so everyone knows and understands the problem.
- Behavior management that increases the chances for success. For example, kids with ADD or ADHD respond best to predictable environments where expectations are clear and consistent, and consequences are known ahead of time. Breaking down instructions or directions into steps and strategies for keeping track of assignments and tasks helps a lot.
- Collaboration between home and school. Parents and teachers should work together to identify the specific attention skills that cause the most trouble. For example, some children have trouble beginning a task because the directions are too complicated. Other kids have no trouble with directions, but have a terrible time making a transition from one activity to another. When everyone knows what skills need the most work, progress is more likely.

The organization Children and Adults with Attention-Deficit/Hyperactivity Disorder has a website, www.chadd.org, which provides information on research, resources, and support groups.

Asperger Syndrome

Stephanie, who had some of the same symptoms as Jeremiah, received an ADHD diagnosis in the second grade. However, the prescription for Ritalin, a common ADHD medication, and the best efforts of her parents and teachers didn't help at all. She was extremely stubborn, seemed to go out of her way to argue with other children, and was openly defiant with her teacher. Her mother, Jan, reported a trait to the school psychologist that helped her figure out what was going on. "Stephanie takes language very literally," she told the psychologist. "If I tell her we'll go to the store in ten minutes she has a complete meltdown and calls me a liar as soon as ten minutes are up. There is no gray with her; everything is black and white."

Stephanie has Asperger syndrome, a neurobiological disorder named for a Viennese physician, Hans Asperger, who in 1944 described children who had autism-like behaviors and serious problems with social and communication skills. Asperger, or sometimes called AS, is not without its share of controversy. Some experts include it as part of the autistic spectrum of disorders while others disagree.

Here is a list of the most commonly seen behaviors associated with AS:

- Trouble getting along with other children from inability to figure out social cues, resulting in the child often playing by him or herself.
- Not interested in what other people think, so the child will stop paying attention as soon as he or she has had their say.
- Assumes everyone knows what he or she is thinking and becomes very impatient when other people don't know what is wanted.
- Emotional overreaction.
- Uncomfortable with eye contact.
- Interprets language literally. He or she is confused by puns, jokes, and idioms like "put your thinking cap on."
- "Meltdowns" occur when there is a change in plan or routine.
- Seen as "marching to their own drummer" and are often considered "odd." I know a little boy, for example, who knows all about insects and lectures everyone he meets about them.
- Often lacks physical coordination.

Researchers agree that Asperger syndrome is brain based. This means that children like Stephanie are not deliberately trying to be difficult. Some brain scientists believe that the "mirror neurons," talked about in chapter 3, don't function properly in an Asperger brain. That would explain why these kids have so many problems reading social cues and having empathy. The scientists still haven't figured out which brain circuits account for the communication and language problems that plague these children.

There is no medication for Asperger, but education and training interventions are proving successful. These children can learn the social skills that seem to come naturally to other children. For example, parents and teachers can teach these kids how to take turns and let other people talk. While most children don't have to learn what an angry face looks like, kids like Stephanie need to learn to identify facial expressions the same way they tackle other school subjects. The good news is that children with Asperger syndrome can learn the skills of friendship.

There is a very helpful website, www.aspergersyndrome.org, where parents can keep up with research and find help.

Childhood Depression

Sally and John came to see me for marriage counseling. Unlike some couples I'd worked with, John and Sally weren't at the point of breaking up. They both just felt there was something missing. Sally explained that she thought they had drifted apart due to the stress of full-time jobs and raising three kids. "We work well together," John agreed. "We seldom fight and coordinate busy schedules without much conflict," he explained. "But we're both worried that the spark in our relationship has gone out. We want to get back on track before it's too late."

Sally and John made quick progress, prioritizing their marriage and making time in their busy lives to pay attention to one another. In our final wrap-up session Sally brought up her concerns about their nine-year-old middle child. "Dr. Walsh," she said, "I'd like to ask you about Spencer. John and I are seeing some changes and are wondering if we should bring him to a counselor."

"Tell me why you're worried," I replied.

"There's been a real change over the past four or five months," Sally began. "He used to enjoy sports, but he just told us last week he doesn't want to join the park board baseball team this spring. He has a lot of trouble falling asleep and his appetite isn't what it used to be." John added, "He spends more and more time alone in his room with his video games. We've put limits on his game time, but he constantly complains he has nothing else to do. He doesn't want to get together with his friends anymore, so we thought that maybe there were some unresolved arguments."

"John works with the father of one of Spencer's friends," Sally explained, "so John talked with him over coffee last week. The other boy's dad said that he wasn't aware of any disagreements between the boys. He told John that his son couldn't figure out why Spencer didn't want to play together anymore."

I was beginning to suspect depression so I asked, "Does Spencer seem more negative than he used to be?"

"Definitely," Sally answered. "That's another real change over the past six months."

"It could be that Spencer is suffering from depression," I said.

"Depressed children are different from depressed teens or adults. They aren't able to articulate their feelings the way older kids and adults can. In fact, he may not even realize that something's wrong. However, you've described enough behavioral cues to cause me to think that it's worth seeing a specialist."

I referred the family to an excellent child psychiatrist I know, and, sure enough, Spencer was suffering from depression. His treatment was a combination of a low dose of Prozac, a medicine that regulates the neurotransmitter serotonin, and therapy with a child psychologist. Spencer responded very well and within months was choosing his friends over video games and looking forward to joining the fall soccer team.

Childhood depression usually shows up in behaviors, not statements, so parents should pay attention to the following signs:

- Cries easily and appears sad most of the time.
- Does not express happiness with special activities or playthings.
- Withdraws from friends and activities they previously enjoyed.
- Becomes unusually touchy and easily upset.
- Change in appetite.
- Sleep problems. Difficulty falling or staying asleep.
- Difficulties concentrating and decision making.
- Underperformance at school.
- Pervasive negative attitude.
- Sluggish and low energy.
- Vague physical complaints.

Mental Health America has an excellent website with information about a wide range of children's behavioral and mental health disorders, www.mentalhealthamerica.net.

Teen Depression and Suicide

Adolescents suffering from depression show the same symptoms as children, but they are often more adept at verbalizing their sadness. It is important to know that there are some significant male-female differences when it comes to depression. The first is the change in depression risk that takes place at puberty. Boys are at greater risk before puberty but the reverse is true afterward. The other distinction is suicide risk.

The increased risk for suicide is probably the most frightening aspect of teen depression. On the rise for over fifty years, the high rate of suicide now makes it the third leading cause of death among teens.

Jeffrey was a smart, popular, and outgoing senior at the high school where I was a counselor. I knew him from classes I had taught, but I had never seen him in the counseling office for either personal or college questions. No one was surprised when word spread that he was accepted into one of the country's most selective colleges. After all, he was a National Merit Scholarship finalist, good athlete, and student government officer. Everyone, however, was completely shocked and devastated when Jeffrey hanged himself two days after getting the acceptance letter in the mail. As I met with groups of grieving classmates the most common statement was some version of "I can't believe it. I can't figure it out. Jeff had everything going for him. He was the nicest guy in the class. Everyone liked him."

As discussed in the chapter about brain-based differences between the genders, the teenage boy is less likely to talk about suicidal feelings than the girl, but more likely to commit suicide. Moreover, he is more likely to choose more lethal methods like guns or hanging. It's important, therefore, to be on the lookout for subtle clues. "Nothing matters." "What do I care? I won't be around forever." "I probably won't see you again." These kinds of statements may be verbal hints that an adolescent—boy or girl—is contemplating suicide. Suicidal teens may start to give away some of their possessions or become preoccupied with songs of sadness and despair. Other signals include neglecting their personal appearance, running away, using drugs or alcohol to deal with emotional pain, withdrawing from friends, and losing interest in pleasurable activities. Teens at risk for suicide often complain of being a bad person or feeling "rotten inside." Whether these signs indicate a real suicide risk or whether they are a call for help is not always immediately clear, but you should always take these symptoms seriously. Seek professional help immediately if you have concerns about your child being depressed or suicidal. Get in touch with your child's high school counselor, pediatrician, or family doctor.

Anxiety Disorders

Dennis had always been shy and retiring. As a preschooler he would cling to one of his parents if other children approached him on the playground. In school he hardly ever raised his hand even though he usually knew the answer. His parents described him as much more "touchy" than his two brothers and were concerned that he had so much trouble falling asleep at night. Dennis was also a worrier. It didn't matter whether it was about homework, tests, a soccer game, or an upcoming birthday party: he could find something to fret about.

Is spite of his protests, Dennis's parents insisted that he attend overnight Boy Scout camp during the summer following fifth grade. Halfway through the week he phoned home begging his parents to pick him up. "All the other kids are mean," he cried. They insisted that he stay for the week. When they picked him up the following Saturday he screamed at them all the way home for being "so mean."

The Scout camp crisis prompted Dennis's parents to take him to see a child psychologist. Within a few sessions the psychologist had diagnosed Dennis with "generalized anxiety disorder." All children become anxious at times, but Dennis had a brain that was so finely tuned to detect danger that it triggered a fear response every time he turned around. He had an "overactive alarm system."

There is a brain chemical called GABA, which stands for *gamma-aminobutyric acid*. I prefer to call it the "brain's tranquilizer." Recent research shows that almost 20 percent of children are like Dennis—born with low levels of GABA, leaving them in a constant state of fear. Of course, they don't know they're anxious, because they have always felt that way. In other words, anxiety is normal for them. Kids like Dennis are often called shy when they are young. That's because they're in a constant state of anxiety, which causes them to hang back and act clingy.

Dennis had a fairly straightforward case of anxiety disorder. Some children or teens have a type of anxiety called obsessive-compulsive disorder, or OCD. They become preoccupied with thoughts that something bad is going to happen to them. They can't shake scary thoughts or images. Children with OCD become fixated on certain behaviors and are terrified that disaster will strike if they don't perform the "rituals."

There are also children who suffer panic attacks, in which their hearts race and they sweat, feel dizzy, and have chest pains. Other children might develop phobias, in which they experience paralyzing fears focused on specific things like enclosed spaces, dogs, bugs, or monsters.

Intense and unfounded fear is the common denominator in all the anxiety disorders. In some cases a physician might prescribe a medication, but it is more common to use counseling techniques that teach relaxation, meditation, and positive self-talk.

Ned Hallowell's book, *Worry* (Ballantine, 1998) is a good resource for parents who suspect their child might have one of the anxiety disorders. In addition, the Anxiety Disorders Association of America has a very good website for parents whose children have "worried brains," at www.adaa.org/living-with-anxiety/children.

What About Medication?

Many parents are understandably nervous about introducing powerful chemicals into a growing brain. Concerns about overprescribing, long-term damage, side effects, and dependency should be taken seriously. Nevertheless, medications can play an important role when brains aren't working properly. Some can be used for a period of time, allowing the child or teen to develop coping strategies that will eventually eliminate the need for medicine. Other conditions might require a lifetime of medication just as a type 1 diabetic needs a lifetime of insulin.

Drugs alone, however, are never the answer. They should only be used if they are combined with counseling and other behavioral and social skills training. Here are my suggestions for parents considering medication.

- Make sure the prescribing physician is an expert in children and adolescents.
- Make sure you get a thorough evaluation before medications are prescribed.
- Know what type of medication is being recommended and how it works.
- Ask how this drug might react with other medication that your child or teen is taking.
- Don't hesitate to ask the doctor how effective this drug has been for other children.

- Ask the doctor to describe the short- and long-term side effects.
- Search out information on the drug in books and on reputable Internet sites.
- Ask the doctor how and how often he or she will monitor side effects and the drug's effectiveness.
- Be sure the doctor describes in clear language any symptoms that you should watch for that might mean trouble.
- Get clear directions about drug administration and storage. Should the drug be taken on an empty or full stomach, first thing in the morning, etc.? Also, find a pharmacist who will answer your questions and listen to your concerns. Pharmacists usually know more about the medications than doctors do.

Tobacco, Alcohol, and Drugs

During the early 1990s I served as the executive director of one of the largest chemical dependency treatment programs for youth in the country at the University of Minnesota Medical Center, Fairview, in Minneapolis. In that role I saw firsthand the devastation that chemicals can cause in the lives and families of adolescents. More recently I have served as a consultant to the National Center on Addiction and Substance Abuse (CASA) at Columbia University on adolescent chemical use, abuse, and addiction. While we have made some progress reducing child and teen tobacco use, it is disturbing that the epidemic of teen alcohol and drug use continues to rage.

Advances in brain research give us more reason than ever to redouble our efforts to prevent youthful chemical use. We know that the adolescent brain is not the same as the adult brain and it should not surprise us that tobacco, alcohol, and drugs affect it differently in three important ways.

1. THE YOUNG BRAIN BECOMES MORE EASILY ADDICTED.

We have known for more than fifty years that the younger a boy or girl is when they start to smoke, drink, or use drugs, the greater the risk for addiction. We used to think the reason was a lack of experience or maturity. Now we know the risk is brain based. More than a mature brain, a growing brain immediately goes to work creating additional receptors for tobacco, alcohol, and drugs. These chemicals all trigger the release of dopamine, the neurotransmitter that makes us feel good; when the receptors are filled with any of these drug molecules, the dopamine level in the brain rises, creating a sense of pleasure. What the young drinker or user doesn't realize is that the brain has created more "docking stations" for the alcohol or drug. When those stations are filled, dopamine levels remain high. When they aren't filled, however, the dopamine levels plummet, resulting in negative feelings. There is a very strong temptation to restore the pleasurable feelings by smoking, drinking, or using again, a process that is more likely to happen in the young brain than in the mature brain.

2. THE DAMAGE THAT CHEMICALS DO IS GREATER, ON A DOSE-FOR-DOSE BASIS, THAN THE SAME AMOUNT WOULD DO IN THE ADULT BRAIN.

Heavy alcohol provides the clearest example of the increased damage caused by substances to growing brains because it interferes with the encoding of new memories. Alcohol interferes with a neurotransmitter called glutamate, which aids the neurons in learning and in storing new memories—when neurons fire together, glutamate helps them wire together, and thus makes them more likely to fire together in the future—which is why it's hard for anyone to remember what happened after a night of heavy drinking. But its effect on glutamate is *most* pronounced in the adolescent brain. Because adolescent brains are furiously blossoming, pruning, firing, and wiring, glutamate is even more crucial to adolescents than it is to people in other age groups. If glutamate effectiveness drops even a little bit, it can have a very negative effect on the sensitive adolescent brain. Research shows that heavy alcohol use can impair adolescent memory function by as much as 10 percent.

Additional evidence shows that heavy-drinking adolescents have a smaller hippocampus, the brain structure that is key to recording new memories, than nondrinkers. Thus adolescents who drink a lot of alcohol have more memory and learning problems than adults who drink the same amount, because their brains are more susceptible to damage. Those problems persist into adulthood.

3. WARNING SIGNALS THAT THE BRAIN'S BEING AFFECTED APPEAR LATER RATHER THAN SOONER.

Young drinkers or users are *over*sensitive to damage and *under*sensitive to the warning signs. For reasons that we do not yet understand, the sedation effects are not as pronounced in the adolescent brain. The impairment of motor coordination is also delayed. That means that adolescents don't experience the two major warning signals that go off in the adult brain—sedation, or tiredness, and motor problems, like slurring words or stumbling—which indicate "Watch out!" It takes an adolescent longer before sedation and motor coordination problems take effect. By then, they can be dangerously in trouble. In the absence of warning signals that tell them to stop, adolescent drinkers tend to drink or use more than adults. Adolescents like to brag that they can "hold their liquor," but just because they're not showing outward signs of alcohol impairment doesn't mean they're *not* doing themselves serious damage.

Parents, the Antidrug

The research is very clear about what parents should do to protect kids from the dangers that chemicals pose. We *have* to stay connected to our kids. Whether or not they ever get involved with alcohol or drugs, adolescents need to know that their parents know about, and care about, what goes on in their lives.

This advice is confirmed by a study from CASA. Researchers found that teenagers with "hands-on" parents are four times less likely to become involved in smoking, drinking, and drug use than kids who don't have hands-on parents. The scary part is that only 27 percent of American adolescents describe their parents as "hands-on."

What does being hands-on really mean? For starters, it means knowing where your kids are. In addition to making sure they have their cell phone, have them leave a phone number where they can be reached. Asking them about their day and knowing where they like to go is important, too.

Being connected means knowing who your kids' friends are. What do they like to do? Where do they like to go together? Why are they friends? These are the kinds of questions to which you should know the answers. When your kids' friends come to your home, try to engage them in conversation. You don't need to grill them to get a good sense of what makes them tick. If your teenager doesn't bring friends by the house, find out why. Make sure your home is a friendly place for your kids' friends. Stock up on some extra snacks so they will be comfortable coming around. Our kids' friends nearly ate us out of house and home, but we got to know them all. And in luring them to our house with food, we were glad to know they were in a safe place instead of out on the street somewhere.

Having curfews and enforcing them can seem to put a barrier between you and your teenager, but curfews are very important. Teens with curfews have a greater sense of accountability. They know their waiting parents are likely to figure out what condition they are in when they arrive home. In addition, if an adolescent knows that curfews are serious business, he is more likely to tell you where he is going if he is lobbying for an extension. Most important, he won't be out all night.

Serious brain problems aren't issues that parents can handle on their own. Many parents feel like they need outside help at some point. That's why it is important to pay attention. As parents we need to look out for the clues and seek help when we are in over our heads.

The disorders I have described in this chapter are some of the most common, but they are by no means the only mental health disorders that afflict children and adolescents. If you are concerned about the mental health of your son or daughter and the patterns you are noticing do not fit onto any of the lists of symptoms in the previous pages, that doesn't mean you should ignore what you're seeing. If you suspect something is seriously wrong, you may need help from a professional to figure out what the problem is—or just to allay your fears.

DO

- ✓ Look for a pattern of symptoms that persist for a matter of months if you are concerned that your son or daughter has a mental health problem.
- ✓ If you're worried, seek advice from a teacher, counselor, coach, family doctor, or other adult who knows your son or daughter.
- ✓ Get recommendations from people you trust for professionals or programs that are competent and caring.
- ✓ If you need professional help, find out exactly what your insurance policy covers and how the system works. Ask as many questions as you need, to know what your options and rights as a parent are.
- ✓ Get recommendations from school counselors, social workers, pediatricians, or family doctors for the best help possible for your son or daughter. If your health plan restricts you to a designated network, get recommendations about the professionals in the network. In addition, find out how to get approvals for care outside the network, even if you have to pay more.
- ✓ Be open to recommendations about medications, but make sure you learn about any side effects.
- ✓ Get help for yourself. There are often support groups for parents and siblings of mentally ill teens. They can provide information and emotional support to get through difficult times.
- ✓ Model responsible use of tobacco, alcohol, and drugs.
- ✓ Have regular conversations about alcohol, tobacco, and drugs and have clear expectations regarding use, and consequences for violating them.

DON'T

- ✗ Don't ignore signs and symptoms of serious mental illness. Just like physical disease, diseases of the brain can strike any family.
- ✗ Don't panic. Tremendous strides have been made in recent years. I have seen adolescents so incapacitated by depression that they could not lift their heads return to a happy productive life in a matter of months.
- ✗ Don't hesitate to ask professionals as many questions as are necessary to understand both the problem and the treatment.
- ✗ Don't accept care from a professional without appropriate credentials to work with children or adolescents.
- ✗ Don't accept care from a professional who seems rushed or unfamiliar with your child's case, doesn't address your concerns, or doesn't communicate well.
- ✗ Don't accept a prescription for medication without asking questions about side effects and effectiveness. Tinkering with the chemistry of the brain is always serious and is still as much an art as it is a science.
- ✗ Don't accept a medication-only treatment plan for an adolescent. The research is clear that medication with some form of counseling is far superior to medication alone. The medication may correct a chemical imbalance in the brain, but it does not rewire the brain to develop more appropriate skills and behaviors.
- ✗ Don't send mixed messages about tobacco, alcohol, or drug use.
- ✗ Don't ignore signs that your son or daughter is drinking, smoking, or using.
- ✗ Never give up hope for a mentally ill child.

What do I want to continue?

____

____

____

What do I want to change?

____

____

____

FIFTEEN

Brain-Wise Daycare, Preschool, and School Decisions

My coworker Heather, who is expecting her second child, recently complained how hard it is to figure out daycare. "It's so stressful to find the best provider, manage the finances, and hope that there's an opening when you need it," she said. "On top of that, my son's provider won't take infants, so Josh and I will run to two different places every morning and evening."

Heather and Josh aren't alone. Besides the emotional difficulty of leaving a baby with a stranger, there are many financial and logistical factors parents consider in selecting daycare. "Working here doesn't help, either," Heather added. "Learning all about brain development just adds to the pressure," Heather explained. "Making a mistake has huge consequences."

In one sense Heather's correct. Knowing how important a child's first years are for his or her future development can make a parent crazy with worry. In another sense, however, knowing more about children's brain development will make young parents very wise consumers as they ask the right questions and evaluate options in a more informed manner.

Brain research tells us a lot about what children need to succeed in school and life. We've covered a great deal of this research in the pages of this book. Some childcare centers make good use of this information, while others don't. The savvy parent will work brain-based knowledge into the complex calculus of a childcare choice. It doesn't necessarily mean there is one "correct" placement. Every family and every child is different. But understanding some of the key elements of brain development enables us to ask more informed questions.

PARENT TOOL KIT

Choosing Childcare, Preschools, and Schools

These questions are designed to help you evaluate your checklist to make sure it includes brain-based information in your childcare and educational choices.

Yes No

☐ ☐ 1. I know that a savvy provider or teacher understands real self-esteem is built through competence and achievement.

☐ ☐ 2. I'm looking for a provider or teacher who is aware of boy-girl brain differences without getting locked into stereotypes.

☐ ☐ 3. I know how critical it is for providers and teachers to truly enjoy their profession.

☐ ☐ 4. I need to know the good nutrition practices of my provider or school.

☐ ☐ 5. I want to make sure daycare or classroom activities are flexible enough to respond to an individual child's needs.

☐ ☐ 6. I know to ask what ongoing training staff members receive so they can stay up with the latest research.

The more yes answers to the questions in this tool kit, the better prepared you are to make a well-informed choice for your child.

Infant Care

To find care for her baby after she returned to work three months later, Heather needed to decide whether to leave her infant with a relative, friend, or licensed or unlicensed provider. Young parents who have grandparents nearby and available are fortunate because grandparents are usually highly motivated to provide excellent care—a loving relationship is, after all, the most important ingredient for healthy brain development. Other relatives are often similarly invested. There are, of course, dedicated professionals who also do a wonderful job. Some are licensed and they follow state-mandated requirements, while others are unlicensed providers whose only accountability is to the parents.

Here are some questions and suggestions for parents to keep in mind no matter what infant care option they are considering.

- What type of experience, training, or background does the provider have with infants?
- What is the ratio of providers to infants? Many states allow licensed daycare centers to staff at a five-to-one ratio; some go as high as six. The lower the better, with many experts recommending one caregiver for every two or three babies under fifteen months.
- What is the turnover rate of infant caregivers? How long have the present providers been on staff?
- Visit the center more than once and ask what their drop-in policy is.
- What is the policy on sick children and how are emergencies handled?
- Observe the staff interacting with the babies and look for games, songs, reading, and lots of talking with the babies.
- Make sure the providers don't let babies lie in their cribs when they're awake.
- Do they take the babies outside when the weather permits?
- Take note of safety and sanitary practices like wearing gloves during diaper changing, sanitizing changing tables, food preparation, etc.
- Observe the physical connection with the babies to make sure they are touched, hugged, and held.

Toddler Daycare

Choosing a daycare center for toddlers and preschoolers raises additional questions to the ones listed above. Here are some additional tips.

- Visit the center more than once and include your son or daughter in at least one visit.
- Check references and ask if you can speak with other parents.
- Ask about the staff-to-child ratio. Avoid any provider where the ratio exceeds ten to one. Once again the lower the better.
- Ask about the experience, background and training, and turnover rates of the staff.
- Find out if and how children are separated by age.
- Ask about the center's philosophy of child learning. What things do they consider the most important?
- Is the environment inviting, interesting, and stimulating?
- Watch how staff and children interact. Is the atmosphere relaxed? Friendly? Comfortable?

- How are media used? Very few states have any policies on the amount of screen time, so it's important to know when and how media are used. If a TV or video screen dominates the room, it's a sign the provider may rely on media as a babysitter.
- Nutrition and physical exercise are important. What's the provider's policy and practice?
- How is discipline handled?
- Get involved as a volunteer. This is a good way to get a firsthand look at your child's experience.
- Is there opportunity for free play?
- The most important question of all is after your son or daughter enrolls: "How does she or he like it?"

Preschool or Nursery School Programs

Like many parents, my wife, Monica, and I spent a lot of time thinking about where to send our first son, Dan, to preschool. We were lucky to have a lot of options, and each promised to set our son up for success in elementary school. We learned each program was quite different, with varying child-instructor ratios, schedules, and philosophies. The only way we could really get a sense of the school was to visit them. Monica, excited to see the schools in action, scheduled a visit for a preschool connected with a highly regarded elementary school. The director showed her around the building, shared the philosophy of the school, and described an average day in the life of their preschoolers.

"We really focus on academics here," she said. "Your child will enter grade school knowing far more skills than many of the other children. Some people don't think that three- and four-year-olds are capable of sitting down for longer periods of time to work through these concepts, but we've been amazed at what they are able to accomplish," the director said.

"Interesting!" Monica replied. "Can I see a classroom?"

"Of course!" said the director.

The director guided her into a brightly lit, cheery room where there were five little tables surrounded by four or five pint-sized chairs. On the table, in front of each chair, lay a paper worksheet and crayon, awaiting the little three- to four-year-olds who would soon grasp them in their tiny hands. Monica knew why the director was excited to show the space off. It was beautiful. Nevertheless, Monica had an uneasy feeling. After chatting a bit more, Monica finished the tour, thanked the director, and told her we would visit other preschools before making a decision. "Don't wait too long," the director added. "There's a lot of demand so we'll be filling up long before summer."

Actually, Monica had already made up her mind. "There's nothing wrong with worksheets," she told me that night. "But from everything I know about child development, preschool is a time for learning with play and imagination! There will be plenty of time for sit-down academic work later. I want a preschool where Dan will be excited to learn!"

After a few more visits we were lucky enough to enroll Dan, and eventually Brian and Erin, in the nursery school at the University of Minnesota's Institute of Child Development. Our kids had some paper-based activities, but their days focused on plenty of free play, group activities, and time exploring outside. The large classrooms had dress-up and construction areas, playhouses, arts and crafts, and books galore. While the staff was trained in child development, it was clear the primary reason they were hired was their warmth and sensitivity with children.

"I remember being so nervous to leave Dan the first day," my wife still remembers. "But I will never forget picking him up that afternoon. After all the tears he shed after I left, I thought for sure he would be waiting for me at the door. Little did I expect he would barely notice my arrival. I scanned the room of children wondering where in the world he was. Then I spotted him.

"He was up in the playhouse, wearing an apron, and cooking a magnificent pretend dinner for a few other children and an attentive group of stuffed animals. I knew we'd made the right choice when I had to drag him away. He chatted the whole way home about all the things he did."

Our experience choosing a preschool illustrates the divergent approaches schools take to child learning and development. Both the preschools described above focused on teaching kindergarten readiness skills like letters, sounds, colors, and numbers. But the schools' guiding philosophies shaped the way these skills were taught to children. It's important that you choose the environment for your child that best fits his or her temperament, learning style, and emotional needs. Some centers and elementary schools emphasize hands-on learning and creativity while other programs are more structured and adult guided. Brain science can't tell you the right choice, but it does highlight experiences that are important to getting children off to the right start.

Ready to Learn

All U.S. presidential candidates since 1982 have made K–12 education reform and improvement a centerpiece of their campaigns for a very simple reason: students in other countries outperform our kids, with dire economic consequences looming. One educational program after another is touted as the remedy, but so far the main beneficiary is the testing industry. Setting standards and measuring progress has become an obsession. The result is children who are tested from the moment they enter school and again repeatedly as they progress from grade to grade. Some states game the system for political reasons by setting low standards. Other states with higher standards put many underperforming schools on lists that trigger remedies ranging from increased funding to state takeover.

Everyone wants smart, successful, and healthy kids. The problem is the abundant conflicting messages on how to accomplish this goal. Testing, charter schools, vouchers, incentive-based compensation for teachers, and more testing all have their champions. I believe brain science helps us cut through the hype and directs us to identify the basic building blocks for academic success. Let's start with the out-of-school factors essential for children's school achievement before turning to school improvement. Every chapter of this book focused on the fundamentals a child needs before he or she ever sets foot in kindergarten.

- The first years of life are critical to later school and career success. It all starts with early childhood experiences. Our schools do a better job if kids arrive ready to learn. Language-rich environments, free play that fosters creativity and imagination, focused attention and memory skills, good nutrition, adequate exercise, and managing stress are all building blocks for a school-ready brain.
- Early childhood education is critical and pays a very good return on investment. In too many school districts, it's an afterthought. In Minnesota, where I live, recent funding cuts to early childhood education were ill advised and counterproductive.
- Self-discipline is twice as strong a predictor of school success as intelligence. While letter, color, and number recognition are important, I explained in chapter 9 that teaching children how to manage their behavior is even more so. Every minute a K–12 teacher spends on behavior is time taken away from critical learning. That's the reason Monica and I created the Say Yes to No Parenting Program—to teach parents the skills to foster this critical trait in their children.
- In chapter 2 I explained how important it is to reinforce effort and hard work. Accomplishments in school and career all require effort and we need to teach this to our children.

Redefining Kindergarten Readiness

What skills do incoming kindergartners need on the path to academic success? A child's first two years in school fundamentally affect his or her future academic performance. If a child comes to kindergarten "ready to learn," then the skills for reading, math, science, and the arts will find fertile ground. Conversely, if a child shows up in kindergarten not "ready to learn," then valuable time and energy will be lost not only for that child, but also for the other children in the room.

Currently kindergarten readiness assessments usually focus on pre-academic skills, such as knowing your first and last name, colors, numbers, etc., to measure if a child will be successful in kindergarten. However, I asked hundreds of kindergarten and first grade teachers which skills were most important for success in their classrooms. Here's what they reported:

- Able to take turns.
- Able to pay attention to a task.
- Able to stick to and finish a task.
- Able to tolerate some frustration.
- Not reaching for another child's belongings.
- Able to follow a two-step direction like "hang up your coat and get your pencils out."
- Able to sit still for a small-group time.
- Maintaining self-control during transition time.
- Not interrupting inappropriately.
- Able to cooperate with other children during play.
- Able to ask for help.
- Able to tolerate short amounts of quiet time.
- Able to wait for short periods.

These executive-function skills prepare any child to learn all the other cognitive and academic skills that will launch them on the road to school success.

K–12 Schools

Children will spend about thirteen thousand hours with teachers between the time they start kindergarten and the moment they stroll across the stage to receive their high school diplomas. Understanding what neuroscience says about brains and learning enables us to have informed conversations with teachers and schools and to lobby school boards and state legislators to make better decisions about school reform.

PHYSICAL ACTIVITY AND SCHOOL PERFORMANCE

Eliminating recess and physical education in favor of "serious academic subjects" has been a mistake. Exercise, as we learned in chapter 7, doesn't detract from learning; it enhances it. Yet 20 percent of elementary schools in the United States abolished recess to increase classroom time and improve academic achievement. The Centers for Disease Control and Prevention report that only a third of high school students get the current recommended levels of exercise.

Brain science shows us that physical activity is the brain food our children need to excel in school. In five experimental controlled studies, students who spent more time in physical education or school-based physical activity maintained or improved their grades and standardized test scores, even though they got less classroom instruction than the control groups. Physically fit children identify visual stimuli more quickly than sedentary ones, concentrate better, are less likely to be disruptive, and can allocate more cognitive resources to a task for longer periods of time. As you might recall, physical activity produces BDNF, what neuroscientist John Ratey calls "Miracle-Gro for the Brain." Another neuroscientist, John Medina, says, "Cutting off physical exercise—the very activity most likely to promote cognitive performance—to do better on a test score is like trying to gain weight by starving yourself."

"CULTURE OF WELLNESS"

David Jones, the principal at Eisenhower Middle School in Everett, Washington, faced enormous challenges, including dismally low standardized test scores, outdated facilities, and a burned-out staff. His school needed major reform and maybe even a "Hail Mary pass" to turn things around. David, convinced the factors affecting student learning extended far beyond the classroom, resisted pressure to focus on raising test scores. He took the all-too-unusual step of asking the kids themselves what got in the way of their learning. They told him they spent most of their day hungry and tired, anxious, unsafe, and depressed. He heard the same story from parent and teachers. He knew cramming in more instructional time would only make things worse for everyone. He knew enough about brain research to realize that stress, poor nutrition, and lack of exercise were taking a toll on classroom performance.

He formed a team to craft a plan to create a "culture of wellness" within the school. They identified three short-term priorities: increase staff member wellness, increase student fitness, and enhance the nutritional value of food and beverages served on campus. They went into the community to form partnerships that resulted in rock climbing events, themed staff dinners where teachers could socialize and connect, and yoga breaks. They raised money to wean themselves off the revenue generated by soda sales. They served more nutritious food in the cafeteria and got the students moving again. Five years later the number of students meeting state standards increased dramatically, school climate was better, and the achievement gap for students of color shrank. The *Seattle Times* recognized Eisenhower Middle School as one of the most improved middle schools in the state and the National Middle School Association honored Jones as a "Team That Made a Difference."

BRAIN-BASED LEARNING STRATEGIES

Our schools are usually organized with age-based levels and curricula. This wasn't always the case. For most of human history, education meant an apprentice who learned from someone with more knowledge and experience. The Industrial Revolution changed that approach into one where children were grouped by age and taught a single, standardized curriculum. While the new system was more efficient and egalitarian, we lost most of the individualized personal instruction that was a hallmark of apprenticeships.

Students enter the classroom with wildly different capacities based on their birth date, their unique brain wiring, the timetable for their brain's cognitive development, and their previous experience. Consider, for example, a school district with a September first cutoff date to enter kindergarten. A girl born later in September has a brain almost 20 percent more developed than her classmate born in August. That's why I discourage parents from applying for early kindergarten enrollment.

In addition to the timing of birth dates, the latest brain science shows that as children progress through cognitive development stages, activity shifts to different circuits. The timing of those transitions, however, varies a great deal. That's why intelligence and screening tests for gifted and talented programs have very poor predictive value for children younger than eleven. Some children who qualify for gifted and talented classes in the first grade, for example, would not qualify if retested in the fifth grade. Conversely some truly gifted students aren't identified because they were tested before their "thinking circuits" stabilized. For these reasons many children do not have brains sufficiently wired to read or achieve other skills at the age level dictated by state standards or for schools to put much stock in testing in preschool and the early elementary grades.

The maturation variability has very profound implications because of how children's brains—actually all of our brains—respond to academic challenges and problems. Human brains enjoy problem solving when they are operating in what we could call the "sweet spot." On the one hand, if the cognitive challenge is too difficult for our brains, we become frustrated and disengage. On the other hand, we also disengage if the tasks are too simple, because our brains become bored.

I recently conducted a teachers' workshop where two questions made the "sweet spot" clear. I asked the one hundred elementary school teachers what they would do if I distributed an advanced calculus problem and directed them to solve it. "I've never had calculus so I'd immediately give up," piped up a young woman. Another added, "I did take calculus, but it was more than ten years ago, so I'd check out, too." Then I asked them what their reaction would be if I asked them to work on sheets of single-digits addition problems, like 2 + 3 and 5 + 4, for thirty minutes. "I'd be bored within a minute," one of the teachers responded. "Would your mind wander?" I asked. "Sure," came her instant reply. "That is how all our brains work," I added. "Our brains disengage if a task is too hard or too easy. On the other hand, our brains get a shot of dopamine, the 'feel good' brain chemical, when they operate in the sweet spot."

Does this mean we should close schools and have completely individualized instruction? Of course not, but successful schools pay attention to individual student needs, providing scaffolding for some students or more advanced materials for others, which is much more effective then assuming all students' brains are at the same developmental milestone. The best approach lets each student encounter new challenges that are keyed to his or her skill level, choose within a range of curriculum focused activities, and make ongoing assessments of their own efforts.

That's also why class size matters. It's no surprise that many studies show smaller class size boosts student performance. Given that each student's brain is wired differently, smaller classes allow teachers to individualize their approach and to know when students are confused, engaged, bored, or excited. That's a lot harder to accomplish in a room of thirty-five students.

New technology can help. Studies show that computer software that tailors exercises for students boosts student performance when used in conjunction with standard reading programs. These programs can fill in the "learning gaps" students inevitably experience in a classroom filled with different brains. When learning gaps are ignored, students get discouraged and eventually disengage. When they are addressed, students can feel part of the classroom community and make progress along with other students. Well-trained, effective tutors may also help fill in these learning gaps outside school hours.

I explained in chapter 4 that we learn best when information is placed in a meaningful context. While rote memory was a mainstay of education for years, it doesn't play to our brain's strong suit. Field trips and hands-on learning, for example, are more than opportunities to blow off steam and reward kids. They are a meaningful way to connect learning to the real world. We retain information a lot better when it is elaborate, meaningful, and contextual. That's why I remember the batting average of my favorite baseball player more easily than that of a random teammate I don't care about.

Too often schools function in silos—students isolated from one another, teachers isolated from one another, and everyone isolated from the real world. Opening up schools to community and business partnerships, experiential learning, and technology-based distance-learning communities helps students connect their learning to real-life situations. It's a lot easier to remember Spanish phrases when a student has a weekly Internet conversation with a friend living in Cuzco, Peru.

Connecting information to real-world examples can help students' recall. Examples and stories are powerful tools because our brain is able to process information much better when it's associated with what we already know. In addition, we can recall information more easily when we are exposed to it multiple times. A student hearing a mini-lecture that includes real-world examples to explain an idea, goes on a field trip where she gets to see the information in action, and then writes a reflection paper where she reviews and processes what she's learned is light-years ahead of a student who only hears the information once in a lecture. Repeated exposure to information in ways that appeal to multiple intelligences reinforces neural pathways that help us retain and synthesize knowledge.

COMPUTERS AND THE INTERNET

Students who type "Thomas Jefferson" into a Google search box will receive 9 million results. Where to start? They won't know unless they become "information fluent." Stephanie Rosalia is a "21st-century librarian" who works with elementary school students in a New York City immigrant neighborhood. She describes herself as a "multi-faceted information specialist." Librarians were always information gatekeepers for students, possessing the keys to unlock the wonders of books, videos, and, more recently, the

Internet. But their job changed dramatically as the amount of available information exploded. Stephanie teaches kids not only how to check out books from the library, but also how to navigate the flood of digital information confronting them on a daily basis.

Being a "multi-faceted information specialist" includes teaching students how to sift through the 9 million hits on Thomas Jefferson in order to find relevant and reliable information. Stephanie describes the world she grew up in compared to her students. "I was in the information desert while they are in the information ocean, and they are drowning!" She recognizes the world of opportunity at her students' fingertips, but also understands they will get hopelessly lost without the tools to navigate this complex and overwhelming information age. The tools include but also exceed reading and book-based research skills. Students need to possess website literacy, the ability to differentiate between trustworthy and sketchy sources, and how to synthesize vast amounts of information. In other words, they need to be "information fluent."

Students today must acquire 21st-century skills to compete in a global marketplace including information and media literacy, critical thinking, creativity, intellectual curiosity, interpersonal, and economic and civic literacy skills. Digital technologies have the capacity to help young learners gain these skills and enhance the educational process. For example, some school districts invest in "portable classrooms" that enable an entire class to be linked to the same network, where they can upload assignments, conduct collaborative research projects, and receive feedback. Interactive whiteboards, or SMART Boards, quickly replace overheads and chalkboards in schools that can afford them. This technology turns computers and data projectors into powerful teaching tools. School administrators use email and online school communities to communicate more frequently with parents. The pace of innovation is exciting and 21st-century teachers, parents, and students should take advantage of it.

I spoke with a high school teacher, Ron, about how technology shapes the learning environment in his school. "Things have really changed," Ron told me. "We received a grant to introduce a laptop program for our juniors and seniors. When I started teaching we didn't even have the Internet. Now technology allows us to do some amazing learning although I have to admit it hasn't always been easy."

"Can you give me an example?" I asked.

"The science class creates its own podcast every week that other students in the school can listen to. Another teacher uses technology to link students with real data sets at the Minnesota Department of Natural

Resources [DNR] to wrestle with real-world problems. Staff from the DNR even came in to the school to work face-to-face with the students."

"That sounds exciting," I replied. "Are there any problems?"

"Oh sure. Some teachers have no interest in integrating technology into the curriculum at all, and barely know how to turn the computers on, much less teach with them. At the other extreme, a few teachers hand over teaching responsibilities to the computers altogether. Their students just plow through electronic learning modules all day long while the teacher sits by and watches."

"Sounds like a mixed bag." I responded.

"Yeah, that's the thing with technology. It all depends how you use it."

The variety of ways in which teachers at Ron's school use technology in the classroom illustrates why schools must adequately train and support their staff. Research shows that students learn best when technology is integrated with high-quality teaching, good assessments, ongoing training, and effective curriculum. In other words, technology alone is not a silver bullet for improving student achievement. Getting the machines, networks, and interactive whiteboards into the school building is one thing. Integrating them into an effectively orchestrated system of pedagogy and instruction is another. With this in mind, it is especially important that schools make judicious decisions about technology and not rush after every new gadget. Budgets should include as much money for training as they do for the hardware.

TECHNOLOGY, HOWEVER, IS A TWO-EDGED SWORD

All of the benefits notwithstanding, there is nothing magic about technology. Some parents lobby for laptops for every student in spite of the fact that there isn't any research showing that giving kids powerful technology automatically enhances learning. This study should give the laptop-for-every-child enthusiasts pause. Cornell University students were divided into two groups. One group was allowed to bring laptops to class, while the other group heard the same lecture without their computers. The nonlaptop group fared much better on a test measuring how much they recalled from the class. A graduate student recently told me the secret to his straight-A success. "I pay attention to the professor while my classmates check their text messages and social networking pages."

As we saw in chapter 13, we have to make sure that students know how to use computers appropriately lest they fall into the distraction trap, end up falling into hyperlink "rabbit holes," or turn into information butterflies whose knowledge is a mile wide but only an inch deep.

GENDER-BASED LEARNING

In chapter 10 we learned about the differences between boys' and girls' brains. These differences sparked an intense debate in education. Should schools or classrooms be separated by gender? Separating boys and girls is not new. Private and parochial schools have done it for generations. Recently, however, many public schools started gender-specific classrooms or schools due, in no small part, to changes in regulations associated with the federal government's No Child Left Behind Act.

People advocate for single-sex education for two basic reasons. One group believes that the brain-based differences between males and females should drive different teaching strategies and separate learning environments. Authors Leonard Sax of *Why Gender Matters* and Michael Gurian of *Boys and Girls Learn Differently* are the champions of this point of view. While both authors point to success stories to bolster their claims, they were criticized by academics for stereotyping girls and boys as well as cherry-picking and misinterpreting research findings.

The second group argues that boys and girls in this country have different social experiences and thus different learning needs. Teachers and administrators in these schools tend to emphasize that in a world where gender disparities continue, single-sex learning environments help children foster a positive perception of self-worth, competency, and strength.

Some educators decided gender-specific education was the answer after studying the research showing girls lose interest in math and science when they reach puberty. More recently there is a growing concern about boys' academic achievement. Boys today get 70 percent of the D's and F's that teachers give out, make up 80 percent of discipline problems, and account for 80 percent of high school dropouts. Many argue that single-sex classrooms allow educators to pay specialized attention to boys' learning needs.

Despite the growing popularity of single-sex education, there are fierce detractors of the philosophy as well. A lawyer from the ACLU Women's Rights Project was quoted in the *New York Times,* "Have you ever heard of Title IX?" The history of separate but unequal in this country makes many wary of educational models based on separating individuals because they are different. Opponents of same-sex education don't deny the brain-based differences between boys and girls. They just don't think that this justifies creating separate educational institutions and pedagogies for each sex. In addition, some neuroscientists argue there are too many exceptions to the "gender rules," that individuals fall along a continuum, to justify separating students based on their sex. It is possible that sorting by gender would no more sort students according to brain-based learning styles then sorting by height. There are differences between the average boy and girl brain, the argument goes. But that's all they are—averages. In other words, the differences within each gender potentially dwarf the variation between boy brains and girl brains. So the jury is out as to whether single-sex education improves student achievement. The U.S. Department of Education released a study comparing single-sex and coeducational schooling, with mixed results. The debate is not likely to end anytime soon.

The debate about single-sex education does not prevent us from applying the latest discoveries in brain science in the classroom for the benefit of all kids. For example, given what we know about the importance of kinesthetic learning, especially for boys, eliminating recess and physical education makes no sense at all. A strong lesson from brain science is to make lessons active and experiential and to keep verbal instructions short. Girls may be more likely to enjoy reading assignments that stress character development, whereas boys may be drawn to action and adventure. While these may be both brain-based and socially reinforced preferences, assigning a mix of both types of readings or allowing students to pick from a range of options ensures that all students stay engaged. The job of 21st-century educators is to weave together the developmental needs, interests, and experiences of both genders. Understanding the brain-based differences between boys and girls should always be paired with a close examination of gender-based teaching to ensure that brain science doesn't undermine gender equity in schools.

AND SO . . .

New discoveries in neuroscience are another tool in parents', teachers', and administrators' tool kits to help kids learn and inform educational policy. After all, schools are in the business of improving young people's brains, so where better to look than brain science for guidance? It can be tempting to follow every fad and encourage teachers to play Mozart in math class or expose kids to unique smells as they commit chemistry to memory. When these methods are only loosely grounded in science, we should be wary of jumping on every bandwagon that comes along. While brain science doesn't have every answer, well-researched insights offer us significant help in our effort to partner with our children's daycare centers and schools to raise healthy, successful, engaged thinkers and leaders.

DO

- ✓ Do consider brain-based information as you evaluate childcare or school options for your child.
- ✓ Do take the role of nutrition and physical exercise seriously in children's development and learning.
- ✓ Do ask about the staff-to-child ratio or teacher-to-student ratio.
- ✓ Do look for the ways staff or teachers reinforce children's effort and hard work.
- ✓ Do understand the basic building blocks for school success and make sure your child is "ready to learn."
- ✓ Do ask schools and programs about their connections to the broader community and look for ways in which students' learning is placed into meaningful, real-world contexts.
- ✓ Do ask schools and programs about the technological resources available to students and how digital technology is integrated meaningfully into a curriculum.
- ✓ Do get on the same page with program staff and teachers and reinforce their work at home.

DON'T

- ✗ Don't harass staff or teachers on behalf of your child or over-rely on brain science to form quick judgments. Ask informed questions and listen openly to their philosophy and instruction style.
- ✗ Don't use brain science to perpetuate gender stereotypes or use them to limit your child's experiences and opportunities.
- ✗ Don't focus strictly on academic outcomes at the expense of free play, exercise, good nutrition, and sleep.

What do I want to continue?

____

____

____

What do I want to change?

____

____

____

SIXTEEN

The 21st-Century Parent

This book explores recent discoveries from brain science that help us understand what's going on inside our own and our children's heads better than ever before. This new knowledge provides scientific information to help us raise successful and healthy kids. But parents have raised kids for thousands of years. Were they just flying blind, hoping for the best? Modern neuroscience reveals that many of their parenting practices, based on instincts and common sense, were very sound. Our new knowledge, however, in addition to helping us understand how wise the previous generations were, helps us make the best decisions where instincts and common sense fall short and gives guidance for the new challenges of the 21st century. Let's take some time-tested parenting mantras and see how modern brain science translates them for the present era.

"It's such a beautiful day. Get outside and play." Twentieth-century parents knew how important fresh air and exercise were for a healthy body. Twenty-first century parents know that vigorous exercise is as important for a fit brain as it is for strong muscles and bones. In addition, neuroscience calls attention to the importance of unstructured play for creativity and imagination.

"Don't sit so close to the TV. It'll ruin your eyes." While science tells us this 20th-century chestnut is not true, it does show that parents have paid attention to the impact of media on kids for a long time. And parents just a few years ago couldn't have imagined the cell phones, iPods, apps, video games, and other Internet wonders that are part of kids' lives today. Twenty-first-century parents are excited about the potential of technology but also know they have to make sure screens don't take over kids' lives and crowd out critical brain-building experiences.

"The hours before midnight count the most. So get to bed." My mother may have heard this bit of folk wisdom from her parents or she may have just made it up herself. In any case, she believed getting to bed early was important for our body and our brain. Today we know how important sleep is to consolidate memories and learning, how the sleep cycles change at different ages, how sleep deprivation damages us, how many sleep hours kids need, and the strategies to ensure enough shut-eye.

"If you keep making that face, it'll freeze that way." I don't think any kid's face actually got stuck in a funny expression, but it showed parents in previous eras sensed habits could become entrenched behaviors. The 21st-century parent knows the significance of the "neurons that fire together wire together" principle. Because a child's brain is "use dependent," the experiences we steer them to have lifelong implications.

"There won't be any dessert if you don't eat those vegetables." Yesteryear's parents knew a balanced diet was important for good health. Twenty-first-century parents know those veggies are essential ingredients in a brain-healthy "rainbow diet" and they also know how proteins, amino acids, good fats, and complex carbohydrates affect brain cell structure and function.

"No, you can't have coffee, because it will stunt your growth." The part about stunting growth isn't true, but yesteryear's parents were right about caffeine. It shouldn't be part of a child's or teen's diet, because it disturbs sleep; can cause headaches, jitteriness, and nervousness; and gives the young person an inaccurate reading of their energy level. There is even evidence that teens who are heavy caffeine consumers run the risk of hypertension. Unfortunately the beverage industry has discovered kids and targets them with an array of colas and "energy drinks" that are laced with high levels of caffeine. The wise parent should steer kids away from caffeinated drinks and toward healthier alternatives like water or smoothies.

"Your eyes are bigger than your stomach." How did our grandparents know how much our visual sense affects how much we eat? Today we know that there are more neurons dedicated to vision than to the other senses combined. Our visual bias affects how much we eat. Our eyes get us into trouble. Subjects will eat 43 percent more jelly beans if offered ten colors instead of seven. We'll eat more off a bigger plate, too. This creates a real challenge in our "supersize me" culture.

"If your friends jumped off a cliff, would you do it, too?" Generations of parents tried to teach children to say no when they need to. Twenty-first-century parents have an even deeper appreciation for the importance of self-discipline. We know from research that self-discipline is twice as strong a predictor of school achievement as intelligence. Self-discipline turns out to be a critical character trait for success and happiness. We also know it's more difficult to foster now than in bygone eras because of the constant drumbeat of "more, fast, easy, and fun" messages.

"You'd lose your head if it weren't screwed on." Today's parents understand that kids are often absentminded because their "brains are under construction." They also know the importance of attention and memory and how to help develop them.

"An idle mind is the devil's workshop." Oops. Our ancestors got this one wrong. The latest research shows that our brain doesn't go into a lower gear when we're not focused on something. The activity shifts to the imagination and creativity parts of the brain. Many of us parents panic when we hear our kids say, "I'm bored." My mother had a remedy for that. She used to say, "If you're bored, I'll give you something to do." We quickly figured out that we were better off finding something to do ourselves than ending up with chores.

"Turn off that radio until your homework is done." My mother never believed in multitasking and neither do the 21st-century scientists who study it. Our brains are designed to pay attention to one complex task at a time. It's a challenge for modern parents to teach kids to concentrate when there are so many distractions.

"If you want to get ahead you have to get along." I'm sure my parents would have scratched their heads at hearing the term *emotional intelligence*. Yet they knew common decency and courtesy were essential to build strong personal relationships and professional success. Managing emotions, along with the ability to interpret and express them, are key 21st-century skills.

"Eat your carrots. They'll help you see in the dark." I'm not so sure about seeing in the dark, but carrots are rich in vitamin A, which is important for good eyesight. Carrots are a good color to add to the rainbow diet we discussed in chapter 5.

"Get down from there. You're going to fall and crack your head open." The image of brains cracking open was supposed to teach kids to assess risk and think ahead. Today's parents realize a "prefrontal cortex under construction" makes kids daredevils. Nevertheless, we still need to get our kids to think ahead. As for brain safety, since our brain is in charge of everything we do, it makes sense to take care of it. Bike helmets, car seats, seat belts, and other safety headgear are smart choices.

"Don't ask me to help you with your homework until you've tried for at least fifteen minutes." Whether it was in regard to doing my homework or tackling a chore, my mother knew that if there was one thing I could control it was effort. She wouldn't have been surprised to learn that Bill Gates put in thousands of hours of effort before he achieved success. Another old favorite to reinforce this message was "A little hard work never killed anybody." Twenty-first-century parents need to ensure the value of effort and hard work for kids facing 21st-century economies.

"Because I said so. That's why." I guess that logic lesson is as valid today as it was for generations past.

"One day you'll have kids, and I hope they turn out just like you." Although it might have been said in exasperation, there is actually a lot of timeless wisdom behind it. Wouldn't it be a wonderful accomplishment if our 21st-century children found value in how they were raised?

The Art of Parenting

This book brings you up to date with brain science discoveries to aid you in the most important job of your life: raising children. But of course, parenting is an art, not a science. Science informs the art, but there is no book anywhere that can dictate the correct answer or strategy for the millions of decisions we make from the moment we embark on our parenting journey to the day we help our kids load up the U-Haul to strike out on their own. We've covered a lot of information, but the art of parenting basics remains the same.

Relax. Children are remarkably resilient. While we want to be informed parents, we don't want to tie ourselves in knots trying to do everything just right. It's hard to enjoy the journey of parenting if we're always worried about making mistakes.

It's all about balance. We can go overboard on anything, even good parenting. We want our kids to eat healthy without us turning into the food police. We want our kids to get exercise without us enforcing morning calisthenics. We want our kids to learn self-discipline and the importance of effort, but we don't want to run their lives like a boot camp. We need to set clear and high expectations without any unhealthy pressure.

Don't make your kids your report cards. It's not fair to tie our self-esteem to our children's performance. It's hard enough just to grow up, never mind also having to make parents look good.

The time we spend with our kids is a better investment than the money we spend on them. We should try to give our kids what they need without providing everything they want. Our consumer culture works hard to convince kids that happiness lies in having more things. It's up to us to teach them we can find fun at the mall, but we won't find happiness there.

Slow down. It takes a lot of slow to grow. Don't drive yourself and your kids crazy trying to fit in every class, activity, camp, or sport, no matter how worthwhile they are.

Remember, parenting is a delayed gratification activity. If we always look for parenting rewards we may be disappointed. In his book *Stumbling on Happiness*, Harvard psychologist Daniel Gilbert asks the provocative question why we choose to become parents when research shows childless couples are happier than parents. What Gilbert overlooks is the research showing that parents are happier and more satisfied in the long run. Raising kids is hard work, with its share of frustration, aggravation, and worry. We should consider whatever rewards we get along the way as bonuses. However, the payoff does come—when our kids turn out to be the kind of adults we can be proud of.

Raising children is not a problem to be solved. It's a mystery to be lived. At the end of the adventure we'll be able to ask ourselves the question, "Who dunnit?" and the answer is, us and our kids together. Then, to paraphrase Dr. Seuss, they'll have places to go and fun to be done. Thanks to you, the game can be won.

NOTES

One: Our Children's Amazing Brains

PAGE

5 *An infant arrives in the world with about 100 billion brain cells:* Marian Diamond and Janet Hopson, *Magic Trees of the Mind* (New York: Plume, 1999), 37.

5 *The late Nobel laureate Francis Crick:* Francis Crick, *Astonishing Hypothesis: Scientific Search for the Soul* (New York: Scribner, 1994), 91–105.

5 *When a baby arrives in the world, however, only 17 percent:* J. Dobbing and J. Sands, "Quantitative Growth and Development in the Human Brain," *Archives of Disease in Childhood* 48 (1973): 757–67.

6 *neuroscientist Jeffrey Schwartz puts it:* Jeffrey Schwartz and Sharon Begley, *The Mind and the Brain: Neuroplasticity and the Power of Mental Force* (New York: HarperPerennial, 2003), 201.

6 *Even thinking wires the brain:* A. Pascual-Leone, A. Amedi, F. Fregni, and L. B. Merabet, "The Plastic Human Brain Cortex," *Annual Review of Neuroscience* 28 (2005): 377–401.

7 *Experiences with the greatest impact on brain wiring:* Diamond and Hopson, *Magic Trees of the Mind.*

8 *The other 90 percent are called glial cells:* Carl Zimmer, "The Dark Matter of the Human Brain," *Discover,* September 2009.

9 *That's why renowned Swedish neuroscientist Torkel Klingberg:* Torkel Klingberg, *The Overflowing Brain* (New York: Oxford University Press, 2008), 11.

10 *It's Not All Experience:* Jerome Kagan, *The Nature of the Child* (New York: Basic Books, 1984).

Two: How to Raise Your Child's IQ

15 *Psychologists call this the "fundamental attribution error," or FAE:* Lee Ross, "The Intuitive Psychologist and His Shortcomings: Distortions in the Attribution Process," in Leonard Berkowitz, ed., *Advances in Experimental Social Psychology,* Vol. 10 (New York: Academic Press, 1977), 173–220.

15 *Malcolm Gladwell doesn't use the term fundamental attribution error:* Malcolm Gladwell, *Outliers* (New York: Little, Brown, 2009).

18 *Harvard psychologist Howard Gardner believes:* Howard Gardner, *Frames of Mind: The Theory of Multiple Intelligences* (New York: Basic Books, 1993).

18 *Daniel Goleman also makes a convincing case:* Daniel Goleman, *Emotional Intelligence: Why It Can Matter More than IQ* (New York: Bantam, 1995).

18 *Sidestepping this never-ending argument:* M. Snyderman and S. Rothman, *The IQ Controversy, the Media, and Public Policy* (New Brunswick, N.J.: Transaction, 1988).

18 *Although, as far as we know, Albert Einstein never took an IQ test:* Alice Calaprice, *Dear Professor Einstein: Albert Einstein's Letters to and from Children* (New York: Prometheus, 2002), 161.

19 *Even though there are too many life variables at play:* Richard Nisbett, *Intelligence and How to Get It* (New York: Norton, 2009), 17–20.

20 *Judith Harris published a bestselling book:* Judith Harris, *The Nurture Assumption: Why Children Turn Out the Way They Do* (New York: Free Press, 1998).

20 *Although Harris popularized this view:* T. J. Bouchard, "Genetic Influence on Human Psychological Traits," *Current Directions in Psychological Science* 13 (2004): 148–51.

20 *University of Michigan psychologist Richard Nisbett:* Nisbett, *Intelligence and How to Get It*, 21.

21 *French scientists conducted a convincing study:* M. Schiff, M. Duyme, J. Stewart, S. Tomkiewicz, and J. Feingold, "Intellectual Status of Working-Class Children Adopted Early in Upper-Middle-Class Families," *Science* 200 (1978): 1503–4.

21 *It all started innocently enough with some fascinating research:* Frances Rauscher, Gordon Shaw, and Katherine Ky, "Music and Spatial Task Performance," *Nature* 365 (1993): 611.

22 *He was shocked to find out American students had finished dead last:* National Commission on Excellence in Education, *A Nation at Risk: The Imperative for Education Reform*, http://www.ed.gov/pubs/NatAtRisk/risk.html (accessed July 3, 2009).

22 *They found that when they ordered the countries:* Erling Boe, Henry May, and Robert Boruch, "Student Task Persistence in the Third International Mathematics and Science Study: A Major Source of Achievement Differences at the National, Classroom, and Student Levels," http://www.eric.ed.gov/ERICWebPortal/custom/portlets/recordDetails/detailmini.jsp?_nfpb=true&_&ERICExtSearch_SearchValue_0=ED478493&ERICExtSearch_SearchType0=no&accno=ED478493 (accessed July 3, 2009).

Three: How the Brain Listens, Speaks, Reads, and Writes

31 *His brain is ready to learn any language:* P. Kuhl and M. Rivera-Gaxiola, "Neural Substrates of Language Acquisition," *Annual Review of Neuroscience* 31 (July 2008): 511–34.

33 *. . . language emerged more than 200,000 years later:* William Calvin, *A Brief History of the Mind: From Apes to Intellect and Beyond* (New York: Oxford University Press, 2005), 48.

34 *Language acquisition is a social process:* Patricia Kuhl, "Is Speech Learning 'Gated' by the Social Brain?" *Development Science* 10(1) (2007): 110–20.

36 *A 2010 study showed that rates are increasing:* Josef Shargorodsky, Sharon Curhan, Gary Curhan, and Roland Eavey, "Change in Prevalence of Hearing Loss in US Adolescents," *Journal of the American Medical Association* 304(7) (August 18, 2010): 772–78.

37 *Recent brain research gives us the explanation:* P. Su, C. C. Kuan, K. Kaga, M. Sano, K. Mima, "Myelination Progression in Language-Correlated Regions in Brains of Normal Children Determined by Quantitative MRI Assessment," *International Journal of Pediatric Otorhinolaryngology* 72 (December 2008) (12): 1751–63.

40 *She would have been happy to learn that the benefits for bilingual children:* Connect (University of Minnesota College of Education and Human Development.) 3(2) (Summer 2010): 16.

40 *Reading aloud promotes children's brain development, yet researchers:* Alice A. Kuo et al., "Parent Report of Reading to Young Children," *Pediatrics* 113(6) (June 6, 2004): 1944–51.

42 *In fact, a study of children with speech and language disorders:* C. S. Hammer, J. B. Tomblin, X. Zhang, and A. L. Weiss, "Relationship Between Parenting Behaviors and Specific Language Impairment in Children," *International Journal of Language and Communication Disorders* 36(2) (April–June 2001): 185–205.

45 *A survey of major corporations found that writing was a "threshold" skill:* College Board, *Writing: A Ticket to Work . . . Or a Ticket Out: A Survey of Business Leaders* (2004), http://www.writingcommission.org/prod_downloads/writingcom/writing-ticket-to-work.pdf (accessed September 12, 2008).

Four: Memory, Attention, and the Rule of Seven

49 *Students of brain science know about H.M.: HM* (patient), from Wikipedia, http://en.wikipedia.org/wiki/HM_(patient) (accessed June 2009).

51 *In fact, their brains are making the most connections:* Sandra Aamodt and Sam Wang, *Welcome to Your Brain* (New York: Bloomsbury USA, 2008), 149.

53 *Reactive attention—responding to movement:* Charles E. Connor, Howard Egeth, and Steven Yantis, "Visual Attention: Bottom-up versus Top-down," *Cognitive Biology* 14 (October 5, 2004): 850–52.

53 *Jeremy's focused attention is located in his prefrontal cortex:* According to MIT neuroscientist Robert Desimone, as quoted by John Tierney, "Ear Plugs to Lasers: The Science of Concentration," *New York Times,* May 5, 2009.

55 *That's why insurance companies consider talking on a cell phone and driving:* Maureen Dowd, "Whirling Dervish Drivers," *New York Times,* July 22, 2009, A21.

55 *According to Ratey, people "get a quick burst of adrenaline":* Matt Richtel, "Driven to Distraction: Drivers and Legislatures Dismiss Cell Phone Risks," *New York Times,* July 18, 2009.

56 *In one of the most cited psychology studies:* George Miller, "The Magical Number Seven, Plus or Minus Two: Some Limits on Our Capacity for Processing Information," *Psychological Review* 63(2) (1956): 81–97.

56 *University of Virginia scientist Daniel Willingham:* Daniel Willingham, *Why Don't Students Like School? A Cognitive Scientist Answers Questions about How the Mind Works and What It Means for the Classroom* (New York: Jossey-Bass, 2009), 33.

57 *Willingham explains that there are four requirements:* Ibid., 18.

58 *Children with attention deficit disorder:* About Kids Health, "When to Worry About Attention and Memory" (November 10, 2006), www.aboutkidshealth.ca/PrematureBabies/When-to-Worry-about-Attention-and-Memory.aspx?articleID=7831&categoryID=PI-nh5-04b (accessed June 2009).

59 *the hippocampus is where memories of facts and events:* Aamodt and Wang, *Welcome to Your Brain,* 150.

61 *become part of the subconscious mind:* Lise Eliot, *What's Going On in There?* (New York: Bantam, 1999), 329.

61 *In fact the basic memory processes in babies:* Mary L. Courage and Nelson Cowan, eds., *The Development of Memory in Infancy and Childhood* (New York: Psychology Press, 2009), 52.

61 *He showed a baby a box, then touched his own forehead:* Alison Gopnik, Andrew N. Meltzoff, and Patricia K. Kuhl, *The Scientist in the Crib: Minds, Brains, and How Children Learn* (New York: William Morrow, 1999), 33.

63 *children reach two language milestones:* Amy M. Boland, Catherine A. Haden, and Peter A. Ornstein, "Boosting Children's Memory by Training Mothers in the Use of an Elaborative Conversational Style as an Event Unfolds," *Journal of Cognition and Development* 4(1) (2003): 39–65.

63 *Loyola University Chicago scientist Catherine Haden:* Catherine A. Haden, Peter A. Ornstein, David J. Rudek, and Danielle Cameron, "Reminiscing in the Early Years: Patterns of Maternal Elaborativeness and Children's Remembering," *International Journal of Behavioral Development* 33(2) (March 1, 2009): 118–30.

63 *the more knowledge a child has:* D. R. Recht and L. Leslie, "Effect of Prior Knowledge on Good and Poor Readers' Memory of Text," *Journal of Educational Psychology* 80 (1988): 16–20.

64 *Here's an idea for a family story game:* Jenny Rachel Wilson, "Memory Exercises for Everyday" (June 24, 2009), http://ezinearticles.com/?Memory-Exercises-For-Everyday&id=2518918 (accessed July 22, 2009).

66 *Researchers David Bjorklund, Charles Dukes, and Rhonda Brown describe several techniques to enhance memory:* David Bjorklund, Charles Dukes, and Rhonda Brown, "The Development of Memory Strategies," in Courage and Cowan, eds., *The Development of Memory in Infancy and Childhood,* 145.

Five: Brain Food: Nutrition and the Brain

70 *a baby's brain at birth, even with complete circuits for basic survival:* Alison Gopnik, Andrew N. Meltzoff, and Patricia K. Kuhl, *The Scientist in the Crib: Minds, Brains, and How Children Learn* (New York: William Morrow, 1999), 183.

71 *Remember, although the brain accounts for:* John Medina, *Brain Rules* (Seattle: Pear Press, 2008), 39.

72 *Studies show that when teens skip breakfast:* Alfredo Flores, USDA Agricultural Research Service, "Breakfast is Key to Achieving Maximum Nutrition," http://www.ars.usda.gov/is/pr/2002/020621.htm (accessed February 8, 2009).

73 *the brain is mostly made of fat:* Nicola Graimes, *Brain Foods for Kids: Over a Hundred Recipes to Boost Your Child's Intelligence* (New York: Delta, 2005).

73 *Each brain cell or neuron has an outer membrane:* Franklin Institute, www.fi.edu/learn/brain/fats.html#fatsbuild (accessed December 6, 2008).

74 *Myelin, around 70 percent fat:* "Brain Food," www.thethinkingbusiness.co.uk/brainfoods.htm (accessed November 6, 2008).

74 *Neuroscientists have found that the brain functions:* Fernando Gómez-Pinilla, "Brain Foods: The Effects of Nutrients on Brain Function," *Nature Reviews Neuroscience* 9 (July 2008), http://www.nature.com/nrn/journal/v9/n7/abs/nrn2421.html (accessed February 9, 2009).

75 *That's why the American Academy of Pediatrics advises moms:* American Academy of Pediatrics, "Breastfeeding," http://www.aap.org/healthtopics/breastfeeding.cfm (accessed October 14, 2008).

75 *The brain uses thirty-eight of the forty-five nutrients:* Lise Eliot, *What's Going On in There? How the Brain and Mind Develop in the First Five Years of Life* (New York: Bantam, 1999), 446.

77 *In fact, there was not one state:* "Vital Signs: State-Specific Obesity Prevalence Among Adults—United States 2009," Centers for Disease Control and Prevention Report, released August 3, 2010, http://www.cdc.gov/mmwr/preview/mmwrhtml/mm59e0803a1.htm?s_cid=mm59e0803a1_wat (accessed August 20, 2010).

81 *Mercury is a known neurotoxin:* David Schardt, "Checking the Mercury," *Nutrition Action Healthletter* (May 2008).

85 "one tablespoon for each year of a child's age": *American Academy of Pediatrics,* "Parenting Corner Q & A: Nutrition," http://www.aap.org/publiced/BR_NutritionABC.htm (accessed October 9, 2008).

85 *A University of Minnesota study:* Gary Small and Gigi Vorgan, *iBrain: Surviving the Technological Alteration of the Modern Mind* (New York: HarperCollins, 2008), 92–95.

86 *Research has linked commonly used pesticides with attention deficit disorders:* B. Eskenazi et al., "PON1 and Neurodevelopment in Children from the CHAMACOS Study Exposed to Organophosphate Pesticides *in Utero,* "*Environmental Health Perspectives,* www.ncbi.nlm.nih.gov/pubmed/21126941 (accessed August 19, 2010).

Six: Play Is Serious Business

89 *one of the brain's four major areas:* Joan Lessen-Firestone, "Building Children's Brains," paper prepared for the Ready to Learn Summit, 1998–99, http://www.mi-aimh.msu.edu/publications/JoanFirestone.pdf (accessed March 18, 2009).

89 *Play is the laboratory where a child's brain:* Dorothy G. Singer and Jerome L. Singer, *The House of Make-Believe: Play and the Developing Imagination* (Cambridge, Mass.: Harvard University Press, 1990), 65.

90 *They also begin pretend play:* Ibid., 66.

90 *play shapes a child's brain in ways:* Melinda Wenner, "The Serious Need for Play," *Scientific American MIND* (February/March 2009), 22–29.

90 *In the 1960s, University of California, Berkeley:* Marian C. Diamond, "Response of the Brain to Enrichment," *New Horizons for Learning,* http://www.newhorizons.org/neuro/diamond_brain_response.htm (accessed February 2, 2009).

91 *scientists found that the thickness of the cerebral cortex:* Lessen-Firestone, "Building Children's Brains."

91 *after times of rough-and tumble-play, brains:* Nakia Gordon et al., "Socially Induced Brain 'Fertilization': Play Promotes Brain Derived Neurotrophic Factor Transcription in the Amygdala and Dorsolateral Frontal Cortex in Juvenile Rats," *Neuroscience Letters* 341(1) (2003): 17–20.

91 *Play is so important for brain development:* Office of the United Nations High Commissioner for Human Rights, Convention on the Rights of the Child, General Assembly Resolution 44/25 of 20, November 1989, www.unhchr.ch/html/menu3/b/k2crc.htm (accessed March 18, 2009).

92 *there seems to be a special benefit for their brains:* Wenner, "The Serious Need for Play."

94 *Yale child psychologists Dorothy and Jerome Singer studied children's play:* Singer and Singer, *The House of Make-Believe,* 269.

94 *Daniel Pink makes a compelling case for creativity in his book:* Daniel Pink, A *Whole New Mind: Moving from the Information Age to the Conceptual Age* (New York: Penguin, 2005).

95 *Another bonus that comes with free play is its contribution: Connect* (University of Minnesota College of Education and Human Development) 3(2) (Summer 2010): 15.

96 *Neuroscientist Michael Gazzaniga:* Lecture by Dr. Michael Gazzaniga, from the Gifford Lecture series at the University of Edinburgh, recorded October 15, 2009, http://www.youtube.com/watch?v=mJKloz2ywlc (accessed August 8, 2010).

97 *"Toys should be 90% child and 10% toy":* "Play Is Under Siege," *USA Today,* December 16, 2004, 23a.

99 *rough-and-tumble play, especially for boys:* Sergio M. Pellis and Vivien C. Pellis, "Rough-and-Tumble Play and the Development of the Social Brain," *Current Directions in Psychological Science* 16 (April 2007): 95–98.

100 *Stuart Brown, the founder of the National Institute for Play:* Stuart Brown, *Play: How It Shapes the Brain, Opens the Imagination, and Invigorates the Soul* (New York: Penguin, 2009).

100 *That startling finding launched:* Wenner, "The Serious Need for Play."

102 *But board games, video games, organized sports:* Torkel Klingberg, *The Overflowing Brain* (New York: Oxford University Press, 2008), 128.

102 *The give-and-take and negotiation:* Singer and Singer, *The House of Make-Believe,* 137.

Seven: Brain Workouts: Why Exercise Is Critical

106 *Years ago, premature infants were wrapped up:* http://www.uci.edu/features/feature_childrenatplay_081028.php (accessed February 5, 2009).

107 *Scientists running these experiments learned:* http://www.usatoday.com/news/health/2007-10-29-exercise-brains_N.htm (accessed August 4, 2008).

107 *The aerobic mice showed impressive brain growth:* Henriette van Praag, Brian R. Christie, Terrence J. Sejnowski, and Fred H. Gage, "Running Enhances Neurogenesis, Learning, and Long-Term Potentiation in Mice," *Proceedings of the National Academy of Science* 96 (November 9, 1999): 13427–31.

108 *Two areas of the brain:* Michelle Ploughman, "Exercise Is Brain Food: The Effects of Physical Activity on Cognitive Function," *Developmental Neurorehabilitation* 11 (July 2008): 236–40.

109 *John Ratey, the author of Spark:* John J. Ratey, Spark: *The Revolutionary New Science of Exercise and the Brain* (New York: Little, Brown, 2008), 40.

109 *BDNF actually stimulates the production:* Ibid., 38–39.

109 *When Maria runs, she causes more neurons to fire:* Charles Hillman et al., "Aerobic Fitness and Cognitive Development: Event-Related Brain Potential and Task Performance Indices of Executive Control in Preadolescent Children," *Developmental Psychology* 45 (January 2009): 114–29.

110 *she's also increasing the amounts of three neurotransmitters:* Ratey, *Spark,* 5.

110 *There is some new research showing that the serotonin squirt:* Gretchen Reynolds, "Can Exercise Moderate Anger?" *New York Times Magazine,* August 15, 2010, 21.

110 *Dr. Charles Hillman at the University of Illinois:* C. H. Hillman et al., "The Effect of Acute Treadmill Walking on Cognitive Control and Academic Achievement in Preadolescent Children," *Neuroscience* 159 (March 2009): 1044–54.

110 *Almost one in three American children weighs too much:* Centers for Disease Control and Prevention, "Overweight Trends Among Children and Adolescents," http://www.cdc.gov/nccdphp/dnpa/obesity/trend/index.htm (accessed March 2009).

110 *For kids ages six to eleven:* "Physical Activity and Academic Performance," *President's Council on Physical Fitness and Sports Newsletter,* (Fall 2008), http://www.fitness.gov/enewsletter/fall2008/featurearticle.html (accessed February 2009).

110 *We know that overweight children are at greater risk:* http://www.obesity.org/information/childhood_overweight.asp (accessed March 2009).

110 *Researchers have found that academic achievement:* Charles Hillman, Kirk Erickson, and Arthur Kramer, "Be Smart, Exercise Your Heart: Exercise Effects on Brain and Cognition," *Nature Reviews Neuroscience* 9 (January 2008): 58–65. Also see Howard Taras and William Potts-Datema, "Obesity and Student Performance at School," *Journal of School Health,* 75(8) (October 2005): 291–95.

111 *In a 2006 national survey:* Centers for Disease Control, "SHPPS: School Health Policies and Programs Study," http://www.cdc.gov/HealthyYouth/SHPPS/ (accessed February 2009).

111 *Another CDC study, the Youth Risk Behavior Survey: Centers for Disease Control,* "Obesity Epidemic and United States Students," *The 2007 National Youth Risk Behavior Survey,* http://www.cdc.gov/HealthyYouth/yrbs/pdf/yrbs07_us_obesity.pdf (accessed January 2009).

113 *Elementary-age children and preteens:* American Academy of Pediatrics, "Prevention and Treatment of Overweight and Obesity," http://www.aap.org/obesity/families.html?technology=1 (accessed March 2009).

113 *As kids progress from elementary school into high school:* Philip Nader et al., "Moderate-to-Vigorous Physical Activity from Ages 9 to 15 Years," *Journal of the American Medical Association* 300(3) (July 2008): 295–305.

114 *Is it any wonder the number of overweight teenagers skyrocketed:* University of California, "Physical Activity Declines in Children Ages 9 to 15," http://www.universityofcalifornia.edu/news/article/18227 (accessed August 31, 2009).

114 *The goal should be to eventually reach 10,000:* American Academy of Pediatrics, "Active Healthy Living: Prevention of Childhood Obesity Through Increased Physical Activity," http://aappolicy.aappublications.org/cgi/content/full/pediatrics:117/5/1834 (accessed April 2009).

Eight: Your Brain's at Work While You Snooze

117 *Dr. Giulio Tononi, a scientist:* Cited in Greg Miller, "Neural Communication Breaks Down As Consciousness Fades and Sleep Sets In," *Science* 309 (September 30, 2005): 2148–49.

118 *Neurons in the brain stem:* Judy Owens and Jodi Mindell, *Take Charge of Your Child's Sleep: The All-in-One Resource for Solving Sleep Problems in Kids and Teens* (New York: Marlowe, 2005).

118 *"Sleep is the most familiar alteration":* Email communication with Dr. Giulio Tononi, May 7, 2009.

118 *All of us, including children, have two sleep states:* American Academy of Sleep Medicine, http://www.aasmnet.org/ (accessed April 15, 2009).

118 *There are actually three stages of non-REM sleep:* Ibid.

118 *For adults this cycle follows a ninety-minute pattern:* National Sleep Foundation, http://www.sleepfoundation.org/site/c.huIXKjM0IxF/b.4809577/k.BA8B/Children_and_Sleep.htm (accessed April 19, 2009).

119 *In our evolutionary history, REM sleep:* Sandra Aamodt and Sam Wang, *Welcome to Your Brain* (New York: Bloomsbury, 2008), 177.

119 *Dr. Robert Stickgold of Harvard University:* Franklin Institute, "Renew—Sleep and Stress," http://www.fi.edu/learn/brain/sleep.html (accessed April 20, 2009).

119 *Stickgold and his colleagues also believe that REM sleep:* Robert Stickgold and Jeffrey Ellenbogen, "Quiet! Sleeping Brain at Work," *American Mind* 19 (August/September 2008): 23–29.

119 *In an interesting German study, Ullrich Wagner:* Cited in ibid.

120 *The team at the University of Wisconsin's:* Giorgio F. Gilestro, Giulio Tononi, and Chiara Cirelli, "Widespread Changes in Synaptic Markers as a Function of Sleep and Wakefulness in Drosophila," *Science* 324 (April 3, 2009): 109–12.

120 *"Much of what we learn in a day":* Email communication with Chiara Cirelli, May 7, 2009. Originally cited by Susan Lampert Smith in "Sleep: Spring Cleaning for the Brain?" http://www.news.wisc.edu/16506 (accessed April 25, 2009).

120 *Researchers at the University of California, San Francisco:* Marcos G. Frank, Naoum P. Issa, and Michael P. Stryker, "Sleep Enhances Plasticity in the Developing Visual Cortex," *Neuron* 30(1) (April 1, 2001): 275–87.

121 *In another animal study, this time with songbirds:* Aamodt and Wang, *Welcome to Your Brain*, 181.

121 *Overall, children will spend 40 percent:* National Sleep Foundation, "Sleep for Kids: Sleep Information for Parents and Teachers," http://www.sleepforkids.org/html/habits.html (accessed May 3, 2009).

122 *At that point they develop a sleep/wake cycle:* Ibid.

122 *The National Sleep Foundation's Sleep in America study:* National Sleep Foundation, "2004 Sleep In America Poll," http://www.sleepfoundation.org/site/c.huIXKjMOIxF/b.2419299/k.BB15/Children_and_Sleep.htm (accessed April 23, 2009).

123 *A University of Louisville study:* Abstract presented at the twenty-first annual meeting of the Associated Professional Sleep Societies, SLEEP 2007, "Sleep Restriction Affects Children's Speech," American Academy of Sleep Medicine, http://www.aasmnet.org/Articles.aspx?id=464 (accessed May 4, 2009).

124 *Dr. Avi Sadeh studies the effects:* Avi Sadeh, Reut Gruber, and Amiram Raviv, "The Effects of Sleep Restriction and Extension on School-Age Children: What a Difference an Hour Makes," *Child Development* 74(2) (March/April 2003): 444–55.

124 *a lack of sleep cuts down on the glucose supply:* Po Bronson, "Snooze or Lose," New York, October 7, 2007.

125 *That explains the results of a recent experiment:* Michael Brondel et al., "Acute Partial Sleep Deprivation Increases Food Intake in Healthy Men," *American Journal of Clinical Nutrition* 91 (2010): 1550–59.

125 *Follow the American Academy of Pediatrics guidelines:* American Academy of Pediatrics Task Force on Sudden Infant Death Syndrome, "Policy Statement," http://aappolicy.aappublications.org/cgi/reprint/pediatrics;116/5/1245.pdf (accessed May 18, 2009).

126 *Researchers have not discovered the exact cause of SIDS:* Kids' Health from Nemours, "Sudden Infant Death Syndrome, SIDS," http://kidshealth.org/parent/general/sleep/sids.html (accessed May 20, 2009).

127 *In fact, Northwestern University scientists:* Franklin Institute Resource for Science Learning, "Children's Sleep Patterns Related to Behavior," http://www.fi.edu/learn/brain/sleep.html (accessed April 23, 2009).

128 *Researchers find that children with sleep disorders:* American Academy of Sleep Medicine, abstracts presented at the twenty-first annual meeting of the Associated Professional Sleep Societies, SLEEP 2007, "AASM to School Bound: Sleep Is the Right Ingredient for Academic Success," http://www.aasmnet.org/Articles.aspx?id=517 (accessed May 4, 2009).

128 *A report from the Johns Hopkins University School of Medicine:* Ann C. Halbower et al., "Childhood Obstructive Sleep Apnea Associates with Neuropsychological Deficits and Neuronal Brain Injury," *Public Library of Science Medicine* 3 (August 2006).

128 *A University of Louisville study found that among 1,500:* David Gozal and Dennis Pope, Jr., "Snoring During Early Childhood and Academic Performance at Ages Thirteen to Fourteen Years," *Pediatrics* 107(6) (June 6, 2001): 1394–99.

129 *In fact, sleep apnea can be misdiagnosed:* Lynne Lamberg, "Sleep-Disordered Breathing May Spur Behavioral, Learning Problems in Children," *Journal of the American Medical Association* 297(24) (June 21, 2007): 2681–83.

131 *Puberty brings about a big change in sleep patterns:* David Walsh, Ph.D., *Why Do They Act That Way? A Survival Guide to the Adolescent Brain for You and Your Teen* (New York: Free Press, 2004), 175–84.

131 *A 2010 study led by Columbia:* J. E. Gangwisch et al., "Earlier Parental Set Bedtimes as a Protective Factor against Depression and Suicidal Ideation," *SLEEP* (2010) 33(1): 97–106.

132 *scientists at Australia's Swinburne:* "Call Me Sleepless," *Scientific American Mind* 19(4) (August/September 2008): 6.

132 *Although it takes caffeine only thirty to sixty minutes:* Donald Townsend, American Academy of Sleep Medicine, August 3, 2006, http://www.sleepeducation.com/Topic.aspx?id=45 (accessed August 8, 2010)

132–33 *However, results from districts that have reset:* Kyla Wahlstrom, "Changing Times: Findings from the First Longitudinal Study of Later High School Start Times," *NASSP Bulletin* 86 (December 2002): 633, http://cehd.umn.edu/CAREI/Reports/docs/SST-2002Bulletin.pdf (accessed May 15, 2009).

133 *A Kansas study found that the decline:* Fred Danner and Barbara Phillips, "Adolescent Sleep, School Start Times, and Teen Motor Vehicle Crashes," *Journal of Clinical Sleep Medicine* 4(6) (December 2008): 533–35.

133 *Vehicle crashes account for 35 percent:* National Highway Traffic Safety Administration, "Teen Drivers," http://nhtsa.gov (accessed May 28, 2009).

133 *According to the National Sleep Foundation:* National Sleep Foundation, "2004 Sleep in America Poll."

Nine: Self-Discipline: The Key to Success

135 *The marshmallow experiment in question:* Y. Shoda, W. Mischel, and P. K. Peake, "Predicting Adolescent Cognitive and Self-Regulatory Competencies from Preschool Delay of Gratification: Identifying Diagnostic Conditions," *Developmental Psychology* 26(6) (1990): 978–86.

136 *A 2005 University of Pennsylvania study showed:* A. L. Duckworth and M. E. Seligman, "Self-discipline Outdoes IQ in Predicting Academic Performance of Adolescents," *Psychological Science* 16 (2005): 939–44.

137 *In 2007, the Maplewood, New Jersey, public library:* Tina Kelley, "Library Decides Not to Close to Thwart Rowdiness," *New York Times,* January 15, 2007.

137–38 *Eden Prairie High School in Minnesota eliminated:* Katherine Kersten, "Why Valedictorians Are a Dying Breed," *Star Tribune,* June 3, 2007.

138 *Bill Gates offered this assessment:* Bob Herbert, "Clueless in America," *New York Times,* April 22, 2008.

139 *Evidence of DDD surfaced outside schools:* Jill Casner-Lotto and Linda Barrington, "Are They Really Ready to Work?" Conference Board Report Number BED-06-Workforce (October 2006).

144 *Daniel Goleman brought the term emotional intelligence:* Daniel Goleman, *Emotional Intelligence: Why It Can Matter More than IQ* (New York: Bantam, 1995).

144 *Whatever the term, establishing a warm:* For a comprehensive treatment of the importance of connection see Thomas Lewis, Fari Amini, and Richard Lannin, *General Theory of Love* (New York: Random House, 2000).

145 *. . . she'd baby-proofed her apartment:* The University of Minnesota Extension Service has an excellent babyproofing guide at http://www.extension.umn.edu/info-u/families/be379.html (accessed June 2, 2009).

146 *Berkeley psychology professor Alison Gopnik:* The experiment is described in Malcolm Gladwell, "Baby Steps," *New Yorker,* January 10, 2000.

Ten: A Brain Under Construction: The Adolescent Years

155 *Puberty, which biologically launches adolescence:* Kathleen Doheny, "Study: Girls Entering Puberty Earlier By Age 7, Breast Development More Common than Reported 10 to 30 Years Ago," http://children.webmd.com/news/20100809/study-girls-entering-puberty-earlier (accessed August 19, 2010).

155 *The more a child weighs the earlier puberty begins:* Paul B. Kaplowitz, "Link Between Body Fat and the Timing of Puberty," *Pediatrics* 121(121) (February 2008): S208–S217.

156 *A big discovery in brain science is that the prefrontal cortex:* J. N. Giedd et al., "Brain Development during Childhood and Adolescence: A Longitudinal MRI Study," *Nature Neuroscience* 2 (1999): 861–63.

157 *Adolescent boys can have five to seven:* Dennis Styne and Donald Pfaff, "Puberty in Boys and Girls," in Donald Pfaff et al., eds., *Hormones, Brains and Behavior,* (San Diego: Academic Press, 2002), 661–716.

158 *Research now reveals that there is a small part:* J. Giedd et al., "Quantitative MRI of the Temporal Lobe, Amygdala, and Hippocampus in Normal Human Development: Ages 4–18 Years," *Journal of Comparative Neurology* 366 (1996): 223–30.

158 *very rich in testosterone receptors:* Jay Giedd et al., "Quantitative MRI of the Temporal Lobe, Amygdala, and Hippocampus in Normal Human

Development: Ages 4–18 years," *Journal of Comparative Neurology* 366 (1996): 223–30.

162 *The adolescent brain, on the other hand:* Deborah Yurgelun-Todd, "Inside the Teenage Brain: One Reason Teens Respond Differently to the World: Immature Brain Circuitry," www.pbs.org/wgbh/pages/frontline/shows/teenbrain/work/onereason.htmn (accessed August 19, 2010).

Eleven: Boy and Girl Brains: What's the Difference?

169 *Lawrence Summers discovered this the hard way:* Marcella Bombardieri, "Harvard Women's Group Rips Summers," *Boston Globe*, January 19, 2005.

169 *Violinists, for instance:* John Medina, *Brain Rules* (Seattle: Pear Press, 2008).

169 *That many skill differences between the sexes shrank:* Joan Littlefield Cook and Greg Cook, *Child Development: Principles and Perspectives* (Boston: Allyn & Bacon, 2009), 362.

171 *three to four times more likely to stutter:* E. Yairi and N. Ambrose, *Early Childhood Stuttering for Clinicians by Clinicians* (Austin, Texas: Pro-Ed, 2005), chapter 7.

171 *On average, girls utter two to three times more words:* Louann Brizendine, *The Female Brain* (New York: Morgan Road, 2006), 36.

172 *females have at least 20 percent more neurons:* J. Harasty et al., "Language-Associated Cortical Regions Are Proportionally Larger in the Female Brain," *Archives in Neurology* 54(2) (1997): 171–76.

172 *Further, the corpus callosum:* K. M. Bishop and D. Wahlsten, "Sex Differences in the Human Corpus Callosum: Myth or Reality?" *Neuroscience and Biobehavioural Reviews* 21(5) (1997): 581–601.

172 *Youth suicide is certainly:* "Suicide: Facts at a Glance, Summer 2008," http://www.cdc.gov/ViolencePrevention/pdfSuicide-DataSheet-a.pdf (accessed August 1, 2009).

173 *Research shows that when girls talk:* Amanda J. Rose, "Co-rumination in the Friendships of Girls and Boys," *Child Development* 73(6) (2002): 1830–43.

174 *The controversy about overall intelligence:* Larry Hedges and Amy Nowell, "Sex Differences in Mental Test Scores, Variability, and Numbers of High-Scoring Individuals," *Science* 269 (1995): 41–45.

174 *data showing that boys' brains favor spatial skills:* M.P. Bryden, D. Voyer, and S. Voyer, "Magnitude of Sex Differences in Spatial Abilities: A Meta-analysis and Consideration of Critical Variables," *Psychological Bulletin* 117 (1995): 250–65.

174 *Ninety-two percent of American engineers are male:* Aleks Cherednichenko, "Female Engineers Are on the Rise," *Daily Barometer*, 2007, http://media.barometer.orst.edu/media/storage/paper854/news/2007/02/15/News/Female.Engineers.On.The.Rise-2721818.shtml (accessed August 1, 2009).

174 *Marcia Collaer and Melissa Hines:* Marcia Collaer and Melissa Hines, "Human Behavioral Sex Differences: A Role for Gonadal Hormones During Early Development?" *Psychological Bulletin* 118(1) (1995): 55–77.

174 *Is it true? It depends:* Joan Littlefield Cook and Greg Cook, *Child Development: Principles and Perspectives* (Boston: Allyn & Bacon, 2009), 362–65.

174 *In one experiment men and women were told:* S. J. Spencer, C. M. Steele, and D. M. Quinn, "Stereotype Threat and Women's Math Performance," *Journal of Experimental Social Psychology* 35 (1999): 4–28.

177 *Recent research reveals that adult males:* Coren L. Apicella et al., "Testosterone and Financial Risk Preferences," *Evolution and Human Behavior* 29(6) (2008): 384–90.

177 *Psychologist Erin McClure found:* Erin B. McClure, "A Meta-Analytic Review of Sex Differences in Facial Expression Processing and Their Development in Infants, Children, and Adolescents," *Psychological Bulletin* 126(3) (2000): 424–53.

177 *psychologist Rebecca Leeb wanted to know:* Rebecca Leeb and Gillian Rejskind, "Here's Looking at You, Kid! A Longitudinal Study of Perceived Gender Differences in Mutual Gaze Behavior in Young Infants," *Sex Roles* 50(1–2) (2004): 1–14.

177 *A University of Texas study also revealed:* Louann Brizendine, *The Female Brain* (New York: Morgan Road, 2006), 16.

178 *researchers Melissa Hines and Gerianne Alexander:* Larry Cahill, "His Brain; Her Brain," Scientific American May 2005, 40–47.

179 *More careful research, however:* J. E. Burr et al., "Relational Aggression and Friendship During Early Childhood: 'I won't be your friend,'" *Early Education and Development* 16(2) (2005): 161–83.

179 *girls produce 60 percent more prolactin than boys:* Ad Vingerhoets, Adult Crying: A Biopsychological Approach (Philadelphia: Taylor & Francis, 2002), 178.

Twelve: Stress and the Brain

184 *These cues include headaches, stomachaches:* Megan Gunnar and Ronald Barr, "Stress, Early Brain Development, and Behavior," *Infants and Young Children* 11(1) (1998): 1–14.

185 *Talk with your children about their worries:* Edward Hallowell, *Worry* (New York: Ballantine, 1998), introduction, xxxiii.

186 *Noted Stanford neuroscientist Robert Sapolsky:* Robert Sapolsky, *Why Zebras Don't Get Ulcers* (San Francisco: W. H. Freeman, 1998).

187 *Upstairs in the brain, cortisol:* J. W. Newcomer et al., "Decreased Memory Performance in Healthy Humans Induced by Stress-Level Cortisol Treatment," *Archives of General Psychiatry* 56(6) (1999): 527–33.

187 *On top of that, the brain produces less:* J. Licinio and M. L. Wong, "Brain Derived Neurotrophic Factor (BDNF) in Stress and Affective Disorders," *Molecular Psychiatry* 7(6) (2002): 515–19.

187 *Scientists at Duke University:* F. Dolcos, K. S. LaBar, and R. Cabeza, "Interaction Between the Amygdala and the Medial Temporal Lobe Memory System Predicts Better Memory for Emotional Events," *Neuron* 42 (2004): 855–63.

188 *Prolonged stress rewires the brain:* N. Sousa et al., "Chronic Stress Causes Frontostriatal Reorganization and Affects Decision-Making," *Science* 325 (2009): 621–25.

188 *Sapolsky believes the same change:* Natalie Angier, "Brain Is a Co-Conspirator in a Vicious Stress Loop," *New York Times,* August 18, 2009, D2.

189 *Because it is frequently studied:* Bonnie Benard, *Resiliency: What Have We Learned?* (San Francisco: WestEd, 2004).

190 *Michael Thompson's book:* Michael Thompson, *The Pressured Child: Helping Your Child Find Success in School and Life* (New York: Ballantine, 2004).

191 *Psychologist Martin Seligman studied optimism:* Martin Seligman, *The Optimistic Child: Proven Program to Safeguard Children from Depression & Build Lifelong Resilience* (New York: Harper Paperbacks, 1996).

Thirteen: Cyber Brains: Parenting in an Online World

197 *one in three teens send 100 text messages a day:* "Teens and Mobile Phones," Pew Internet & American Life Project, April 20, 2010, http://pewinternet.org/Reports/2010/Teens-and-Mobile-Phones.aspx (accessed August 9, 2010).

199 *Today the average American school-age child spends:* "Generation M: Media in the Lives of 8- 18-Year Olds," report from the Kaiser Family Foundation, January 20, 2010, http://www.kff.org/entmedia/entmedia012010nr.cfm (accessed August 23, 2010).

201 *This research shows, for example:* Douglas Gentile and Ronald Gentile, "Violent Video Games as Exemplary Teachers," *Journal of Youth and Adolescence* 37 (2007): 127–41.

201 *that certain video games can teach prosocial behaviors:* Douglas Gentile et al., "The Effects of Prosocial Video Games on Prosocial Behaviors: International Evidence From Correlational, Longitudinal, and Experimental Studies," *Personality and Social Psychology Bulletin* 35 (2009): 752–63.

201 *violent video games can also teach aggressive:* Craig Anderson and Brad Bushman, "The Effects of Media Violence on Society," *Science* 295 (2002): 2377–78.

202 *For example, a recent study used functional MRI:* Gary Small and Gigi Vorgan, *iBrain: Surviving the Technological Alteration of the Modern Mind* (New York: HarperCollins, 2008).

202 *For example, a researcher in the United Kingdom:* Ibid.

203 *A Stanford University study found:* Norman Nie and D. Sunshine Hillygus, "The Impact of Internet Use on Sociability: Time Diary Findings," *IT & Society* 1 (2002): 1–20.

203 *On a similar note, a recent poll from the Annenberg:* USC Annenberg Center for the Digital Future, "Family Time Decreasing with Internet Use," 2009, http://www.digitalcenter.org/pdf/cdf_family_time.pdf (accessed August 8, 2009).

203 *According to the 2010 Pew:* "Teens and Mobile Phones," Pew Internet & American Life Project.

204 *Research from the University of California's Digital:* Mizuto Ito et al., *Living and Learning with New Media: Summary of Findings from the Digital Youth Project* (Berkeley, Calif.: MacArthur Foundation, 2008).

204 *Studies show that adults who use computers:* K. Renaud, J. Ramsay, and M. Hair, " 'You've Got Email': Shall I Deal with It Now?" *International Journal of Human-Computer Interaction* 21(3) (2006): 313–32.

204 *The research is conclusive:* Nicholas Carr, *The Shallows: What the Internet Is Doing to Our Brains* (New York: Norton, 2010), 139–43.

205 *MIT professor of social studies and technology Sherry Turkle:* "Here and Now," *Public Radio International,* July 3, 2009, http://www.pri.org/health/texting-affects-teenagers-development1467.html (accessed July 3, 2009).

205 *KARE11, the local NBC:* Joe Fryer, "Teen Tech Experiment: Can Teens Survive Without Their Cell Phones?" KARE11.com, 2008, http://www.kare11.com/news/news_article.aspx?storyid=524397&catid=2.

206 *Although he doesn't use that term:* Carr, *The Shallows.*

207 *Researchers with the University of California's Digital:* Ibid.

209 *A study from Tufts University:* Katherine A. Coon et al., "Relationship Between Use of Television During Meals and Children's Food Consumption Patterns," *Pediatrics* 107 (2001): e7, http://pediatrics.aappublications.org/cgi/content/full/107/1/e7 (accessed July 8, 2009).

209 *preschool children watching more than two hours:* J. A. Mendoza, F. J. Zimmerman, and D. A. Christakis, "Television Viewing, Computer Use, Obesity, and Adiposity in U.S. Preschool Children," *International Journal of Behavioral Nutrition and Physical Activity,* 2007, http://www.ijbnpa.org/content/4/1/44 (accessed June 17, 2009).

209 *Research conducted at Baylor:* Children's Nutrition Research Center, "TV Eating Up Family Mealtime," 2004, http://www.bcm.edu/cnrc/consumer/archives/tveating.htm (accessed July 8, 2009).

209 *A disturbing report:* Jeffrey Levi et al., *F as in Fat: How Obesity Policies Are Failing in American 2009* (Washington, D.C.: Trust for America's Health and the Robert Wood Johnson Foundation, 2009).

210 *One group of researchers discovered that children playing Wii Sports:* Lee Graves et al., "Comparison of Energy Expenditure in Adolescents When Playing New Generation and Sedentary Computer Games: Cross Sectional Study," *British Medical Journal* 335 (2007): 1282–84.

212 *Recent data shows that one in five youth sext:* Donna Leinwand, "Survey: 1 in 5 Teens 'Sext' Despite Risks," *USA Today,* June 24, 2009, http://www.usatoday.com/news/nation/2009-06-23-onlinekids_N.html (accessed June 25, 2009).

213 *another study in which 86 percent:* Jerry Hirsch, "Teens, Driving and Texting Are a Bad Mix," *Los Angeles Times* blog, August 2, 2010, http://latimesblogs.latimes.com/technology/2010/08/teens-driving-and-texting-bad-mix.html (accessed August 10, 2010).

213 *Brain research explains why cell phones and driving:* "Cell Phones and the Hazards of Driving While Chatting," interview with David Strayer and Steven Yantis on Minnesota Public Radio, July 30, 2009, http://minnesota.publicradio.org/display/web/2009/07/30/midmorning2/ (accessed August 20, 2009).

215 *My friend and colleague Douglas Gentile:* Douglas Gentile, "Pathological Video Game Use Among Youth 8 to 18: A National Study," *Psychological Science* 20 (2009): 594–602.

Fourteen: Wired Differently: Special Needs Brains, Mental Illness, and Chemical Use

219 *As neuroscientist Aditi Shankardass says:* Aditi Shankardass, TED lecture, http://www.ted.com/talks/aditi_shankardass_a_second_opinion_on_learning_disorders.html (accessed August 21, 2010).

Fifteen: Brain-Wise Daycare, Preschool, and School Decisions

242 *Yet 20 percent of elementary schools:* David Satcher, "Healthy and Ready to Learn," *Educational Leadership* 63 (2005): 26–30.

242 *The Centers for Disease Control and Prevention report:* Centers for Disease Control and Prevention, "Youth Risk Behavior Surveillance—United States," 55 (2006): 1–108.

242 *In five experimental controlled studies:* Stewart Trost, "Active Education: Physical Education, Physical Activity, and Academic Performance," prepared for the Active Living Research program of the Robert Woods Johnson Foundation, 2007.

242 *Another neuroscientist, John Medina:* John Medina, *Brain Rules* (Seattle: Pear Press, 2008).

242 *David Jones, the principal at Eisenhower Middle School:* David Jones, "Healthy and Smart: Using Wellness to Boost Performance," *Principal Leadership* (December 2007).

243 *In addition to the timing of birth dates:* K. H. Lee et al, "Neural Correlates of Superior Intelligence: Stronger Recruitment of Posterior Parietal Cortex," *NeuroImage* 29(2) (2006): 578–86.

243 *That's why intelligence and screening tests:* Po Bronson, *Nurture Shock: New Thinking about Children* (New York: Twelve, 2009), 98–109.

243–44 *many children do not have brains sufficiently wired:* Medina, *Brain Rules.*

244 *Studies show that computer software:* Ibid.

245 *Stephanie Rosalia:* Motoko Rich, "In Web Age, Library Job Gets Update," *New York Times,* February 15, 2009, http://www.nytimes.com/2009/02/16/books/16libr.html?_r=1 (accessed August 18, 2009).

247 *Research shows that students learn best:* Partnership for 21st Century Skills, "21st Century Learning Environments White Paper," 2009, http://www.21stcenturyskills.org/documents/le_white_paper-1.pdf (accessed July 26, 2009).

247 *This study should give the laptop-for-every-child:* Helene Hembrooke and Geri Gay, "The Laptop and the Lecture: The Effects of Multitasking in Learning Environments," *Journal of Computing in Higher Education* 9 (September 2003): 179–91.

248 *Recently, however, many public schools:* Elizabeth Weil, "Teaching Boys and Girls Separately," *New York Times,* March 2, 2008, http://www.nytimes.com/2008/03/02/magazine/02sex3-t.html?pagewanted=2&_r=1&ref=magazine (accessed August 16, 2009).

248 *Leonard Sax:* Leonard Sax, *Why Gender Matters* (New York: Random House, 2005).

248 *Michael Gurian:* Michael Gurian, *Boys and Girls Learn Differently* (New York: Jossey-Bass, 2001).

248 *Boys today get 70 percent:* Ibid., 56–57.

249 *The U.S. Department of Education released a study:* Fred Mael, Alex Alonso, Doug Gibson, Kelly Rogers, and Mark Smith, *Single-Sex Versus Coeducational Schooling: A Systematic Review,* prepared for the U.S. Department of Education Office of Planning, Evaluation, and Policy Development, 2005, http://www.ed.gov/rschstat/eval/other/single-sex/single-sex.pdf (accessed July 15, 2009).

Sixteen: The 21st-Century Parent

252 *It shouldn't be part of a child's or teen's diet:* Natan Gadoth et al., "Caffeine as a Risk Factor for Chronic Daily Headache: A Population-based Study," *Neurology* (2005) 65: 180.

252 *There is even evidence that teens who are heavy caffeine consumers:* Margaret Savoca et al., "The Association of Caffeinated Beverages with Blood Pressure in Adolescents," *Archives of Pediatric and Adolescent Medicine* 158 (2004): 473–77.

252 *Subjects will eat 43 percent more jelly beans:* Food Addictions Seminar presented by Institute for Natural Resources, July 22, 2010, Minneapolis.

253 *The latest research shows that our brain:* Jonah Lehrer, http://scienceblogs.com/cortex/2010/05/vacation_2.php, (accessed on August 21, 2010).

255 *In his book* Stumbling on Happiness: Daniel Gilbert, *Stumbling on Happiness* (New York: Knopf, 2007), 241.

ACKNOWLEDGMENTS

First and foremost I want to acknowledge my partner in life, parenting, and this book. My wife Monica's imprint is on every page—from idea to finished drafts. Thousands of hours of discussion, research, writing, revising, and editing went into this project. Her weekends and evenings were as dedicated to bringing this volume to life as mine. It was a joint project in every sense of the word, except for the ultimate responsibility for what you read. Any mistakes are mine.

Monica and I learned the joys, tribulations, and challenges of everyday parenting from our three kids. Dan, Brian, and Erin—all now adults—along with their partners and our grandchildren, continue to bring richness to our lives. In addition, Erin was an active contributor to this book, especially chapters 13 and 15.

Monica and I are so glad that we made a decision many years ago to create an extended family of support for ourselves and our kids. Thank you to all our close friends. Sharing ideas, suggestions, support, and encouragement over the years has been a rare gift.

I owe a great deal of appreciation to my literary agent, Marly Rusoff, who has been so helpful in bringing my work to the publishing world for the past eight years.

This is my third project with a gifted editor, Leslie Meredith. In fact, this book was her idea. She suggested it shortly after Free Press published my last book. I appreciate her guidance and always helpful suggestions. I have benefited greatly from her guidance as well as the contributions of her colleagues at Free Press, especially Donna Loffredo, Leslie's assistant editor, and my publicist, Christine Donnelly.

I have been fortunate enough to have counseled thousands of families and taught and led workshops for thousands more. Their stories are sprinkled throughout these chapters. I am indebted to them for so much of what I have learned about children, parenting, and family life.

INDEX

ABOUT THE AUTHOR

David Walsh, Ph.D. has emerged as one of the world's leading authorities on children, teens, parenting, family life, and the impact of technology on children's health and development. He spent ten years teaching and coaching high school students before joining Fairview Health Services in Minneapolis to develop and direct innovative counseling programs for youth and families. In 1995, he founded the internationally renowned National Institute on Media and the Family, which he led until 2010. Dr. Walsh has presented workshops to parents, educators, and professionals throughout the world. He is currently launching a new company called Mind Positive Parenting™ to coincide with the release of this book. A consultant to the World Health Organization and the ministries of education in Japan and South Korea, he has testified before congressional committees on numerous occasions. Dr. Walsh has also authored columns on numerous topics and his articles have appeared in newspapers across the country, including the *Washington Post* and *Los Angeles Times*.

A frequent guest on national radio and television, Dr. Walsh has appeared on NBC's *Today* show, *Good Morning America,* the CBS *Early Show, PBS NewsHour with Jim Lehrer, Dateline NBC,* ABC's *20/20,* and National Public Radio's *All Things Considered* and *Morning Edition,* and has been featured on three nationally broadcast PBS specials. He has been the recipient of numerous awards, including the Council on Family Relations' *Friend of the Family Award.*

He received his B.A. degree from Mount Carmel College, his M.A. degree from the University of St. Thomas in St. Paul, and his Ph.D. in educational psychology from the University of Minnesota. He is on the faculty of the University of Minnesota, is a senior advisor at Search Institute, and has published many articles in the professional and general press. He is active in many professional associations, is a licensed psychologist, and has been the recipient of awards and an honorary doctorate. He and his wife, Monica, live in Minneapolis and have three adult children and a growing number of grandchildren.